Ezequiel L. Posesorski

Between Reinhold and Fichte

August Ludwig Hülsen's Contribution to the Emergence of German Idealism

EuKlId

Europäische Kultur und Ideengeschichte

Studien. Band 5

Herausgeber: Bernd Thum, Hans-Peter Schütt
Institut für Philosophie, Karlsruher Institut für Technologie (KIT)

Eine Übersicht über alle bisher in dieser Schriftenreihe erschienenen Bände finden Sie am Ende des Buchs.

Between Reinhold and Fichte

August Ludwig Hülsen's Contribution
to the Emergence of German Idealism

by
Ezequiel L. Posesorski

Impressum

Karlsruher Institut für Technologie (KIT)
KIT Scientific Publishing
Straße am Forum 2
D-76131 Karlsruhe
www.ksp.kit.edu

KIT – Universität des Landes Baden-Württemberg und nationales
Forschungszentrum in der Helmholtz-Gemeinschaft

KIT Scientific Publishing 2012
Print on Demand

ISSN: 1867-5018
ISBN: 978-3-86644-861-2

For Ariane

Acknowledgements

I would like to thank my family and friends for their continuous support over my research period.

This essay has been originally submitted in fulfillment of the requirements for the degree of "Doctor of Philosophy" to the Philosophy Department at the University of Haifa. I would like to express my hearty gratitude to my advisor Dr. Franz G. Nauen, whose invaluable teachings, encouragement, guidance, and support throughout the years enabled me to develop an understanding of German idealism.

I owe a big debt of gratitude to Prof. Dr. Manfred Frank for receiving me as a guest researcher at the Eberhard-Karls-Universität Tübingen, and for his precious advice and continuous support. I am deeply thankful to Prof. Dr. Hans-Peter Schütt for his constructive suggestions and comments, and for publishing this essay in the EuKlid series.

Special thanks also to Axel Müller and Barabara Brachmann for their infinite hospitality.

The research for this dissertation could not have been carried out without the generous support I received from the University of Haifa, the Switzerland-Israel Philosophical Fund, and the Bucerius Institute for Research of Contemporary German History and Society.

TABLE OF CONTENTS

Table of Contents

Zwischen Reinhold und Fichte:
A.L. Hülsen's Beitrag zur Heraufkunft des Deutschen Idealismus

Zusammenfassung

Zwar hat August Ludwig HÜLSEN (1765–1809) zur Entstehung des Deutschen Idealismus Entscheidendes beigetragen, doch sein Name und sein Werk sind den meisten Gelehrten, die dieses Feld beackern, bis auf den heutigen Tag fast gänzlich unbekannt. Diese Arbeit diskutiert die historische Bedeutung von HÜLSENs *Prüfung der von der Akademie der Wissenschaften zu Berlin aufgestellten Preisfrage: Was hat die Metaphysik seit Leibniz und Wolf für Progressen gemacht?* (1796), seiner einzigen Buchpublikation, die zur Entstehung des Deutschen Idealismus beigetragen hat und im besonderen zum Denken von REINHOLD und FICHTE während der 1790er Jahre.

Üblicherweise wird die *Wissenschaftslehre* und mit ihr die Heraufkunft des Deutschen Idealismus als FICHTES „Antwort" auf die von SCHULZE-AENESIDEMUS gegen REINHOLDS frühe *Elementarphilosophie* erhobenen skeptischen Einwände in den Blick gerückt. Diese „Antwort" war indes, wie FICHTE selber 1798 bemerkt hat, weit davon entfernt vollständig zu sein. Meine These ist, daß HÜLSEN als Fichteaner gerade jene Aspekte von REINHOLDS System zu restrukturieren und neu zu begründen suchte, die FICHTE selber unberührt gelassen hatte: im besonderen REINHOLDS nahezu vergessenen Entwurf einer rationalen Geschichte der Philosophie. 1797 nahm FICHTE die Ergebnisse, die HÜLSEN erzielt hatte, zum Anlaß, dessen Schrift in den *Annalen des philosophischen Tons* als Einführung in seine *Wissenschaftslehre* zu empfehlen. Das ist, wie mir scheint, ein gutes Indiz dafür, daß FICHTE in HÜLSEN einen Partner bei der Vervollständigung seines noch unvollständigen Systems anerkannt hat. Entsprechend besteht die historische Bedeutung von HÜLSEN's Schrift darin, daß sie FICHTES Versuch komplettiert, den REINHOLDschen Standpunkt zu überwinden und dadurch zur Entstehung des Deutschen Idealismus beigetragen hat.

Between Reinhold and Fichte:

A. L. Hülsen's Contribution to the Emergence of German Idealism

Abstract

August Ludwig HÜLSEN (1765–1809) was a contributor to the emergence of German idealism. Notwithstanding, his name and works are up to this day almost entirely unknown to most scholars in the field. This essay discusses the historical importance of HÜLSEN's *Prüfung der von der Akademie der Wissenschaften zu Berlin aufgestellten Preisfrage: Was hat die Metaphysik seit Leibniz und Wolf für Progressen gemacht?* (1796), his only book, for the emergence of German idealism, especially the thought of REINHOLD and FICHTE during the 1790's.

The usual way of focusing on the *Wissenschaftslehre,* and hence, on the emergence of German idealism, is as a "response" of FICHTE to the skeptical objections of SCHULZE-AENESIDEMUS to REINHOLD's early *Elementarphilosophie.* This "response", as FICHTE himself recognized in 1798, was far from complete. My thesis is that HÜLSEN, a Fichtean thinker, restructured and re-grounded those aspects of REINHOLD's system that FICHTE left intact: in particular, REINHOLD's almost forgotten approach to the rational history of philosophy. In 1797, HÜLSEN's achievement prompted FICHTE's recommendation of HÜLSEN's book in *Annalen des philosophischen Tons* as an introduction to his *Wissenschaftslehre.* This indicates, I hold, that FICHTE recognized HÜLSEN as a partner in the development of his incomplete system. Accordingly, the historical importance of HÜLSEN's book is that it completed FICHTE's attempt to overcome REINHOLD's standpoint and contributed to the emergence of German idealism.

Introduction

August Ludwig Hülsen (1765-1809) was a contributor to the emergence of German idealism. Notwithstanding, his name and works are up to this day almost entirely unknown to most scholars in the field. During the last five years of the 18th century, the short period of time in which he was active, some leading German philosophers considered Hülsen a prominent contributor to the development of critical philosophy. Fichte, whose standpoint Hülsen originally shared, emphatically recommended the reading of Hülsen's only book as an introduction to the *Wissenschaftslehre*.[1] Fichte's *Philosophisches Journal,* one of the leading German journals of the time, became the vehicle of publication of two of Hülsen's subsequent short essays.[2] Fichte's recognition of Hülsen's achievement not only persuaded him to offer Hülsen to collaborate with him at the University of Jena,[3] but also named him godfather of his son Immanuel Hermann.[4] Schelling, to whom Hülsen was personally introduced by Fichte in 1797 on the occasion of Fichte's first personal meeting with Schelling, rated Hülsen's book as the expression of one of those "superior spirits" that "so uncommonly excel in the field of philosophy".[5] After Hülsen's death in 1813, Schelling published and wrote the afterword to Hülsen's *Literarischem Nachlaß* in his *Allgemeine Zeitschrift von Deutschen für Deutsche.*[6]

Hülsen's work also received a considerable amount of respect and interest from the early German romantics. From 1798 and until 1800, after some significant changes in his original philosophical position,

---

[1] See: FICHTE GA I-4, 317
[2] These were the 1797 *Philosophische Briefe an Hrn. v. Briest in Nennhausen. Erster Brief. Ueber Popularität in der Philosophie,* and the 1798 *Ueber den Bildungstrieb.*
[3] See: FUCHS 1978 ff., 6,1, 272
[4] See: FICHTE GA III-3, 37
[5] See: SCHELLING 1971, I 298
[6] *Philosophische Fragmente, aus Hülsens literarischem Nachlaß,* in: HÜLSEN 1971, 267-97. For Schelling's afterword see: SCHELLING 1971, I 298–302

Hülsen became a contributor to the *Athenäum*.[7] Novalis reacted to Hülsen's book in his *logologischen Fragmente*. He included Hülsen among the five members of the "philosophical directorate" of Germany.[8] Friedrich Schlegel — by far, the most enthusiastic early romantic reader of Hülsen—, described his only book in *Athenäum* fragment 295 as an "extremely rare work in philosophy"; as "a work in the strictest sense of the word", that is, as "a work of art", "only second to Fichte in dialectic virtuosity".[9] On March 25 1798, Schlegel reported to his brother August Wilhelm that he considered Hülsen a more important philosopher than Schelling.[10] Both Schleiermacher and August W. Schlegel showed interest in Hülsen's work and corresponded with him.

In this dissertation only Hülsen's *Preisschrift*, his only book, not his later essays in *Philosophisches Journal* or in *Athenäum* will be discussed, and *Preisschrift* only in so far as it relates to the history of early German idealism, especially the thought of Reinhold and Fichte during the 1790's. The importance of Hülsen's writings, including *Preisschrift* for the understanding of Schelling and Hegel and the early German romantics, especially Friedrich Schlegel, Novalis and Schleiermacher must be postponed for a later occasion.

Preisschrift relates to the ongoing debate, which began in the 1790's on the significance of Kant's achievement. By the end of the 1780's the *Kritik der reinen Vernunft* was the subject of intense controversy between Kantian and anti-Kantian philosophers.[11] The situation had not changed dramatically by 1792. The ongoing rivalry among the contending parties prompted the Berlin Academy of Sciences to intervene. The academy's intention was to end the controversies by bringing about "philosophical peace".[12] The academic authorities decided to

---

[7] These were the 1799 *Ueber die natürliche Gleichheit der Menschen*, and the 1800 *Natur-Betrachtungen auf einer Reise durch die Schweiz*.

[8] See: NOVALIS, SCH II, 529, n. 25

[9] See: SCHLEGEL, KA II, 241-2

[10] For Schlegel's letter, see: SCHLEGEL, KA XXIV, 113

[11] For the controversial situation of critical philosophy during the end of the 1780's, see: REINHOLD 1963, 1-68

[12] See: HÜLSEN 1796, 37

organize a philosophical contest. Scholars were requested to discuss the progress that has been achieved in philosophy due to the conflict of the schools. The academy demanded that all discussions consider two fundamental concepts: (1) historical progress and (2) the history of philosophy. The organizers formulated these two requirements under the following task-question: What progress has metaphysics achieved since Leibniz and Wolf? Only a few essays reached the organizing committee. The authorities decided to postpone the contest. A new contest was announced in 1795.[13] The second contest attracted the attention of the most outstanding thinkers of the time including Kant himself, who wrote but did not submit his own contribution. Karl Leonhard Reinhold, Johann Heinrich Abicht, and Johann Christoph Schwab were the three winners.[14]

Hülsen, who had in 1792 already planned to take part of the event, seems to have handed in his essay for the second 1795 contest. Hülsen's paper reached the organizing committee some time after the stipulated dead line.[15] In 1796, Hülsen added a preface and a supplementary section to his manuscript and transformed it into a book. It appeared in print under the title *Prüfung der von der Akademie der Wissenschaften zu Berlin aufgestellten Preisfrage: Was hat die Metaphysik seit Leibniz und Wolf für Progressen gemacht?* in 1796, J. F. Hammerich, Altona.

Hülsen wrote *Preisschrift* under the strong influence of Fichte's early idealism.[16] Fichte taught that critical or "scientific" philosophy (*Wissen-*

---

[13] See: FLITNER 1913, 26

[14] For Schwab, Reinhold and Abicht's essays see: SCHWAB/REINHOLD/ABICHT 1971

[15] See: KRÄMER 2001, 287-8

[16] Existing research on Hülsen's achievement is cursory. The most extensive studies of it are:
   - ... *meine Philosophie ist kein Buch: August Ludwig Hülsen (1765–1809), Leben und Schreiben eines Selbstdenkers und Symphilosophen zur Zeit der Frühromantik* (2001) by Ulrich KRÄMER,
   - *August Ludwig Hülsen und der Bund der freien Männer* (1913) by Willy FLITNER,
   - *August Ludwig Hülsen: Seine Schriften und seine Beziehungen zur Romantik* (1910) by Karl OBENAUER.

schaft) must be self-conscious of itself and not have hidden or *unjustified* premises. Hülsen's position was that one should make an inquiry into the transcendental possibility of *grounding* and *solving* the prize-question *systematically*; a point that the Academy of Sciences in its announcement completely overlooked. Hülsen also stressed the "*spirit*" (as opposed to the "*letter*") of Fichte's early idealism. One of Hülsen's major purposes was to ground systematically the historical intellectual process that led to the *Wissenschaftslehre*. At a certain stage of his transcendental deduction, Hülsen "injects" an *inherent temporal dimension* to Fichte's *logical-dynamic a priori* concept of rationality. For Fichte the transcendental system of all knowledge is an *ever-existing system. What takes place in time is the philosopher's personal self-reflective articulation or derivation.* The rational being creates his own system, Fichte holds, by following the *supra-historical* producing course of action of the Absolute I. Hülsen expanded Fichte's antinomic concept of reason into a historically developing agent. Hülsen's position was that a system of knowledge is *simultaneously produced and articulated*

Manfred FRANK's *Unendliche Annäherung* (1998), Alfred LANGEWAND's *Moralische Verbindlichkeit oder Erziehung* (1991), Dieter KLAWON's unpublished *Geschichtsphilosophische Ansätze in der Frühromantik* (1977), Helmut GIRNDT's *Die Differenz des fichteschen und hegelschen Systems in der hegelschen „Differenzschrift"* (1965), and Rudolf HAYM's *Die romantische Schule* (1870) dedicate some pages to the discussion of Hülsen's system. — *Preisschrift* is also the topic of the following articles:
- *August Ludwig Hülsens erster Beitrag zur philosophischen Frühromantik* (1998) by Guido NASCHERT,
- *Geselligkeit und absolutes Sein* (1990) by Christoph JAMME,
- *Ansätze des Prinzips der Einheit von Logischem und Historischem im Übergangsfeld der fichteschen Transzendentalphilosophie zum objektiven Idealismus: J.G. Fichte — A.L. Hülsen* (1984) by Klaus FREYER and Jürgen STAHL,
- *Das romantische Bild der Philosophiegeschichte* (1926) by Hans HESS.
Passing references to *Preisschrift* are also found in *Dimensionen der Transzendentalphilosophie* (1990) by Steffen DIETZSCH, *Was soll die Schweiz dem Athenäum* (1988) by Friedrich STRACK, *Geschichte der kant'schen Philosophie* (1987) by Karl ROSENKRANZ, *August Ludwig Hülsen 1765–1809* (1983) by Christian TILLITZKI, *Hülsens idealistische Romantik* (1979) by Martin OESCH, and *Studien zur Wirkungsgeschichte Fichtes als Pädagoge* (1970) by Rudolf LASSAHN.

in time. System to Hülsen appears as the final *self-reflectively developed* outcome of a *universal history of reason*, the necessary ending "chapter" of which contains *the entire history of philosophy.* Hülsen was the first post-Kantian idealist philosopher to resort to a logical method based on the resolution of contradictions to explain the causation of historical events. Hülsen's inquiry into the systematic possibility of grounding and solving the prize-question pushes the topic intended by the academy into the background. His historically augmented version of Fichte's system is his central topic.[17] Although Hülsen's own approach mainly concentrates on the systematization of the history of philosophy, it also contains brief explanations for the emergence of other rational-historical events such as mythological thought, the establishment of the family, and the genesis of social bonds.[18]

In the preface to *Preisschrift*, Hülsen claims that he had sketched ideas for a systematic approach to the history of philosophy in 1792. Three years later, however, Hülsen's basic premises had undergone a radical change. By 1795, Hülsen was familiar with Fichte's early idealism. Although Hülsen claims in his preface of 1796 that many of his early ideas had not survived this radical change,[19] in the supplementary section of *Preisschrift* he makes a number of statements revealing his early philosophical convictions. What these statements disclose is the

---

[17] The systematization of the rational history of philosophy was the topic of some essays written earlier than *Preisschrift*. The most prominent among these works are REINHOLD's *Ueber den Begrif der Geschichte der Philosophie: Eine akademische Vorlesung* (1791), Salomon MAIMON's *Über die Progressen der Philosophie* (1793), and Wilhelm Gottlieb TENNEMANN's *Uebersicht des Vorzüglichsten, was für die Geschichte der Philosophie seit 1780 geleistet worden* (1795). What distinguishes *Preisschrift* from its forerunners is the innovative possibility of logical-historical progress.

[18] Although there is no direct evidence that Hülsen influenced Schelling and Hegel on any of the points discussed in this paragraph, the history of ideas could still record HÜLSEN's *Preisschrift* as a predecessor of SCHELLING's *System des transcendentalen Idealismus* and of HEGEL's *Phänomenologie des Geistes*. The discussion of these interesting topics, however, transcends the limits of this monograph.

[19] See: HÜLSEN 1796, pp, I-II

substantial role that Karl Leonhard Reinhold, one of Hülsen's philosophy teachers,[20] played in his philosophical education. In the appendix
of *Preisschrift*, Hülsen argues that he spent many years studying Reinhold's writings. His teacher's thoughts, he adds, guided him in his
careful reading of Kant's *Kritik*. Owing to Reinhold's philosophy, Hülsen improved his understanding of the "spirit" of critical philosophy.
Reinhold's concept of critical systematicity, and his systematic approach
to the rational history of philosophy, seemed to satisfy Hülsen's early
demands.[21] One of my basic conclusions is that Hülsen's acquaintance
with Fichte's early idealism brought about a significant rethinking of
many of these early convictions but not their complete rejection.[22] In the
appendix of 1796, Hülsen stressed that Reinhold's early *Elementarphilosophie* played a significant influential role in the articulation of his
historically enlarged *Wissenschaftslehre*. Hülsen writes:

Hierin [i.e., in Reinhold's philosophy] *liegt überhaupt das Prinzip für alle
Geschichte der Philosophie. Die Philosphie als Wissenschaft ist das reine
Selbsterkenntniss in uns. Dieses in seiner empirischen Entwickkelung unter-
sucht giebt uns den Geist aller Zeiten und einzelnen Selbstdenker. Reinhold
sahe schärfer als irgend einer der Kantianer seiner Periode. Er fasste den
Begriff eines Systems und wandte ihn an auf die Vernunftkritik. Da leuchtete
ihm ein, was noch immer nur wenigen einleuchten will, dass das keine Philosophie als Wissenschaft sey. Diese klare Einsicht brachte ihn zu Versuchen —
und der Genius der Philosophie konnte ihn nicht besser führen, als dadurch,
dass er ihn auf die Theorie des Bewusstseyns führte. Reinhold forderte Einheit* [i.e., critical systematicity], *und dadurch brachte er einen neuen Geist in
das Studium der Kritik.*[23]

Existing research of *Preisschrift* does not discuss Reinhold's significant
influence on Hülsen. An adequate exposition demands, in my opinion,
not only a very specific survey of Fichte's early idealism, but also a
scrutiny of those relevant aspects of Reinhold's philosophy that con-

---

[20] In 1794, Hülsen enrolled at the University of Kiel, where Reinhold was prominent.
[21] See: HÜLSEN 1796, 199-200
[22] In 1795, Hülsen moved to Jena and became a student of Fichte.
[23] HÜLSEN 1796, 198

ditioned Hülsen's standpoint. I will attempt to prove that Hülsen was not only another "devotee" of Fichte's *Wissenschaftslehre*. Through the idealistic influence of Fichte, Hülsen restructured and grounded many unjustified or rather uncritically established aspects of Reinhold's system: in particular, his systematic approach to the rational history of philosophy. Thus, Hülsen succeeded in offering new solutions to some of Reinhold's main concerns. It is in this context, as we shall see, that Hülsen's *Preisschrift* emerges as a still unnoticed, though considerably relevant contribution to the emergence of German idealism.

The usual way to focus on the *Wissenschaftslehre,* and hence, on the emergence of German idealism, is as a "systematic response" of Fichte to the skeptical objections of Schulze-Aenesidemus to Reinhold's *Elementarphilosophie*.[24] Fichte's "response", as he himself recognized in 1798, was far from complete.[25] In the preface to the 1794-5 *Grundlage der gesammten Wissenschaftslehre* Fichte refers to his system as a plan. Fichte writes that he does not tell everything to his reader, that he wishes to leave him something to think about, that he encourages independent thought, and hopes that on further consideration, parts of his system continue to change and renew themselves. The plan of the *Grundlage,* Fichte adds, should provide the reader with a complete view of *how to erect further systematic construction upon its foundations.* Suggestions from other philosophical authors, he concludes, are welcome.[26] Hülsen "picked up this gauntlet". Hülsen directs his efforts at rearticulating and developing some significant, though critically deficient aspects of Reinhold's system that Fichte left almost intact. Hülsen's historical enlargement of the *Wissenschaftslehre* is an attempt to "fill" the "empty spaces" left by Fichte's incomplete rearticulating of Reinhold's early *Elementarphilosophie.* Traces of Fichte's intention to develop the historical dimension of the *Wissenschaftslehre*

---

[24] It should be recalled that the amendment of some Kantian positions, as well as the skeptical objections posed to Kant by Salomon Maimon, played an important role in Fichte's re-structuring of critical philosophy. The discussion of these interesting topics, however, transcends the limits of this monograph.

[25] See: FICHTE, GA, I-2, 162

[26] See: FICHTE, GA I-2, 252-4

are found in the so-called *Programmschrift,* i.e., the 1794 essay in which Fichte outlined the program of his forthcoming system.[27]

Both Fichte and Hülsen agree that the concept of the *Wissenschafts-lehre* is not a *"literal"* but a *"spiritual"* concept, a standpoint that de-mands *personal* and *independent explanation,* or rather *self-adaptable normative completion* of its critical plan.[28] Hülsen does not consider his divergent inclusion of an inherent temporal dimension in Fichte's *a priori* concept of rationality as a step beyond the *Wissenschaftslehre.* Nor did it seem to be such to Fichte, who in his 1797 *Annalen des philosophischen Tons* comes to Hülsen's defence against an hostile reviewer, and rates his *Preisschrift* as *"Eine Schrift, die ich zur Er-leichterung des Studiums der Wissenschaftslehre recht sehr empfehlen kann".*[29] Although in some specific aspects the positions of Hülsen and Fichte do not entirely concord, they both mutually refer to each other as developers of the same philosophical project. Fichte's identification of *Preisschrift* with the *Wissenschaftslehre* indicates that *Fichte reco-gnized Hülsen as a partner in the development of his incomplete system.* The historical importance of Hülsen's achievement is that *it completed Fichte's attempt to overcome Reinhold's standpoint, and contributed to the emergence of German idealism.* This point has been entirely over-looked by scholars.

Hülsen begins his inquiry in *Preisschrift* by discussing the human condition. Resistance to moral perfection characterizes the history of humanity. Nature and the rational being are engaged in a persisting *heteronomous* relation of *self-contradiction.* Although humanity has already achieved critical or "scientific" knowledge in the *Wissenschafts-lehre,* most philosophers ignore this achievement. Ignorance of critical knowledge is the cause behind the rational being's historical inability to determine his will *autonomously.* The *Wissenschaftslehre* taught that moral improvement demands personal striving after self-conscious

---

[27] I will discuss this topic in section 2.7.
[28] This, as far as I know, is an unnoticed aspect of Fichte's thought. I will discuss it in section 2.9.
[29] FICHTE, GA I-2, 317

8

determination or *self-identity*. Hülsen argues that self-interest, which is commonly called selfishness, or ignorance of critical knowledge gives vent to a widespread state of philosophical controversies. The latter take place among different disputing parties or sects. Their exclusive object of dispute is the true universal concept of philosophy. None of these rival factions can critically exhaust the derivation or justification of their respective foundational premises, for Hülsen a key distinctive feature of true philosophy. Ignorance of critical knowledge results in the simultaneous mistaken assertion of the *particular* standpoints of all these parties as the exclusive *universal* representatives of the only true possible philosophy, and hence, their irreconcilable disputes. Insight into the nature of disputes reveals that all rival factions share a common implicit goal: philosophy must be a "scientific" discipline. This means for Hülsen that all factions tacitly argue in favour of the overcoming of the state of disputes. Now, this historical state of *discrepancy* or *disunity* worsens humanities' moral situation. For it prevents an *integrative coordination* among contending rivals. The recognition of the universal standpoint of the *Wissenschaftslehre*, of the true possibility of increasing self-determination, not only enables a dramatic improvement of the moral situation of man. If understood, it enables a *universal consensus* as to the undisputable concept of philosophy, the practical result of which will be a *self-determined improvement* of the communal relations of man.

The purpose of Hülsen's *Preisschrift* is pedagogic. Hülsen's main intention is to teach his reader how to achieve moral perfectibility through self-determined coordinated consensus. For this, a *reconstruction of the systematic possibility of consciousness* is needed. Hülsen proves that the philosophical knowledge attained in the *Wissenschaftslehre* is the accurate tool for achieving this moral goal. Its self-determining insight, opens up the road for a self-conscious understanding of the efficacy of nature (Not-I) as an unendingly self-posited product of reason. Its universality, assures an exclusive and therefore *unquestionable* philosophical position. The *Wissenschaftslehre* consequently enables a withdrawal from the sphere of partisan disputes, namely the achievement of exhaustive philosophical consensus.

Hülsen shares Fichte's absolute holistic point of departure. Hülsen, like Fichte, is committed to the contention that philosophy must be based on a single first principle. Hülsen however holds that from a certain stage on, the system of all knowledge ceases to be a purely *a priori* or *supra-historical* system. It emerges as the *necessary outcome* of a *simultaneous rational-temporal process of practical-theoretical development*, the closing "chapter" of which steps through the history of philosophy. The critical reconstruction of reason's history and of its concluding "chapter" is Hülsen's way to justify (1) the necessary emergence as well as (2) the consensual overcoming of the morally adverse epoch of partisan disputes. The achievement of moral perfection in the broad sense of the word emerges as the true and inevitable spiritual-historical vocation (*Bestimmung*) of man.

Hülsen's reconstruction of human consciousness is: reason, a dynamic *Geist,* is in its original supra-historical moment a purely or absolutely self-posited agent; both its absolute positing and being coincide. *Qua* pure reason, reason immediately appears to itself as a self-identical agent. The emergence of consciousness (mediation) however demands that this original identity be limited or counter-posited. Hülsen hence holds that in its original proto-conscious moment, reason cannot recognize itself as the universal self-determined source of its absolutely self-posited being. Its pure immediacy prevents it from achieving real autonomy. That compels pure reason to develop a system of knowledge. Through it, reason will try to return to itself, achieve a *mediated* self-positing of itself as reason, and attain thereby critical self-determining knowledge of its *originally* and *autonomously* self-posited being. The innate self-pursuing, and hence self-reflective nature of reason's practical-theoretical activity, determines the *necessary circular-teleological* character of its entire course of development.

Reason's next step is to oppose a determining Not-I to itself. Methodical considerations reveal that two additional simultaneous procedures are necessary to proceed with the construction of the transcendental system of knowledge: (1) counter-positing and (2) synthesis. One of the ensuing results of their establishment is the *concrete* emergence of the imaginative ability of intuitional representation. For Hülsen the system of all knowledge cannot be developed *in abstracto.* It is this *actually developed* theoretical ability to self-limit itself through the practical self-positing of a *spatiotemporal determining object,* which determines *reason's abandonment of its pure supra-historical sphere and its inevitable entrance into the empirical realm of historical development.* Reason now emerges as a necessary *logical-historical* developing agent. Pure reason is transformed into *empirical* or *progressing reason* (*empirische* or *fortschreitende Vernunft*). The actual procedure of self-limitation results in a simultaneous transformation of reason into a *universally self-particularizing* agent. Thus, the transcendental ground of all *individuation* is established. From this stage on, the *general* developing history of reason coincides with the epistemic historical development of the *concrete* individual.

Reason first appears in history as a conditioned representing being (*vorstellendes Wesen*). Its empirical standpoint is characterized by a *heteronomous* determination of *concrete objectivity,* that is, by a Not-I that is not yet perceived as a subjectively self-posited object. Progressing reason's next step is to resort to the spontaneous self-reflecting activity of the imagination, and begin the logical-historical construction of a faculty of judgment. This transcendental faculty, judgment, enables the rational being to recognize, discursively, the theoretical efficacy of the Not-I as its own practically self-posited product. Expanding the sphere of its self-determining activity, the rational being frees himself from his first heteronomous historical situation. The activity of the imagination makes possible self-reflecting *in concreto* on an intuited object. Progressing reason accordingly subsumes the concrete stage of intuitional representation under its free self-positing power. It so determines the ground of *the first real possible discursive knowledge.* Progressing reason establishes all subsequent transcendental levels of the faculty of judgment by repeating this concrete self-reflective procedure. The three correlative discursive steps that progressing reason takes are the: (1) positing of concrete objective reality (thetic judgment), (2) counter-positing of concrete objective reality (anti-thetic judgment), and (3) synthesis of concrete objective reality (synthetic judgment). Each one of these concretely taken steps determines a logical-historical epoch in the discursive intellectual development of humanity.

The faculty of judgment furnishes the ground of *the first real discursive synthesis*. Thus, the transcendental possibility of *systematic thought* is established. Humanity is now able to start the aforementioned "freeing" ascending systematization (discursive self-subsuming and unification) of the coercive action of the Not-I. The task of systematization, the logical-historical result of which will be critical or "scientific" knowledge, takes place through the concrete accumulative repetition of the judging stages of thesis, anti-thesis, and synthesis. Each new judging stage appears as a higher self-posited form of systematic thought. Accordingly, each concrete systematic synthesis results in a higher concrete systematic thesis, the concrete counter-positing of which takes place through an ensuing systematic anti-thesis. Qualitatively, the logically-historically active faculty of judgment cannot develop any further.

For Hülsen judgments or rather the concretely developing systematic positions enabled by them, are more than mere logical-historical acts of discursive self-positing. Every possible judgment simultaneously expresses a *constitutive procedure* of *asking-answering*; a conclusion that Hülsen reaches after a preliminary inquiry into the essential nature of questions and answers. All discursive *self-reflective* stages of this developing system emerge as answered questions, or rather as *self-posited question-answer-standpoints* of progressing reason. As in the case of judgment, every concrete synthetic question-answer-standpoint results in a higher concrete thetic question-answer-standpoint, the concrete counter-positing of which, takes place through an ensuing anti-thetic question-answer-standpoint. The establishment of the mechanism of judgment as a simultaneous mechanism of asking-answering opens a new epoch in the systematic history of progressing reason: *the history of philosophy*. Progressing reason is so transformed into "philosophizing reason" (*philosophierende Vernunft*).

Hülsen's reconstruction shows that the concrete or objective determining action of the Not-I affects philosophizing reason in a number of concrete *quantitative* ways. Personal intentionality, a particular or dissimilar empirical representation of reason's being, establishes the possibility for the articulation of different philosophical systems. All systems of philosophy emerge as *ascending* and hence *not entirely universally determined* judging attempts of philosophizing reason at a definitive attainment of critical knowledge (self-consciousness). *Each represents a partial self-reflecting stage of practical-theoretical development within a single, universal, and historically extended attempt of philosophizing reason at a production and portrayal of a system of knowledge.* Methodical reconstruction furthermore shows that an empirically reachable, though not fully self-aware ideal of philosophical perfection orients philosophizing reason's teleological course of evolution throughout the epoch of pre-critical thought.

All systems of philosophy attain the status of representative stages of the philosophical progress of humanity as a whole. The fact that the same single *universal* agent strives through different concrete thinkers after critical knowledge confers a *collective* character to each possible *particular* effort in a rational history of philosophy. Accordingly, in their *personal* practical strivings, all finite rational beings meet the same historically emerging standpoints in philosophizing reason's *universal* course of development. The ongoing practical activity of a reduced number of avant-garde philosophers opens up the road for the subsequent general progress of the human species. Progress however demands *personal practical reproduction* of this avant-garde philosophizing. The necessarily emerging self-conscious standpoint of critical philosophy is reproduced as a personal standpoint. In principle, to strive for oneself is tantamount as to strive for all other rational beings and conversely. So the systematic possibility for a simultaneous development of the intellectual histories of the concrete rational being and humanity is consolidated.

In addition, reconstructive thought finds in the history of philosophy logical-historical ascending answers to the question of *how metaphysics (or the system of all knowledge) is possible.* Each personal answer emerges within the antinomically developing form of a rationally self-posited system of philosophy.

The history of philosophy is so divided in epochs. In each one of these epochs, philosophizing reason synthetically counter-posits a determinate number of its ascending systems or products. In Leibniz's epoch, one finds a *synthetic counter-positing* between the *thetically self-posited* Leibnizian system — the epoch-making system — and the *anti-thetically self-posited* systems of his contemporary opponents. Each thetically self-posited system appears as an *unprecedented practical advancement* of philosophizing reason towards the exhaustive determination of the system of all knowledge. Thetic systems inaugurate new logical-historical stages in the rational history of philosophy. They establish higher forms of synthetic unity, the self-reflected or self-subsumed objects of which are the synthetically given, though not entirely reconciled counter-positions of their preceding epochs. Apart from the universal and non-counter-positable system of critical philosophy, each new thetically posited system is counter-posited by its contemporary opponents; *uncritical* or *non-universally determined representatives* of the only true possible "science" as well. This inherent antinomic situation compels philosophizing reason to strive forward, and attempt to achieve the universal self-reconciling idea of philosophy.

The antinomically developed character of all systems of philosophy was until Hülsen an unnoticed phenomenon. Throughout its history, philosophizing reason is not a self-conscious agent. It does not grasp itself as the *universal relational* agent behind its logical-historical production. Its *synthetically counter-positing* activity, as Hülsen tries to show, is mistaken for a *non-contextually* established *opposition* or *contradiction* among mutually excluding systematic positions, which appear to the observer only as *atomic* facts. That is the reason why what is found throughout this pre-moral epoch of humanity is a persisting dissociating state of philosophical disputes.

According to Hülsen, the *self-conscious insight* of critical philosophy first enables an uncovering of the universally self-grounded character of philosophizing reason. Through it, the rational being attains concrete theoretical knowledge of how metaphysics or rather the logically-historically developed system of all knowledge has been established. He accordingly gains insight into the self-pursuing (teleological) ability of striving whereby reason has attained critical knowledge. All disputing systems first appear as *relative self-posited products,* or rather as *anti-nomically developed stages* of philosophizing reason's *exclusive* and *universally self-posited* system of philosophy. The epoch of partisan disputes emerges as a historical material condition for the logical production and articulation of the system of all knowledge. The universal integrative insight of philosophy results in a *contextual synthesis,* the concrete object of which is philosophizing reason's entire pre-critical production. Reason thus suppresses all possible partisan atomicity, a theoretical result of its multiple and disparate course of practical development, and thereby achieves *reconciling self-unity.*

According to Hülsen, only the logical-historical *qualitative* evolution of the system of all knowledge, and hence of its inherently contained history of philosophy, is exhausted with the emergence of the distinctive self-conscious insight of critical philosophy. The *regressive* uncovering of the original and absolutely self-grounded I (reason), shows that no additional *progressive* instances of *transcendental* or *qualitative* cognition can be added. The logical-historical development of this qualitative conditions, is carried out, in each one of its concrete self-subsuming stages, through an ascending handling of a spatio-temporally expanding, though ultimately finite quantity (a Not-I). What develop are the logical-historical conditions of the system of knowledge but not their inherently self-posited quantities. This enables the systematic production and portrayal *in concreto* of the *universal conditions of experience,* that is, the transcendental grounding of critical philosophy. What remains is a *quantitative* expansion of these qualitative self-determining conditions for all possible posited objects of experience: a necessary ensuing procedure demanded for the completion of the self-subsuming of the coercive action of the Not-I. Quantitative expansion therefore is humanity's empirical way to attempt to reach the *originally, immediately,* and *identically* self-posited foundational act of the Absolute I, and thereby achieve exhaustive autonomy. The inexhaustible holistic being of the Absolute I, compels an unending *logical-historical striving task of quantitative self-determining approximation.*

A revised *Wissenschaftslehre* according to Hülsen enables an *integration* of philosophizing reason's entire practical production with the *universal qualitative unity of reason*. All mutually excluding systems appear as logical-historical developing stages of a necessarily resulting reconciling concept of critical philosophy, which paves the way for an innovative *systematic articulation* of the history of philosophy as the inherent concluding "chapter" of the logically-historically developed system of all knowledge. The history of philosophy emerges as the "science of the becoming science" (*die Wissenschaft von der werdenden Wissenschaft*). Its self-reflective articulation enables an accurate reproduction of philosophizing reason's entire course of production. The logical-historical epoch of partisan disputes is the *only object* of this concluding chapter. Neither *achievement of self-determining autonomy*, nor *withdrawal from the subordinating sphere of partisan disputes*, is possible prior to the articulation of the rational history of philosophy. This task of articulation is not fulfilled with the self-conscious insight of a revised *Wissenschaftslehre*. It demands that a universal concept be retrospectively employed as a reconstructive criterion in the analytic evaluation of each logically-historically emerged pre-critical standpoint.

Since its entrance into the realm of historical development, reason is transformed into a universal self-particularizing agent. Philosophy's standpoint is a *general-personal expression* of the logical-historical activity of reason. Philosophy emerges as *a concretely self-determined* manifestation of this practical-theoretical activity, which spontaneously appears to itself under *the necessary discursive form of a self-related spiritual agent*. The attainment of philosophical knowledge demands the *personalized performance of a self-reflecting act*. Only such an act assures that the only possible content of philosophy, the concretely developed system of knowledge, emerge as a *real content*. The universal character of philosophy cannot be divorced from one's own personalized act of self-reflection, without which the *theoretical* character of the former is reduced to a *mere abstraction*. Philosophy is meaningless without its relation to the concrete individual. "Spirit" (*Geist*) is Hülsen's term for this act. No philosophy must be possible without spirit. This means that no printed text can express true philosophical knowledge. No printed letter can convey this required personal spiritual act. Philosophical books have for Hülsen only a *propaedeutic* or *instructive* status. Their exclusive function is to teach readers how to begin their own spiritual series of logical-historical self-reflective production and reach concrete philosophical knowledge.

The systematic articulation of the history of philosophy is a *personal spiritual task,* to be pursued exclusively by "scientifically" cultivated men. Ignorance of critical philosophy precludes the recognition of the teleological direction of philosophizing reason. Prior to the emergence of the revised *Wissenschaftslehre,* neither the establishment of systematic order among philosophizing reason's unilateral products, nor the attainment of an accurate idea of its contextual condition is possible. All systems of philosophy emerge as *atomic facts.* Only critical insight enables a clear apprehension of the true systematic idea of the inherently self-posited history of philosophy. Self-determination is the result of a *personal critical understanding* of the logical-historical spiritual relation of philosophy to all its general-personal evolutionary stages, and hence, the resulting self-determined ability to reach universal coordinated consensus.

Articulation requires that each single philosopher employ his spiritually attained concept of philosophy as a *retrospective, universal and reconstructive criterion.* Comparison and contrast enables a personal evaluation of the proportional amount of developing truth contained in each logical-historical pre-critical standpoint of philosophizing reason. Personal evaluation assures that all antinomically developed outcomes gain a definitive logical location within a systematic portrayal of reason's historically extended course of development.

According to Hülsen, his revised *Wissenschaftslehre* is the *common universal* outcome of all the previous disputed strivings of philosophizing reason for critical philosophy. Personally attained self-conscious insight reveals the spontaneously self-grounded character of reason. The true spiritual concept of philosophy fits the concept of an unendingly self-determining or morally improving subject. *Heteronomously determined* logical-historical relations are transformed into *autonomously self-determining* relations. The consensual character of philosophy makes possible the *unanimous coordination* of all "scientifically" educated men in the infinite spiritual task of quantitative approximation. Hülsen combines Kant's concept of the "categorical imperative" (moral perfection) with his own concept of practical progression after regulative theoretical self-determination (self-identity). As the opposite of heteronomy, the latter attains the status of an *autonomously expanding self-harmony –happiness* for Hülsen. The resulting possibility of moral improvement is furthermore characterized as an unprecedented epoch of *increasing "highest good"*, a synthesis of moral virtue and happiness. The unending attainment thereof appears as the inevitable spiritual vocation of man. The qualitative end of the history of philosophy opens an unprecedented epoch of moral perfection.

According to Hülsen, "scientific" knowledge has additional implications for the role of self-determination and for the scope of personal philosophical independence. The general-particular character of all rational activity assures the universal validity of personally attained autonomy. Hülsen characterizes each autonomously self-determining subject as a "self-thinker" (*Selbstdenker*), a well-known *Aufklärung* epithet that designated those thinkers who by appealing to reason's universality determined their own autonomous stances and extended the personal scope of their philosophical *independence*.[30] Hülsen's argument for a necessary autonomous production and articulation of a logically-historically developing system of all knowledge is a clear exposition and development of this independent spirit of the *Aufklärung*. The particularly expressed universal spiritual nature of the rational being, which is the exclusive object of all philosophical self-reflection, enables an identification of the concepts of "man" and "philosopher". *To be a philosopher is tantamount to fulfilling one's own practical spiritual nature and conversely.* This identification by Hülsen makes philosophical knowledge concrete and available to all human beings, and in this specific sense, *"popularizes"* it. Full intellectual autonomy transforms *academic freedom* into a real not formal concept. Academic affiliation is not a necessary requirement for a self-thinker,

---

[30] See: BAUM 1974, 86

and morality compels self-thinkers to avoid any subordination of their wills to academic institutions. Still the established possibility of purposive self-determined coordination enables Hülsen to sketch the idea of *a true academy of sciences*; a modern institution in which self-determined members autonomously congregate to achieve a joint coordinated striving after regulative morality. One of the roles that the self-thinker will play within this institution is to instruct uncritically educated students. As the ethically best man of his time, his pedagogic mission is to promote and facilitate the personal, independent, and spiritual self-knowledge of his pupils. The self-thinker is the true moral educator of humanity. It is as a plea for a *"popularizing philosophical education"* that the *Preisschrift* should be interpreted.

1. Reinhold

1.1 Reinhold's Influence

Records of Hülsen's early university years are scarce. In 1794, Hülsen left the University of Halle and matriculated at the University of Kiel. Hülsen probably moved to Kiel because of Reinhold.[1] Apart from Hülsen's statements about Reinhold's influence in *Preisschrift*, an additional explanation for his seeking of Reinhold can be found in Johann Georg Rist's *Lebenserinnerungen*. Rist, one of Hülsen's friends, reported in his memoirs that long before his arrival to Kiel Hülsen concerned himself both with Kant's *Kritik der reinen Vernunft* and with the history of philosophy.[2] It is probable that Hülsen moved to Kiel to learn more about Reinhold's approach, in which the critical forerunning model of his own connection of system and history of philosophy can be found. Other specific aspects of Reinhold's thought such as the concepts of "philosophical disputes" and "self-determined consensus", the importance of formulating correct critical questions, the key pedagogic activity of the self-thinker, and its popularizing task in the moral improvement of the human species remained strong commitments of Hülsen even after his conversion to Fichte's standpoint.

1.2 The Crisis of Critical Philosophy

By the time Hülsen began to philosophize, Karl Leonhard Reinhold (Vienna, 1758–1823) was already one of the most prominent critical philosophers in Germany. The enormous successes of Reinhold's *Briefe über die kantische Philosophie* from 1786–1787, made him one of Germany's leading Kantians,[3] which prompted the academic authorities at

---

[1] Hülsen matriculated at the Christian-Albrecht University on May 22, 1794 under a false name: Franciscus Jacobus Hegekern. For a historical account of Hülsen's stay in Kiel, see: KRÄMER 2001, 48-67

[2] See: Christian HÜLSEN 1934, 96

[3] In the *Briefe*, Reinhold accomplished two major tasks: (1) the popularization and the assertion of the systematic character of the Kantian philosophy, and (2) the

the University of Jena to offer him the chair of critical philosophy. In the fall of 1787, Reinhold delivered his first academic lectures on Kantian philosophy. The attendance was massive. However, after a short time, Reinhold noticed that only a few of his students had read Kant. Most of those misunderstood the *Kritik*. Some others, *Aufklärung* advocates, attacked Kant and accused him of unintelligibility.[4] A conflict of schools broke out among Reinhold's pupils.

Reinhold, himself an *Aufklärer,* for whom universal principles and comprehensibility were essential, realized that the philosophical assumptions of *die Aufklärung*, German Enlightenment, were seriously discredited. Morality, religion, political and civil right, etc, were endangered. Reinhold insisted that a true universal philosophy, a grounding discipline of all disciplines was necessary to base these on a rigorous, secure and legitimate foundation.[5] According to Reinhold, the obscurity and the idiosyncratic terminology of Kant's *Kritik* prevented this. For a devote *Aufklärer* like Reinhold this implied that Kant's philosophy unamended cannot provide a sound basis for social consensus.[6]

Reinhold tried to reassert the enlightened "spirit" of Kant's philosophy by complementing it with a universally accepted (*allgemein-geltende*) ground of deduction. Reinhold hoped to transform critical philosophy into an undisputed discipline capable of establishing a philosophical and social consensus (*Einverständnis*)[7], subsequently a key feature of Hülsen's thought.

Reinhold was the first post-Kantian thinker to refer to the possibility of reformulating Kant's philosophical standpoint while keeping its "spirit" intact. Critical philosophy requires, as later in Fichte's,

---

formulation of a reconciling solution to the knowledge-faith conflict rose by Friedrich Heinrich Jacobi's objections to Kant in the famous pantheism controversy. For a concise analysis of the letters, and of Reinhold's position regarding Jacobi's claims, see: PINKARD 2002, 90-9

[4]   See: FRANKS 2005, 215. The charge of unintelligibility was of course a serious objection to the enlightened character of Kant's philosophy.

[5]   See: REINHOLD 1978, XIII-IV

[6]   See: FRANKS 2005, 215

[7]   See: REINHOLD 1978, VI-VII

Schelling's, and Hülsen's thought, a stepping back from the "printed letter" of the *Kritik* by *normatively* while systematically establishing a ground of deduction.[8] Reinhold tried to accomplish this enterprise in his *Elementarphilosophie*.[9]

According to Reinhold, objections against an "improved" critical philosophy come from four different philosophical positions: skepticism, dogmatism, empiricism, and rationalism. Reinhold claimed that all of these parties, or "sects", share a common object of inquiry: philosophical truth, though *unaware* they make half-true/half-false systematic assertions regarding the *universal* character of this truth.[10] Consequently, each party gains only a *partial* or *unilateral* insight into their common object of inquiry.[11]

Den Grundsätzen aller andern Partheyen, der seinigen ausgenommen, Allgemeingültigkeit absprechen, und seine Parthey für das einzig ächtphilosophische Publikum ansehen, setz wahrlich eben keinen Scharfsinn voraus. Wer sich von der unumstösslichen Wahrheit seiner Behauptung überzeugt hält, der braucht nur zu wissen, dass die Behauptung eines andern das Gegentheil der Seinigen ist, um dieselbe für falsch, und durch die Gründe seiner eigenen Behauptung für wiederlegt zuhalten.[12]

A philosophical dispute (*Streit*) or misunderstanding (*Missverständnis*) arises consequently among the opponent parties. None of the parties

---

[8]   See: HORSTMANN 1991, 47-8

[9]   The first phase of the *Elementarphilosophie* (the one that concerns us here) comprehends three major works: *Versuch einer neuen Theorie des menschlichen Vorstellungsvermögens* (1789), *Beiträge zur Berichtigung bisheriger Mißverständnisse der Philosophen* (vol. 1) (1790), and *Ueber das Fundament des philosophischen Wissens. Nebst einigen Erläuterungen über die Theorie des Vorstellungsvermögens* (1791). It furthermore includes an almost neglected part: *Ueber den Begrif der Geschihte der Philosophie. Eine akademische Vorlesung* (1791). I will discuss this essay in section 1.5.

[10]   As Frederik BEISER (1987, 227) comments, "without consciousness of the principles and procedures of transcendental reflection, we have no guarantee of the truth of the theory based upon them. We proceed in no less blind and dogmatic a fashion than the old metaphysicians."

[11]   See: REINHOLD 1963, 43

[12]   REINHOLD 1963, 125

can fully justify its basic claims; their partial or relative assertions provoke inevitably counter-assertions. Unilateralism, as Hülsen will later
hold, prevents any possible reconciliation. According to Reinhold,
what is lacking is an exclusive and universally accepted transcendental
ground of deduction. Only this will guarantee a full systematic determination or true derivative exhaustion of each partially true assertion.
It also will secure a rigorous removal of all undetermined inconsistencies, and so shed light on the ground of disputes. The establishment
of such a ground, Reinhold concludes, will end all partisan affiliation
by producing a universal philosophical consensus.[13] Hülsen, as we will
see, will learn this strategy and adapt it to his Fichtean standpoint.

Reinhold claims that the assertion of this ground presupposes a
study of the metaphysical nature of reason. For some of the litigant
factions reason's possession of such a capacity is an open question.[14]
For Reinhold however this is the main question (*Hauptfrage*, or *grosse
Frage*) that philosophy has to answer.[15] A rigorous *critically oriented
answer* has to provide the required ground. Reinhold confers a cardinal
importance to the correct formulation of philosophical questions, and
especially to the one mentioned above. The crucial reassertion of
critical philosophy depends on it.[16] From Reinhold Hülsen learned the
importance of determining reason's ability to ask and reply by making
a preliminary inquiry into the essence of questions and answers. Reinhold argues that one of the main reasons philosophers engage in
disputes is because they do not agree on the philosophical questions
that they have to ask. Lacking is a general awareness of the true sense
of the point of questioning (*Sinn der Fragpunkte*),[17] namely of the
decisive role that questions play in the orientation of philosophical

---

[13] See: REINHOLD 1963, 43-44, 142-43, and REINHOLD 2003, I 46-47
[14] See: REINHOLD 2003, I 164-65
[15] See: REINHOLD 2003, I 256. See also REINHOLD 1978: 12-3, and REINHOLD 1963,
     129. In *Ueber das Fundament*, Reinhold also refers to this question as reason's
     big problem (*grosen Problems*). See: REINHOLD 1978, 135
[16] See: REINHOLD 2003, I 247, and REINHOLD 1978, 13
[17] See: REINHOLD 1963, 8-9

thought.[18] All litigant factions formulate questions according to their own specific standards and arbitrary interests. Reinhold calls such non-critical questions, "disputing-questions" (*Streitfrage*).[19] Through them, the philosophical disputes persist, as they move philosophers away from the main question (*Hauptfrage*). Reinhold consequently warns the opponents of critical philosophy: *"Das Resultat aller eurer bisherigen Streitigkeiten war immer nur eine neue Streitfrage."* [20] Hülsen's later Fichtean characterization of all systems of philosophy as ascending self-posited answers that reason gives to the question about the possibility of metaphysics is an attempt to solve this problem systematically.[21]

---

[18] Note the following passage from *Ueber das Fundament*: "*Leibniz, Locke, Hume und Kant, die vier grösten neuern Schriftsteller, welche die Gründe des mensch-lichen und inbesondere des philosophischen Wissens, zum Gegenstand besonderer Untersuchungen gemacht haben, sind daher auch von der Frage über der Ur-sprung der Vorstellungen ausgegangen, und ihre Antworten auf diese Frage sind die eigentlichen Bestimmungsgründe ihrer Uberzeugung von der Natur, den Gränzen und letzten Gründen des philosophischen Wissens gewesen.*" REINHOLD 1978, 13

[19] See: REINHOLD 1963, 140

[20] REINHOLD 2003, 247

[21] The fact that all disputing parties determine their concepts in an imprecise or arbitrary way is an additional cause behind quarrelling. The lack of a universally accepted ground of deduction, Reinhold claims, prevents a rigorous conceptual determination. What follows is mutual misunderstanding among partisan stand-points. According to Reinhold, Kant is also to blame for a similar conceptual imprecision. The disputes that spread around the truth and the meaning of the *Kritik* also rise in Reinhold's opinion due to the arbitrary interpretations that a significant number of Kant's contemporaries make of his ambiguous concepts. Reinhold concludes that quarrelling on the *Kritik* will not cease before it can be reformulated on a universally accepted ground of deduction, that is, converted into a rigorously determined philosophical theory [See: REINHOLD 2003, 1 231-2]. I however will not discuss this point, as it is no necessary precondition for understanding *Preisschrift*. HÜLSEN only tackles it in his 1797 *Philosophische Briefe an Hrn. v. Briest in Nennhausen. Erster Brief. Ueber Popularität in der Philosophie.*

1.3   The *Elementarphilosophie*: "Scientific" Systematicity

Reinhold believed that the reformulation of critical philosophy required a complete conceptual deduction of the meaning and the scope of the elements of consciousness that Kant took for granted in his *Kritik der reinen Vernunft*. Reinhold's main point is that Kant's vague concept of representation (*Vorstellung*), the fundamental element in human knowledge, is the reason for most disputes regarding the *Kritik*. In addition, Kant employs the concept of *Vorstellung* in an entirely new fashion pertaining to objects of cognition. Reinhold consequently demanded a renewed discussion of the transcendental act of representation.[22]

Reinhold's own epistemology influenced Hülsen's *Preisschrift* only indirectly; Hülsen was a strong supporter of Fichte's "improved" *Elementarphilosophie*. Reinhold's epistemology will however help us understand some aspects of his systematic approach to the history of philosophy (section 1.5), Hülsen's major topic of interest in the *Elementarphilosophie*. It also will help us understand Hülsen's initial interest in Reinhold as well as his subsequent shift to Fichte's standpoint (section 1.6).

Reinhold believed that the *Kritik* provides an insufficient ground of deduction for the transcendental elements involved in the theory of knowledge (*Erkenntnisslehre*). Also according to Reinhold, reason's practical part is ungrounded in the *Kritik*. Reinhold consequently called for a fundamental deductive grounding of both the theoretical and the practical faculties of reason (*Vernunftvermögen*).[23] According to Reinhold, Kant's basis of metaphysical knowledge is only propaedeutic. Only the establishment of a universal and integrative ground

---

[22]   See: REINHOLD 1963, 62-8, 48-50

[23]   REINHOLD 2003, I 233: "*Ich erkläre daher doch einmal, daß ich unter Elementarphilosphie das einzig mögliche System der Prinzipien, auf welche sowohl theoretische als praktische, sowohl formale als materiale Philosophie gebaut werden muß, verstehe. Daß es bisher keine solche Wissenschaft gegeben habe, ist Tatsache.*" For a sketch of Reinhold's complete program see the closing section of *Über den Begriff der Philosophie* in: REINHOLD 2003, I 62-5

of deduction will transform Kant's propaedeutic into an indisputable theory of the faculty of knowledge (*Erkenntnissvermögen*).[24] The question that Reinhold tries to answer in his grounding inquiry, as Kuno Fischer indicates, can be formulated as follows: How is the *Kritik* as a metaphysical system possible?[25]

The *Kritik's* lack of a universal grounding principle leads Reinhold to make a major methodological shift, the implications of which will be crucial for the subsequent achievements of German idealistic philosophy including *Preisschrift*. According to Reinhold, many philosophers, including Kant, derive their fundamental concepts in an inverted way.[26] Kant's concept of derivation, as Manfred Frank points out, means

[...] *etwas wie ›Rechtfertigung‹ von Geltungsansprüchen, aber nicht auf dem Wege einer syllogistischen Deduktion aus Definitionen und Prinzipien. [...] Was es im klassischen kantischen Falle zu rechtfertigen gilt, ist [...] die universelle Geltung der Kategorien für alle Anschauungen.*[27]

Reinhold objected that even Kant *inducted* his grounds by moving from given consequences. Critical philosophy required a *deductive* movement from a first universal ground to its consequences; a move that Hülsen endorsed strongly even after Schulze-Aenesidemus's objections to the *Elementarphilosophie,* and which explains his subsequent commitment to Fichte's *Wissenschaftslehre*. According to Wolffian terminology, Reinhold demanded a methodological shift from the *analytic* to the *synthetic* form of derivation.[28] It can be argued that Reinhold's intention was to return to the logical paradigm of the Cartesian-Wolffian school.[29] The synthetic shift enables a linear syllogistic-deductive de-

---

[24] See: REINHOLD 1978, 62-3
[25] See: FISCHER 2000, 24
[26] See: REINHOLD 1978, 5-6
[27] FRANK 1998, 157
[28] According to Joh. Ch. HOFFBAUER, "*Die sätze, auf welche der analytische Beweis in seinem Fortgange kommt, sind immer Prämissen, schon vorher aufgestellter Conclusionen, also Gründe derselben. Bey dem synthetischen Beweise verhält es sich umgekehrt. Dieser geht von den Prämissen zu den Conclusionen, von Gründen zu den Folgen fort.*" Cited in: FRANK 1998, 448
[29] See: FRANK 1998, 161

monstration that the *Kritik* lacks.[30] In the Cartesian-Wolffian tradition, a deduction designs

[...] *eine wohlgeformte Kette von Syllogismen, deren Prämisse eine universell geltende und* a priori *einsichtige Inferenzregel ist (,Wenn etwas ein x ist, dann ist es ein y') — und zwar möglichst so, daß sie die Conclusio unmittelbar aus sich hervorbringt, ohne Vermittlung eines (auf zusätzlicher Information beruhenden) Untersatzes, der womöglich empirisch wäre.*[31]

According to Reinhold, the synthetic reformulation of philosophy demanded (1) an original and universally accepted propositional principle (*allgemeingeltenden erster Grundsatz*); through it, philosophy can be (2) transformed into a complete and consistent discipline. (3) All its branches can be fully derived from this *Grundsatz* in a rigorous syllogistic way. (4) Thus, philosophy can first attain a formal and undisputed systematic unity. Those are, according to Reinhold, the basic conditions that philosophy has to supply to become critically grounded or "scientific",[32] the same basic criteria that Fichte will reformulate, and which Hülsen will embrace.

According to Reinhold, a *Grundsatz* is an indispensable requisite to any discipline, which like philosophy is supposed to assure universal and necessary knowledge. The only possible way to attain this sort of

---

[30] One of Reinhold's main objections to Kant was that his analytic deduction of the categories assures neither their rigorous completeness, nor their necessary triadic organization under the forms of quantity, quality, relation, and modality [See: REINHOLD 2003, I 215]. Regarding the terms "analytic" and "synthetic", Richard FINCHAM (2005, 301) reminds us that in his 1764 *Untersuchung über die Deutlichkeit der Grundsätze der natürlichen Theologie und der Moral*, "[...] Kant himself employs these terms to describe the same distinction. However, he clearly believes that the analytic method is the correct procedure of all philosophy, whereas the synthetic method describes the correct procedure of mathematics."

[31] FRANK 1998, 161. Martin Bondeli's studies show that apart from the linear syllogistic method, Reinhold resorted in *Beiträge vol. 1* to a parallel, though not entirely acknowledged method of circular inference. This method only attained importance in the opening essay of *Beiträge vol. 2*, a work that Hülsen will reject. For Reinhold's parallel methods of inference see: BONDELI 1995, 108-53

[32] See: REINHOLD 2003, I 82-4

knowledge is through thinking or judging. Hence, what philosophy demands at its ground is a propositional expression. *A Grundsatz* is for Reinhold an original, universal and certain proposition capable of formally determining or *a priori* deriving other subordinated propositions. *The Grundsatz* cannot be dependent, or determined by any other higher proposition. It has to supply the first unquestioned link in the chain of deductions. Hence, it cannot attain its certainty from any other principle but only from itself. It has to be self-certain. The original and exclusive character of *The Grundsatz* should prevent philosophy from being established on ungrounded propositions. *The Grundsatz* endows philosophy with a necessary formally monistic and autonomous character. Subordinated propositions ought not be originally contained in it. Its content also is not dependent on subordinated propositions. Only *The Grundsatz* determines all ensuing necessary logical (syllogistic) interconnections. Through *The Grundsatz*, all propositions obtain a certain, necessary and unifying form. In addition, this procedure avoids all arbitrary (and disputed) propositional interrelations.[33] Reinhold concludes:

Indem er [i.e., The *Grundsatz*] *durch die ihm zunächst untergeordneten Grundsätze, deren Notwendigkeit einzig in ihm gegründet ist, der mittelbare Grund der Notwendigkeit aller übrigen ist; so verdankt ihm das ganze Gebäude der Wissenschaft, das nur durch ihn systematisch wird, seine ganze Festigkeit, die nur durch den durchgängigen Zusammenhang aller Sätze, und durch Zurückführung aller auf Einen möglich ist.*[34]

Such *A Grundsatz* must propositionally express an undisputed and self-certain principle. Originality must exempt this principle from any prior logical derivation. *The Grundsatz* must not only supply the propositional expression of a *universally valid (allgemeingültiges)* or true principle; it should express a *clearly transparent* and therefore *universally accepted (allgemeingeltendes)* principle.[35] A key condition to

---

[33] See: REINHOLD 2003, I 82-4
[34] REINHOLD 2003, I 84
[35] According to REINHOLD (1963, 71) the following is the case: "*Das allgemeingeltende Princip in der Philosophie unterscheidet sich von dem Allgemeingültigen*

attain universal acceptance is that the principle in question is immediately self-grounded. Paul Franks summarizes Reinhold's self-grounding criteria:

First, the first principle must be "self-explanatory": it (or rather its subject matter) must provide itself with its own *ontic ground*, the reason why it is the way it is. Second, the first principle must be self-evident: it must provide itself with its own *epistemic ground* or reason for being believed, without relying inferentially on the evidence of some other truth. Third, the first principle must be "self-determining": it must provide its own *semantic ground* or introduce its own terms clearly and unequivocally, without relying on prior definitions.[36]

Reinhold insists that only an unquestionable "fact of consciousness" (*Tatsache des Bewustseyns*) can fulfil these criteria and provide universally accepted validity.[37] Reinhold argues that even the most extremist sceptic opponent cannot deny the factual existence of consciousness:

Der Grund, auf welchen die neue Theorie angeführt werden konnte und mußte, besteht allein aus dem bey allen Menschen nach einerley Grundgesetzen wirkenden BEWUSTSEYN, *und dem, was unmittelbar aus demselben erfolgt und von allen Denkenden wirklich eingeräumt wird.*[38]

---

    dadurch, daß es nicht nur, wie dieses, von jedem der es versteht als wahr befunden, sondern auch von jedem gesunden und philosophirenden Kopfe **wirklich** *verstanden wird.*" [my bold]

[36] FRANKS 2005, 229. Frederik BEISER (1987, 245) comments that "Reinhold draws an important conclusion about the nature of the first principle. Namely, it cannot be a logical formula, concept, or definition. All conceptualization or definition destroys immediate truth, for it introduces the possibility of mistakes and conflicting interpretations about phenomenon to be explained or defined."

[37] As FRANKS (1997, 318) explains, the word "'*Tatsache*' was not an ordinary German world in the late eighteen century, although it has become one since. Instead, '*Tatsache*' was a philosophical term introduced in 1756 by J. J. Spalding to translate one of the central terms of Bishop Butler's Analogy: 'matter of fact'. This term carried with it a legal background and entered German in the context of Enlightenment theology. A *Tatsache* was a deed or occurrence whose actuality was not inductively or deductively demonstrable but was nevertheless well-established on the basis of reliable testimony."

[38] REINHOLD 1963, 66

Facticity is for Reinhold the feature that "immunizes" consciousness from being inferential, both inductively and deductively; it assures its *immediateness,* the condition required to determine the ontic, epistemic, and semantic self-evident character demanded by a first principle of philosophy. It however should be noted that the facticity that Reinhold has in mind is not an empirical, but a *transcendental facticity.*

For Reinhold, consciousness or knowledge is the result of a complex process. It synthesizes the two foundational branches that the *Kritik* left ungrounded: intuition and thought. The fact of consciousness supplies these branches with a universal synthetic ground. Reinhold argues that *The Grundsatz* has to express that which furnishes consciousness with its *spontaneous* possibility; that which Kant integrally presupposed but did not explain. This requires an elemental analysis of the faculty of representation (*Vorstellungsvermögen*); for what can be *really* cognisable, presupposes the active possibility of being represented.

According to Reinhold, the original act of representation is comprised of a *spontaneous-representing* (*Vorstellendes*) and a *receptive-represented* (*Vorgestelltes*) component. These two are distinguished in consciousness from the form of representation (*Vorstellung*) that contains and relates them. Reinhold argues that reflection on the fact of consciousness immediately confirms the original and necessary character of representation. Analysis of this act opens the road to the propositional version of the reconciling *allgemeingeltende Princip.*[39] Reinhold puts the fact of consciousness in the following propositional form: "*Die Vorstellung wird im Bewustseyn vom Vorgestellten und Vorstellenden unterscheiden und auf beyde bezogen*".[40]

---

[39] See: REINHOLD 1963, 190, 200

[40] REINHOLD 2003, I 99. Reinhold's focus on representation as the ground of philosophical consensus is not accidental. As Paul FRANKS pointed out, for Reinhold the conflict of pre-Kantian philosophy is a quarrel between rationalist supporters of inborn ideas (Leibnizians) and empiricist supporters of sense-impressions (Lockians). Representation is a universal *mediating concept;* it fuses Leibnizian *a priority* and Lockian *a posteriority,* namely the partial true insights gained by each one of these parties. Representation is aimed at grounding the Kantian thesis that empirical objects of cognition are representations grounded

Reinhold names it the "proposition of consciousness" (*Satz des Bewusstseins*). It constitutes *The Grundsatz* of all philosophy. The proposition of consciousness provides the *Kritik* with the synthetic foundation that it lacks. It is the resulting propositional expression of the original pre-cognitive act of representation, which enables the subsequent systematic syllogistic grounding of the theory of consciousness (*Erkenntnisslehre*), the remaining part of the system of knowledge. As philosophy's original principle, the proposition of consciousness determines the entire spectrum of epistemic states. All concrete cognitive states relate to it as particular derivative modifications. According to Reinhold:

Dieser Satz gilt allgemein, sobald er verstanden wird, und er wird verstanden, sobald er mit Reflexion gedacht wird; indem durch denselben nichts behauptet wird, als die Handlung die im Bewustseyn vorgeht, und die jeder durch Reflexion über dasselbe unmittelbar als wirklich anerkennt. Jeder weiß, daß er das Objekt seiner Vorstellung von der Vorstellung selbst, und vom Subjekte unterscheidet, und dieselbe Vorstellung sich, d.h. dem Subjekte sowohl, in wie ferne er sich dasselbe als das Vorstellende denkt, beimesse, daß heißt, daß er die Vorstellung auf Subjekt und Objekt beziehe.[41]

Reinhold holds that the fact expressed in the proposition of consciousness is not an *empiric fact*. It is neither a product of inner or of outer experience. Its disclosure depends on personal reflection.[42] This proposition emerges immediately as the *ontic* or *material* expression of a *pre-*

---

on things-in-themselves, and settle the quarrel between skeptics and dogmatists, and between empiricists and rationalists. See: FRANKS 2005, 215-6

[41] REINHOLD 2003, I 99

[42] Reinhold was here inconsistent. Personal reflection transforms *The Grundsatz* into a derived product of self-consciousness. Reinhold undermined the original status of his first principle. This also shows, as Richard FINCHAM (2005, 306) indicates, "[...] that the dichotomy of analytic and synthetic methods may be a false one. For one could argue that [...] the Elementarphilosophie involves some kind of 'analytic' component, insofar as the 'proposition of consciousness' *qua* proposition is not something of which we are immediately aware, but rather a 'truth' which we ascertain through a process of reflection upon our qualitatively diverse conscious states."

cognitive transcendental fact.[43] In this context, Bernhard Mensen pointed out, Reinhold made an important contribution: he insisted on the *material* character of *The Grundsatz.*[44]

The proposition of consciousness gives philosophy an unquestionable ground of assertion. It expresses the original pre-cognitive act that furnishes consciousness with its possibility. It consequently functions as consciousness' most extensive transcendental genus (*Gattung*). All particular forms of representation relate to it as its specific subsumed species (*Arten*). The specific differences that define each one of these species are not originally contained in the genus. The genus is responsible for their logical systematic integration. Among these particular forms of representation, there are sensations, perceptions, thoughts, concepts, ideas, etc. As specific or narrower transcendental conditions of the empiric process of cognition, they express different derived kinds of possible interconnections between the subject and the object.[45] Both subject and object are neither transcendent to the process of representation, nor originally contained in it. Their possibilities emerge through deduction as two necessary moments in the theory of representation.[46]

---

[43] Nikolai HARTMANN (1960, 10) clarifies: "*Das vorstellende Bewußtsein aber weiß unmittelbar sowohl um diesen Unterschied als um diese Zusammengehörigkeit. Das heißt aber, der Satz des Bewußtseins ist ein selbstverständlicher, in sich selbst evidenter Satz. Er ist in der einfachen Tatsache des Bewußtseins gegeben.*"

[44] A distinctive feature of *The Grundsatz*, Mensen comments, is that it does not express a mere *formal* proposition as Leibniz's logical law of contradiction (*Satz des Widerspruch*) does. [See: MENSEN 1974, 124] REINHOLD (2003, I, 102-3) maintains that "*ihn* [i.e., *The Grundsatz*] **wirklich** *jedermann verstehen muß, der sich durch ihn nicht den bloßen Satz des Bewustseins und folglich kein Philosophisches Theorem über Objekte, die Vorstellung, und das Vorstellende denkt, welches freilich der Satz an sich nicht verhindern kann. Ich nenne ihn allgemeingeltend nur in wieferne er das Bewustsein ausdrückt*". [my bold].

[45] See: REINHOLD 1963, 195-220

[46] As Frederik BEISER (1987, 251) comments, "A theory of representation goes seriously astray, Reinhold insists, if it attempts to determine the nature of representation from subject and object. We know the subject and object only from the representations that we have of them, so that to infer the nature of representation

Reinhold's next derives the theory of knowledge (*Erkenntnisslehre*) from the original act of representation. He shows how the transcendental elements that the *Kritik* left undetermined relate to the precognitive act expressed in the proposition of consciousness. For Reinhold the grounding of this part impels a derivation of the transcendental mechanism of representation embodied in the faculty of representation.[47] Subsequently, Reinhold derives the faculty of knowledge (*Erkenntnißvermögen*), the instance that exhausts the system of philosophy. In this way, Kant's propaedeutic gains its final synthetic ground. I however will not discuss Reinhold's epistemology in detail, as it is not necessary precondition for the understanding of Hülsen's system.

1.4 The *Elementarphilosophie*: a "Popular" and Pedagogic Discipline

The *Preisschrift* should be interpreted as a philosophy of education. Hülsen's major purpose is to promote and enable a moral improvement of the human species. What is presupposed in Hülsen's pedagogic position is that both a universally recognized philosophy and the ensuing consensual withdrawal from the sphere of partisan disputes are results of a personal, independent, and directly accessible self-conscious portraying insight into the autonomous nature of the human spirit. Reinhold's *Elementarphilosophie*, as we shall see in this section, is where Hülsen seems to have learned some of his practical stances.

---

from the nature of subject and object is to put the less certain and mediately known before the more certain and immediately known. Further, knowledge of the subject and the object consists in distinct class of representations, and these cannot be sufficient for explaining the concept of representation in general, which is not reducible to this or that species of representation."

[47] Reinhold 2003, I 119: "*Das Vorstellungsvermögen ist dasjenige, wodurch die bloße Vorstellung, das heißt, was sich im Bewußtsein auf Objekt und Subjekt beziehen läßt, aber von beiden unterschieden wird, möglich ist, und was in der Ursache der Vorstellung d.h. in demjenigen, welches den Grund der Wirklichkeit einer Vorstellung enthält, vor aller Vorstellung vorhanden sein muß.*"

According to Reinhold, the *Satz des Bewusstseyns* emerges immediately as a necessary propositional expression through a personal act of self-reflection on the fact of consciousness. This intimate act confers the proposition of consciousness *direct accessibility* and *real evidence*, and hence *universal acceptance*.[48] Karl Ameriks suggests that originally Reinhold developed his concept of certainty independently of any rigorous epistemological inquiry. What Reinhold demanded, this commentator holds, is an express *universally accepted certainty available not only to philosophers, but to the great mass*.[49] Ameriks claims that this personalised strategy enables Reinhold to make philosophical knowledge concrete, and bring it into direct independent relation (at least in principle) with what people already implicitly believe (common sense). In this specific sense, Ameriks concludes, Reinhold's system attempts to achieve "popularity".[50] Hülsen will follow a similar independent "popularizing" strategy. Fichte's *Wissenschaftslehre* will help him rearticulate and stress Reinhold's combination of personal insight and universally recognized systematicity by deducing first the particularized or self-reflecting nature of reason, and by identifying next the spiritual vocations of "man" and the "philosopher".

Reinhold's position endorses his strong commitment to the *Aufklärung*. The essential goal of its reforms was to give common people the possibility of determining themselves independently through rationality, and thus achieve *universal autonomy* by freeing themselves from the heteronomic power of natural forces and traditional authorities.[51] Reinhold promotes this practical "spirit" of the Enlightenment through the immediately certain, universally recognized, and "popular" character that his fundamental "scientific" claim attains through *direct*

---

48 See: REINHOLD 2003 I, 99, 102-3
49 See: AMERIKS 2000, 96
50 See: AMERIKS 2000, 86. Reinhold's project should not be mistaken for the anti-systematic projects of some of his contemporary *Popularphilosophen* such as Feder or Nicolai. This party, whose arguments Reinhold emphatically rejected, denies the existence of universally accepted principles. For Reinhold's attitude to this propagated movement see: REINHOLD 1963, 133-4
51 See: AMERIKS 2005, XIV

personal self-reflection;[52] a strategy that Hülsen will attempt to follow. The purpose of Reinhold's grounding project was, as Ameriks holds, to replace

[...] methodological, ethical, religious, and political authoritarianism by a philosophy that can bring about and secure enlightened and universal self-determination.[53]

Here, the source of another major conviction of Hülsen is revealed. Reinhold ascribes to the self-thinker (*Selbstdenker*), an Enlightenment ideal who exclusively appealed to reason to determine his own independent stances, a key guiding role in the enabling and promotion of moral improvement. Self-thinkers were according to Reinhold only a minor sector of the community of scholars. However, only these *truly determined* self-thinkers, a position gained through progressive philosophical analysis, can be promoters of a personally enlightened "scientific" culture.[54] For they alone can gain full systematic insight into the *a priori*, *spontaneous*, and *universally autonomous* nature of the human spirit.[55] This direct *causal coincidence* between the *personal* theoretical account of the self-thinker and the true *a priori* system of knowledge enables that the former *self-determine* his practical stances *universally* and *independently*, or in Reinhold's language, that he be in self-agreement with his true spiritual nature.[56] Self-agreement alone is the key to leave

---

[52] In that respect, AMERIKS (2005, XIV) comments that from "the time of his earliest writings, the most distinctive feature of Reinhold's commitment to the Enlightenment was his insistence on finding a way to support social reform with a philosophy that met the double demand of being popular and systematic in the best sense."

[53] AMERIKS 2000, 87

[54] See: REINHOLD 1978, V-VI. See also: BONDELI 1995, 105

[55] As to the accounts of those non-entirely determined self-thinkers, REINHOLD (2003, I 46-7) explains: "*Jede bisherige Erklärung, die ein Selbstdenker über Philosophie aufgestellt hat, enthält etwas unstreitig Wahres, und ist nun in so ferne unrichtig, als sie unbestimmt ist, und zwar, als ihr ein wesentliches Merkmal fehlt, wodurch sich die Philosophie von allem, was nicht Philosophie ist, unterscheidet.*"

[56] As AMERIKS (2003, 87) adds, "the general reproach of the era, that Kant was insufficiently "scientific" tended to focus on two central systematic demands: that

behind all non-universal affiliations.[57] Only it assures a definitive withdrawal from the sphere of partisan disputes.[58] Self-determination emerges for Reinhold as the condition *sine qua non* for universal enlightened consensus; undoubtedly, a conviction that Hülsen will rework through Fichte's idealism.

Reinhold's *Elementarphilosophie* provides a faithful account of the *a priori* system of knowledge. Reinhold hence holds that a sound self-determined consensus will only take place after all self-thinkers independently agree on the universality of *The Grundsatz*.[59] As self-determined advocates of true Enlightenment, Reinhold infers, they are implicitly committed to his critically grounded approach. Hülsen will replace this with his historically augmented *Wissenschaftslehre*. — In Reinhold's words:

Das Problem der reinen Philosophie oder Wissenschaft des Absolutnotwendigen und Unveränderlichen würde seiner vornehmsten Bedingung nach aufgelöset sein, wenn es ein letztes Merkmal des Absolutnotwendigen und Unveränderlichen gäbe, worüber sich alle Selbstdenker vereinigen könnten und müßten.[60]

Reinhold ascribes a key instructive role to the self-determined self-thinker. His *Elementarphilosophie* is a sort of *philosophical education*, the enlightened purpose of which is to end up all possible partisan disputes and promote personal-universal self-determined consensus; a key pedagogic stance that Hülsen will improve and emulate. Reinhold summarizes this position later in 1794 in his *K. L. Reinhold an seine in*

---

philosophy provide for a) a refutation of skepticism and b) for a unity of theoretical and practical philosophy based on a clear general account of freedom. These are precisely the issues that Reinhold thought his *Elementarphilosophie* could solve at once by basing everything on a supposedly self-evident, ever-present, and absolutely spontaneous power of representation."

[57] See: REINHOLD 1963, 126, 128-9
[58] See: REINHOLD 1978, XV–XVII. See also: REINHOLD 2003, I XIII
[59] See: REINHOLD 2003, I 96-7
[60] REINHOLD 2003, I 81. As AMERIKS (2000, 123) comments, "Reinhold does not think that the mere existence of a philosophical community is sufficient for change. What is specifically required is a reorganized community of philosophers *qua Selbstdenker*, i.e., strong advocates of Critical philosophy."

Jena zurückgelassenen Zuhörer. According to Reinhold, it should be kept in mind that

[...] *sich nur von dieser Philosophie ohne Beynamen* [i.e., the *Elementar-philosophie*] *unter den redlich gesinnten Selbstdenkern diejenige Eintracht erwarten lasse, ohne welche dieselben, einander immer entgegenarbeitende, die Ihnen zukommende Lenkung der öffentlichen Überzeugung (opinion publique) sich selber vereiteln müssen — und durch welche ein Volk allein zu derjenigen bestimmten festen Überzeugung gelangen kann, die den Charakter der mit sich selbst einstimmigen gemeinschaftlichen Vernunft und des allgemeinen Willens hat.*[61]

Reinhold's promotion of universal consensus through direct and independent enlightened self-determination, as Fichte will argue, served a major end: the moral improvement of man through philosophy.[62] Hülsen will keep this commitment of the self-thinker throughout his short philosophical career.

---

[61] REINHOLD 1794, 320

[62] In a letter from April 22, 1799, Fichte praised Reinhold for his practical enlightened intentions. FICHTE (GA III-3, 327) wrote: "*Sie haben vom Anfange Ihrer philosophischen Schriftstellerei an eine praktische Wärme im Philosophieren gezeigt,* [...] *die Ihnen nicht aus der Kantischen, sondern aus Ihrer vorherigen philosophie kam, welche vielmehr Sie zur Kantischen, von der Sie sich einen besseren praktischen Effect versprechen, geleitet hat. Sie haben immer die Hoffnung gehegt, und hegen sie noch, die Menschen durch Philosophie zu bessern, und zu bekehren, sie über ihre Pflichten in diesem Leben, und über ihre Hoffnungen in jenen zu belehren.*"

1.5 The *Elementarphilosophie* and its Systematic Connection with the History of Philosophy

A distinctive feature of *Preisschrift* is the systematization of the history of philosophy. The systematic reconstruction of reason's history and its "concluding chapter" in particular, is Hülsen's way to justify the necessary emergence and the consensual overcoming of the morally adverse epoch of partisan disputes. As we shall see in this section, Reinhold's almost entirely forgotten approach to the history of philosophy is one of Hülsen's major sources.

Both German and Anglo-Saxon studies of Reinhold have not paid sufficient attention to the *systematic connection* of the *Elementarphilosophie* with the history of philosophy. Reinhold understands his own system as the last historical step of a *purposive philosophizing activity of reason* that ends the history of philosophy and enables the accomplishment of the true Copernican revolution. Reinhold discusses different aspects of this self-understanding in the writings of 1789-1791. The *Versuch* and *Beiträge vol.1* contain passing statements. The opening pages of *Ueber das Fundament* discuss a key aspect of it by introducing the theory of representation as the resulting product of a systematic history of philosophizing reason (*philosophierende Vernunft*). Reinhold explicitly develops this approach in a neglected and not republished essay from 1791: *Ueber den Begrif der Geschichte der Philosophie. Eine akademische Vorlesung.*[63] The complete picture of Reinhold's approach to the history of philosophy emerges only after the respective arguments of the *Versuch, Beiträge vol.1, Ueber das Fundament*, and *Ueber den Begrif* are methodically integrated.[64] The

---

[63] The essay appeared in print on May 1791 in the first issue of Georg Gustav Fülleborn's journal *Beyträge zur Geschichte der Philosophie*. By the time of the publication, Fülleborn, a distinguished student of Reinhold, was seriously committed to the *Elementarphilosophie*. The purpose of his journal was to introduce Reinhold's theory as the culminating event of the history of philosophy.

[64] This reconstructive task is only partially accomplished in Karl Ameriks' *Reinhold on Systematicity, popularity, and the Historical Turn; Reinhold, History,*

Elementarphilosophie so understood is the conclusive step of a rational process that ends the evolutionary course of philosophizing reason and enables the final historical articulation of the system of all knowledge. In addition, *Ueber den Begrif* fulfils another function; it reveals the role that the theory of representation plays in the construction of the rational history of philosophy.

Let us precede the discussion of the relevance for Hülsen of this almost forgotten aspect of Reinhold's system with a number of preiminary remarks. One can *prima facie* argue that Reinhold only attaches a minor importance to his approach to the history of philosophy. In his writings concerning the *Elementarphilosophie*, Reinhold devotes most of his efforts to the articulation of his critical system. Reinhold's claim that both the settlement of the philosophical disputes concerning Kant's *Kritik* and the grounding of morality, religion, political and civil right, etc., demand a synthetically grounded system of philosophy, may explain his concern on the task of articulation. His less developed preceding philosophical account of the rational historical process that preceded and contributed to the emergence of the *Elementarphilosophie* ought however not to be considered marginal. Reinhold justifies and complements the discussion of his system by commenting on the historical need of reforming critical philosophy. Reinhold in fact introduces his *Versuchschrift* by discussing the efforts made by pre-Kantian philosophers to determine the uncritical foundational premises (*Grundsätze*) of their respective systems. In *Beiträge vol.1* and in the *Fundamentschrift* in particular, the systems of Leibniz and Locke appear as constant points of reference. Paul Franks already pointed out the impact that the systematic efforts of these two thinkers had on Reinhold's *mediating-reconciling* position.[65]

---

and the Foundation of Philosophy; and in Marion HEINZ's *Untersuchungen zum Verhältnis von Geschichte und System der Philosophie in Reinholds Fundament-schrift*.

[65] See: FRANKS 2005, 215. For Reinhold's own account of the impact that the history of philosophy had on his own philosophical development, see: REINHOLD 1963, 51–68

There are additional reasons to think that Reinhold's presentation of his own philosophical theory as a product of a systematic history of philosophizing reason is not marginal. In the preface to the first edition of the *Kritik*, Kant already had introduced his own inquiry by implying the impact that the history of philosophy had on his philosophical position. Kant sketches a sort of rudimentary historical model in which his critical system emerges as an intermediate stance between dogmatism and skepticism.[66] Equally suggestive are the opening words of the last section of the *Kritik*, *"Die Geschichte der reinen Vernunft"*, in which Kant implies in passing the rational connection of his system with the preceding efforts made throughout the history of philosophy. Kant writes:

Dieser Titel steht nur hier, um eine Stelle zu bezeichnen, die im System übrig bleibt, und künftig ausgefüllet werden muß. Ich begnüge mich, aus einem bloß transzendentalen Gesichtspunkte, nämlich der Natur der reinen Vernunft, einen flüchtigen Blick auf das ganze der bisherigen Bearbeitung derselben zu werfen, welches freilich meinem Auge zwar Gebäude, aber nur in Ruinen vorstellt.[67]

Kant's statement that this part of his system is incomplete may have persuaded Reinhold to justify the history of philosophy as a project necessary to complete the normative grounding of the *Kritik*. Reinhold's approach to the history of philosophy provides, I hold, a supplementary perspective on the *rational historical background process* that enabled, conditioned, and justified the innovative articulation of the *Elementarphilosophie*. One therefore can think of it as a pertinent *systematic introduction* to his approach.[68]

---

[66] See KANT, *KrV* A IX–XXII: WW II, 12–19

[67] KANT, *KrV* A 852 = B 880: WW II, 709

[68] Manfred Frank also noted this rational-historical introductory character. For his short discussion, see: FRANK 1998, 449-50. Additional evidences of Reinhold's persisting interest in such an introductory history, though from a different systematic perspective can be found in *Über den Unterschied zwischen dem gesunden Verstande und der philosophierenden Vernunft in Rücksicht auf die Fundamente des durch beide möglichen Wissens*; the opening essay of *Beiträge vol. 2*. See: REINHOLD 2003, II 13, 17, 28. The 1795 *Was hat die Methaphysik seit Wolff und*

Hülsen learns from Reinhold that philosophy's historicity is the product of a rational activity. Reinhold contends that the given data of this history (philosophical systems) are derived outcomes of a productive activity of the understanding. Rational correlation is according to him an exclusive feature of the history of philosophy, an idea that Hülsen expands to all historical phenomena. History, in turn, is restricted to sensual determination. The correlation of events is established in it through the contingent unity of time.[69]

At first glance, Reinhold's concept of rational historicity seems to be problematic. In *Ueber den Begrif,* Reinhold claims that his philosophical theory of representation provides a universal explanation of the necessary *a priori* set of acts whereby the eternal nature of the human spirit apprehends its cognitive objects. Reinhold consequently argues that the object of all philosophical cognition is the rational being's *unchangeable* and *historically independent* spiritual nature[70], a position that Hülsen modifies by deducing a constitutive evolving nature of reason. Reinhold's argument suggests that an "historical turn", to use Karl Ameriks' words, is a systematic inconsistency. As Ameriks points out

The whole idea of the *Elementarphilosophie* and the project of a philosophy resting on a single transparent "*Grundsatz*" would seem to presume that philosophy can and should seek a ground with an ever accessible certainty that would make all historical considerations irrelevant and distracting.[71]

Reinhold's contribution to the history of philosophy has been overlooked because from the perspective of the subsequent achievements of critical philosophy, his concept of philosophical historicity, embodied

---

Leibniz gewonnen? is additional evidence of Reinhold's persisting interest in the history of philosophy. Neither *Beiträge vol. 2,* nor *Was hat die Metaphysik* influenced Hülsen.

[69] See: REINHOLD 1791, 12

[70] See: REINHOLD 1791, 12-6. Consider in addition the following passage from Beiträge vol.1: "*Nur durch den Charakter der Wissenschaft des Unveränderlichen wurde die Philosophie von der Geschichte, die auf das Verändliche eingeschränkt ist, unterschieden.*" REINHOLD 2003, 178

[71] AMERIKS 2004, 116

in what he calls philosophizing reason (*philosophierende Vernunft*), is a presupposed and unexplained notion. Reinhold discusses neither its transcendental possibility nor its mechanism of development. All one can possibly argue in Reinhold's favour is that he does not conceive his theory of representation in static terms. Knowledge in Reinhold's *Elementarphilosophie* is the product of a spontaneous activity of the human spirit. As Marion Heinz points out, historical development occurs in Reinhold's approach only at the level of philosophizing reason's necessary progressive analytic understanding of its own eternal transcendental laws.[72]

In the opening pages of *Ueber das Fundament* Reinhold introduces the history of philosophy as an ascendant or accumulative logical-historical process. Each developing stage of this process enables both the logical and the historical possibility of a subsequent step.[73] Reinhold argues that ongoing philosophizing activity results in a rectification of the very concept of philosophy.[74] Reinhold conceives his critical theory of representation as a result of this rational-historical activity. Hülsen will adapt this stance to his historically extended *Wissenschaftslehre*. — In Reinhold's own words:

Jeder weitere Fortschritt der philosophierenden Vernunft sezt die vorhergegangenen voraus, und ist nur durch sie möglich. Die in ihren Principien vollendete Philosophie geht nicht dem Geschäffte der philosophierenden Vernunft vorher, sondern ist das Produkt derselben.[75]

Philosophizing reason is the *universal* agent behind this *collective* introductory process. It historically manifests itself *exclusively* through the *particular self-determining positions* of different self-thinkers by formulating demands (*Forderungen*).[76] As Hülsen in *Preisschrift*, self-thinkers push philosophizing reason forward by progressively attempting to satisfy these historical demands. Reinhold writes:

---

[72] See: HEINZ 2002, 337
[73] See: HEINZ 2002, 339
[74] See: REINHOLD 1978, 8
[75] REINHOLD 1978, 9-10
[76] See: REINHOLD 1978, 62

Man ist darüber einig, daß die Philosophie ein Produkt des menschlichen Geistes ist, das nicht plötzlich, sondern nur nach und nach, und durch große Anstrengungen, durch vereinigte Arbeit vieler Selbstdenker, durch vielfältige mißlungene Versuche zu Stande kommen kann.[77]

Although Reinhold argues that the only concern of the history of philosophy is philosophy's "inherent fate", it is not clear in Reinhold's account how the course of history can potentially affect philosophizing reason's logical-historical development.[78] Still, Reinhold's formulation of the idea of philosophizing reason has a crucial importance for both the history of critical philosophy and for the understanding of *Preisschrift*. Reinhold is the precursor of the logical-historical approach to reason.

Throughout his writings, Reinhold employs the term philosophizing reason as referring to the historical development of philosophy. Reinhold paid full attention to the *self-enlightening* historical process only when he wrote the closing pages of *Ueber den Begrif* referring to his logical-historical agent as a self-knowing philosophizing reason (*sich selbst erkennende philosophierende Vernunft*).[79] For Reinhold, philosophy's development ends with the emergence of the *Elementarphilosophie*. Reinhold's system enables a final recognition and articulation of the eternal pure laws of reason, of its ultimate truth. It is free from all particular partisan limitations and historic eras.[80]

---

[77] REINHOLD 2003, I 22. Or as REINHOLD (2003, I, 78) alternatively puts it: "*Alles Philosophieren war von jeher ein allgemeines, fortwährendes, unaufhaltsames Bestreben der Selbstdenker, das Unveränderliche im Gebiete des Vorstellbaren von dem Veränderlichen zu unterscheiden, und durch bleibende unveränderliche Merkmale festzuhalten. Das letztere muß freilich so lange mißlingen als nicht der letzte vorstellbare Unterscheidungsgrund des Notwendigen vom Zufälligen entdeckt und auf ein allgemein Evidentes gegen alle Mißverständnisse gesichertes letztes Prinzip zurückgeführt ist.*"

[78] See: REINHOLD 1791, 27. Note for example Reinhold's statement that philosophizing reason can only emerge in the era of civil society, that is, in the transition from a natural state to a rational enlightened society. See: REINHOLD 1791, 35, and AMERIKS 2004, 135. The same statement can be found in: REINHOLD 2003, I 71

[79] See: REINHOLD 1791, 33

[80] See: AMERIKS 2004, 126

Wird nun das völlig bestimmte gemeinschaftliche Merkmal des Absolut-
notwendigen entdeckt; und läßt es sich auf einen allgemeingeltenden gegen
alles Mißverständnis gesicherten Grundsatz zurückführen, so hört von dieser
Zeit an die Veränderlichkeit der reinen Philosophie auf, oder es geht vielmehr
damit die Epoche an, wo reine Philosophie aufhört eine bloße Idee zu sein.[81]

Reinhold believed that through his formulation of the theory of representation, his introductory systematic approach to the history of philosophy was based on sound philosophical criteria. Reinhold explains
philosophy's historical course by purging it of all non-philosophical
contents:

Mein Kriterium ist der philosophische Sinn einer Vorstellungsart. Lässt irgend
ein Lehrsatz, der einem auch noch so berühmten Philosophen zugeschrieben
wird, durchaus keinen solchen Sinn zu, so gehört er gar nicht in das, was ich
für Geschichte der Philosophie halte. Lässt er aber einen solchen Sinn zu, so
gehört die Entwickelung desselben zu demjenigen, was ich die Form der
Geschichte der Philosophie nenne, weil ein solcher Lehrsatz nur durch einen
solchen Sinn zu einem tauglichen Stoffe dieser Wissenschaft wird.[82]

Reinhold's explanation excludes from the sphere of the history of
philosophy the histories of humanity, of sciences, of the personal lives
and opinions of the philosophers, etc.[83] His approach provides a rigorous concept for

[...] *der dargestellte Inbegrif der Veränderungen, welche die Wissenschaft*
des nothwendigen Zusammenhanges der Dinge von ihrer Enstehung bis auf
unsre Zeiten erfahren hat.[84]

In this way, Reinhold's position explains all previous philosophical
systems as derived products of a necessary logical-historical self-expli-
cative activity of reason. Hülsen will preserve the strict rational character of this argument by rearticulating and transforming it as the key to
all historical phenomena.

---

[81] REINHOLD 2003, 180
[82] REINHOLD 1791, 30-1
[83] See: REINHOLD 1791, 21-30
[84] REINHOLD 1791, 20

In *Ueber den Begrif*, Reinhold claims that all philosophizing activity is the product of an innate desire of the human spirit: the knowledge of "scientific" philosophy. This desire motivates philosophizing reason's historical development.[85] Philosophizing reason appears in the history of philosophy as striving necessarily after (1) the final recognition of critical truth and (2) the definitive establishment of universal consensus (suppression of all possible philosophical disputes); unfulfilled according to Hülsen if not supplemented by Fichte's practically self-grounded idealism.

Die wissenschaftliche Philosophie blos die Resultate eines Nachdenkens begreift, das die Erkenntnis der Wahrheit um ihrer Selbstwillen, das geistige Bedürfnis der Vernunft selbst, den beabsichtigten Zusammenhang der Dinge zum Zweck hat. [...] Die Geschichte der Philosophie [...] zeigt uns den menschlichen Geist, beschäftiget mit einem einzigen und bestimmten Zwecke, im bestreben sich über den Zusammenhang der Dinge Rechenschaft zu geben, und seine Begriffe von demselben zu erweitern und zu berichtigen.[86]

Reinhold fails to analyze the status of this goal of reason. It is clear however that it is not simply a regulative idea of reason. In fact, reason's goal in Reinhold's *Elementarphilosophie* is an achievable logical-historical objective. The fact that philosophizing reason sets itself the goal of historically pursuing true philosophy and consensus implies that its logical development is necessarily teleological. While *Ueber den Begrif* lacks a discussion of philosophizing reason's *modus operandi*, Reinhold briefly states in the opening pages of *Ueber das Fundament* that in pre-critical philosophy philosophizing reason seems to act by chance. Ignorance prevents it from uncovering the productive-teleological character of its own systematic activity. Notwithstanding, philosophizing reason advances by analyzing its own original nature. Still, all pre-critical philosophy is controversial for philosophizing rea-

---

[85] In the closing section of the *Versuch*, Reinhold argued that representation is set into motion by willing. Reinhold did not connect this possibility to philosophizing reason.

[86] REINHOLD 1791, 14, 22

son's attempts to reach true philosophy are imperfect.[87] According to Reinhold,

Während dieser Periode und bis zu jener Entdeckung [i. e., of the foundation] *muss die Vernunft durch jeden ihrer späteren Fortschritte für unzureichend er-klären, was sie durch den unmittelbar Vorhergegangen als zureichend befunden hat; bis dahin muss sie durch einzelne Selbstdenker verschiedene Lehrgebäude, die für ihre Urheber Wissenschaften, für die eigentliche Philosophie selbst aber blosse Hypothesen sind, aufstellen, in welchen* […] *Materialen für die künftige Wissenschaft gesammelt, und aus dem Rohen herausgearbeitet sind;* […].[88]

For Reinhold the correct formulation of philosophical questions is cru-cial. Questions not only orient philosophical thought; they also deter-mine philosophy's resulting answer-conclusions. In the opening pages of *Ueber das Fundament*, Reinhold argues that Leibniz, Locke, Hume and Kant (i.e., philosophizing reason) attempted to answer unsuccess-fully the same single question, namely how representation is possible.[89] Reinhold concludes that philosophizing reason's final attainment of its goal (critical philosophy) and the consequential ending of its necessary historical development are dependent on a prior "mysterious" agree-ment on the critical formulation of the above-mentioned question.

Die philosophierende Vernunft musste über diese Frage mit sich selbst einig werden, bevor sie an eine eigentlich wissenschatliche Philosophie durch Ent-deckung des letzten Grundes derselben denken konnte.[90]

Reinhold argued that pre-critical philosophers were not able to re-cognize fully the eternal pure laws of the human spirit. The inability to identify the transcendental mechanism of representation caused the philosophical disputes that motivated his reformulation of critical philosophy. From the definitive perspective of philosophizing reason,

---

[87] See: REINHOLD 1978, 10-1
[88] REINHOLD 1978, 11. See also: REINHOLD 1963, 143, and REINHOLD 2003, 113
[89] See: REINHOLD 1978, 13
[90] REINHOLD 1978, 13. Reinhold's argument is problematic. It is not clear how this preliminary agreement on critical questions can follow. If the correct for-mulation or determination by the parties is dependent on a shared universal ground, then Reinhold's argument is of course circular.

this inability means that prior to the necessary emergence of *The Grundsatz* philosophy evolved inevitably by attempting to articulate "unscientific" and controversial systems.[91] Reinhold associates philosophy's historical development with an incomplete concept of philosophy, an insight that Hülsen will develop through his deduction of a temporally evolving reason. Reinhold writes:

Zwar sehr oft, aber nichts weniger als jederzeit, sind Kurzsichtigkeit des Geistes, Unwissenheit, Übereilung, verblendende Leidenschaft usw. die Veranlassung solcher versteckter Mißverständnisse, welche das Gebiet der Philosophie bisher zu einem Kampfplatz gemacht haben, auf dem so viel gestritten, und so wenig ausgemacht worden ist. Es gibt Mißverständnisse unter den Philosophen, die schlechterdings auf die Rechnung der Philosophie selbst, oder wenn man lieber will, der Stufe der Entwicklung gehören, auf welcher sich die philosophierende Vernunft bei ihrem allmählichen Fortschritte befindet. Hierher zähle ich vor allen diejenigen, die ihren Grund im dem bisherigen leidigen Zustande, oder vielmehr gänzlichen Mangel der Elementarphilosophie, haben.[92]

According to Reinhold, the discovery of the *Elementarphilosophie* closes the epoch of partisan controversies. What characterizes this epoch is philosophizing reason's ascending from particular and arbitrarily established convictions to general grounding proofs. Due to the discovery of the theory of representation, philosophizing reason reaches a reconciling epoch of synthetic thought. Hülsen will develop this thought by relating it to Fichte's self-grounded standpoint.

[...] so muss die philosophierende Vernunft auf dem analytischen Wege noch einen Schritt weiter fortrücken, als sie in der Kritik der Vernunft gekommen ist; und dieser Schritt ist dann der letzte, den sie auf dem analytischen Wege zu höhern Principien thun kann. Durch ihn und nur durch ihn allein, ist das letzte und eigentliche Fundament der Philosophie entdeckt.[93]

According to Reinhold, Kant's *Kritik* paved the way for a new synthetic epoch in which an exhaustive revision of philosophy's grounding procedure was possible. Recognition of the ever-existing laws of the

---

[91] See: REINHOLD 2003, I 9
[92] REINHOLD 2003, I 232
[93] REINHOLD 1978, 72

human spirit replaces the purely logical analysis of pre-critical philosophy.[94] Analytic thought, and its resulting historical state of disputes, emerged in the systematic history of philosophy as a necessary introductory phase, which enables the definitive establishment of philosophy with the *Elementarphilosophie*. All historic partisan assertions lose their raison-d'être. What follows is universal philosophical consensus. Reinhold concludes that no mutual "enlightened" understanding should be possible prior to the historical securing of philosophy.[95] This resulting consensus has for Reinhold a crucial importance for the definitive grounding of morality, religion, political and civil right, etc. Hülsen will develop, reformulate, and incorporate these arguments in his own historically augmented *Wissenschaftslehre*.

The validation of the universally accepted (*allgemeingeltend*) character of philosophy enables that man become fully aware of his practical nature. This historical moment is determined as later on in *Preisschrift* by the evolutionary logic of philosophizing reason. Only after philosophy has been achieved, can the principles of practical reason appear under a universally accepted theoretical form. In this way, reason determines the possibility for the achievement of full moral potentiality.[96]

The discovery of this synthetic foundation makes the historical assertion of the universal (enlightened) spirit of critical philosophy possible. Reinhold consequently holds that the final accomplishment of Kant's Copernican revolution will take place only after philosophizing reason has reached the culminating evolutionary stage of the *Elementarphilosophie*.[97]

---

[94] See: REINHOLD 2003, I 91-2
[95] See: REINHOLD 1978, V–X
[96] See: HEINZ 2002, 343 [Hülsen not mentioned]
[97] See: REINHOLD 1978, XIV, 10, 12. Reinhold's focus on the securing of philosophy as an historical millstone confirms once again the enlightened spirit of his thought. As Werner SAUER comments, "Enlightenment is the realization of reason in history. Since the initially always dogmatic-naïve stance of reason leads unavoidably to antinomies, an antinomic situation must arise in the process of Enlightenment. And just as, in the narrower domain of theoretical thought, these antinomies provide the occasion of surmounting the dogmatic-naïve view

Philosophizing reason manifests itself exclusively through *particular* historical positions. Its ability to display its full practical potentiality, its enabling of enlightened *self-determined consensus,* is dependent on *personal insight* into the synthetically grounded system of knowledge. Only such an insight can assure an autonomous derivative correction and exhaustion of the partial grounds and concepts apprehended and coined by the disputing parties.

Sollten die neuen Principien wahrhaft allgemeingültig, und ihrer Natur nach dazu gemacht seyn allgemeingeltend zu werden, so müssten sie jeder bisherigen philosophischen Sekte volle Gerechtigkeit wiederfahren lassen, mit der grössten Bestimmtheit das Wahre, das in den respektiven Grundsätzen jeglichen Systems enthalten ist, in sich fassen, das Falsche ausschliessen, und dadurch ein System aufstellen, welches jedem Selbstdenker das, was er aus seinem Gesichtspunkte richtig gesehen hat, wieder finden liesse.[98]

Reinhold's position evinces that reason's entire pre-critical course of development was necessary to reach the logical-historical stage from which the *principle of consciousness,* the touchstone of the early *Elementarphilosophie,* can first emerge as transparent principle. Philosophy's pre-critical crises were necessary to pose the problem which Reinhold's system solves. As Karl Ameriks explains:

[...] Reinhold held that the principle [i.e., the principle of consciousness] has not only a critical historical *purpose* in providing the sole means for the possibility of a truly enlightened society, but it also itself requires a historical *foundation* in its mode of exposition. That is, the principle, must be presented in a way that makes clear how it alone can resolve the crises of modern philosophy that have led in the past to the endless seemingly unprogressive disputes about philosophy as a true science and about reason as a guide to life in general. This means that it must reconstruct a picture of what

---

in favour of the critical one, so too the Enlightenment will, with increasing insight into the peculiarity of its crisis, base itself on the critical concept of reason, thereby resolving its crisis and removing legitimation from the tendencies running counter to Enlightenment." Cited in: VON SCHÖNBORN 1999, 53

[98] REINHOLD 1963, 22-3

these crises hae been, so that it can be universally convincing in its argument for why a solution can finally appear imminent.[99]

Reinhold adresses this topic in the closing pages of *Ueber den Begrif.* Reinhold argues that the systematic reconstruction of the history of philosophy, i.e., the rational subsuming and overcoming of reason's pre-critical crises, demands a "philosophy without nicknames" (*eine Philosophie ohne Beynamen*), a rigorously determined concept. For the history of philosophy, Reinhold's *Elementarphilosophie* is a universal reconstructive (or interpretative) vehicle.

Hat er [i.e., the self-thinker] *es mit seiner Untersuchung des Vorstellungs-, Erkenntnis- und Begehrungs-Vermögens noch nicht so weit gebracht, sich über alle partheyen zu erheben; [...] so wird er die Philosopheme älterer und neuerer Zeiten, nicht nach den bisher verkannten allgemeingültigen Principien der allen Menschen gemeinschaftlichen Vernunft, sondern nach den aus unentwickelten Begriffen gezogenen schwankenden Grundsätzen einer einzelnen Secte beurtheilen; [...].*[100]

Reconstruction demands that this universal criterion be employed retrospectively in the analysis of all relevant logical-historical data. Prior to the historical securing of philosophy, no rigorous recognition of reason's inherent goal or of the inherent correlative character of its history is possible. Throughout this, all emerging systems appear to the observer as atomically given products. For this reason, Reinhold argues that only a truly determined self-thinker can perform the personal task of reconstruction. Only a self-determined self-thinker is familiar with the universal concept of philosophy.[101] Reinhold claims:

Ich halte daher die Bekanntschaft mit der Natur des menschlichen Vorstellungs-, Erkenntnis- und Begehrungs-Vermögens für eine [...] wesentliche Bedingung für das Studium der Geschichte der Philosophie [...].[102]

The task of reconstruction demands that *each single truly determined self-thinker* determine the proportional amount of truth contained in

---

[99] AMERIKS 2009, 119

[100] REINHOLD 1791, 35

[101] See: REINHOLD 1791, 32-3

[102] REINHOLD 1791, 34

each relevant historical product of philosophizing reason by contrast-
ing it with the pure concept of philosophy. Only in this way can the
systematic explanation of philosophizing reason's necessary introductory course achieve a rigorous rational meaning. The personal means
employed for the definitive logical location of each relevant analytic
point of view within this reconstructive model, is comparative critical
insight into the historical expression of the question-answer procedure
of philosophical thought. According to Reinhold,

[...] *wenn er selbst* [i.e., the self-thinker] *nicht weiss, was er über diese oder
jene Frage, die sich dieser oder jener Weltweise zu beantworten versuchte, zu
denken habe; wenn er nicht diejenige Antwort gefunden hat, welche die sich
selbst erkennende philosophierende Vernunft nicht aus dem einseitigen Ge-
sichtspuncte dieser oder jener Secte, sondern nach den Gesetzen der ursprünglichen Einrichtung des menschlichen Geistes ertheilen muss; so wird er die
Lehre, die er beurtheilt, nie verstehen, so wird er das Wahre, was sie neben dem
Falschen enthält, nie angeben, so wird er ihren vernünftigen Sinn nie
entdecken können.*[103]

Reinhold argues that only those works that mark historic epochs should
be contained in the history of philosophy,[104] those that provide an ex-
plicative model for all those significant evolutionary changes that the
theory of representation underwent from pre-critical times until the
present.[105] The systematic reconstruction of the history of philosophy
integrates all relevant analytic-relative standpoints as evolutionary stages
of a *single historically formulated synthetic philosophy.*[106] The full teleological character of philosophizing reason can appear to the self-thinker
only after the completion of the task of reconstruction. The *Elementarphilosophie* is that historical step in which philosophizing reason

---

[103] REINHOLD 1791, 33
[104] Reinhold does not explain how this division in epochs should be established. All
he argues is that the history of philosophy should only include those works that
caused substantial changes in the form of philosophy. See: REINHOLD 1791, 29
[105] REINHOLD 1791, 21, 33
[106] "[...] *den einzigen Gesichtspunkt* [...] *der alle verschiedenen vereinigt und das
Problem auflöset; bis dahin muss es Philosophieen, aber keine Philosophie, geben.*"
REINHOLD: 1978, 12. See also: REINHOLD 1963, 135-6

suppresses all possible contradictions and accomplishes a definitive and reconciling self-unity. The history of philosophy is completed at this point. Philosophizing reason's allegedly atomically given products (systems), reach an ultimate limit and achieve a definitive rational or universal "measurement".

Neither *Ueber den Begrif*, nor *Ueber das Fundament, Beiträge vol.1*, and the *Versuch* offer a reconstruction of a chapter of the history of philosophy. *Ueber den Begrif* provides only a sketch for the critical method of historical reconstruction. Nonetheless, Reinhold's concept of enlightened self-determined consensus is wider than what is ascribed to it by most scholars. Its attainment demands *personal understanding of the historical relation of philosophy to all its introductory analytic stages*. A personal articulation of the history of philosophy enables withdrawing fully from the sphere of partisan disputes. *Ueber den Begrif* has another unnoticed function in Reinhold's *Elementarphilosophie*. Its closing arguments reveal the key role, which the scientific theory of representation, will play in the systematic construction of the history of philosophy. Hülsen will reformulate and incorporate Reinhold's reconstructive criteria in his own historically augmented system.

1.6 The Crisis of the *Elementarphilosophie* and Hülsen's Shift to the *Wissenschaftslehre*

The multiple coincidences between *Preisschrift* and the *Elementarphilosophie* reveal Reinhold's crucial influence on Hülsen. Hülsen reformulated Reinhold's ideas and completed Fichte's rearticulating of the *Elementarphilosophie*. This section discusses the alleged causes behind Hülsen's shift to Fichte's *Wissenschaftslehre*.[107]

Not long after his arrival to Kiel Hülsen found that Reinhold's system had undergone a radical change. Already in 1792, the *Elementarphilosophie* was in deep crisis due to the rigorous objections that Carl

---

[107] Records of these causes are significantly small. My explanation is mainly based on speculation.

Immanuel Diez, one of Reinhold's students, raised in class during the lecturing of the *Elementarphilosophie*. According to Diez, there were serious methodical inconsistencies in Reinhold's synthetic mode of deduction. Reinhold himself reported to Johann Benjamin Erhard on June 18, 1792, that Diez's objections called for a basic reconstruction of his theory.

Ich sehe nun deutlich ein[,] das[s] in dem Ersten Theil der Fundamentallehre der Elementarphilosophie, Theoreme vorkommen[,] bey denen ich selbst hatte ausdrücklich zeigen sollen[,] daß sie nicht unmittelbar aus dem Satze des Bewußtseins[,] sondern nur vermittelst anderer Sätze[,] die ich in dieser Elementarlehre ohne Beweis als Aussprüche des sens[us] commun[is] aufstelle[,] erfolgen, und welche Sätze mir dann erst erweisliche Aussprüche der philosophierenden Vernunft werden können, wenn die übrigen Sätze als Beweisgrund aufgestellt und entwickelt sind. Z.E. das Theorem, daß der Stoff gegeben[,] die Form hervorgebracht[,] die Vorstellung erzeugt sey, wobey Selbstbewußtseyn und bewußtseyn der Selbstthätigkeit, das nicht im Bewußtseyn überhaupt liegt[,] vorausgesetzt wird. Allein jene Aussprüche des gemeinen Verstandes müssen schlechterdings lemmatisch in der Elementarphilosophie angenommen werden; da nur vom gemeinen Verstand zur philosophierenden Vernunft übergegangen werden kann; aber sie müssen durch die letztere in der Folge gerechtfertigt werden.

Das Fundament der Elementarphilosophie sind lauter Fakta des Bewußtseyns, unter denen das eine ⟨?⟩ [,] das den Satz des B.[ewußtseins] überhaupt ausdrückt[,] der allgemeinste und in sofern im System der erste ist. Die Elementarphilosophie stellt erst ⟨die [?]⟩ Principien der Philosophie auf, kann also von keinen solchen Principien ausgehen[,] sondern von blossen Thatsachen[,] die sich durch ihren Unterschied und Zusammenhang erläutern, und aus denen jene Principien alsdann von selbst hervorgehen.[108]

As Reinhold's letter confirms, in a revised version of the *Elementarphilosophie*, *The Grundsatz* must be kept to guarantee the systematic character of the transcendental mechanism of cognition. However, it no longer can fundamentally justify the entire system of philosophy; *The Grundsatz* losses its self-justificatory status. Diez has objected that to validate *The Grundsatz* a complete different mode of grounding

---

[108] Cited in: FRANK 1998, 398

(justification) is needed. Reinhold understood, as the letter to Erhard shows, that the system of philosophy could be grounded only through a preliminary analytic regress to *The Grundsatz* from pre-cognitive *facts* of consciousness or given *statements* of common sense (*Lemmata*).[109] It can be concluded with Richard Fincham that

prior to the *Systemkrise*, Reinhold is a proponent of the synthetic method insofar as he endeavours to justify the objective validity of our *a priori* possessions by means of their connection with a first principle, but, after the *Systemkreise*, he is a proponent of the analytic method, insofar as he argues that the objective validity of these *a priori* possessions must be justified by an analytic regress from common sense convictions.[110]

A close familiarity with Diez objections, and Reinhold's analytic shift, seem to have persuaded Hülsen to leave Kiel after one academic semester. As Rist's *Lebenserrinnerungen* confirm, Hülsen questioned Reinhold's new philosophical position.[111] Hülsen's rejection of the new *Elementarphilosophie* and his subsequent shift to the *Wissenschaftslehre* becomes even clearer from Fichte's letter to Christian Gottlob Voigt from November 8, 1795. As Fichte reported some time after Hülsen's departure from Kiel to Jena,

Hegekern, [i.e., Hülsen] *ein Mann von gesetzen Jahren, der schön längst seine Studien vollendet hatte, und Hofmeister war, wurde [durch] das unüberwindliche Streben, Einheit in sein Denken zu bringen, getrieben, alles zu verlaßen, und zuerst Reinhold, dann abermals mit wichtigen Aufopferungen, mich aufzusuchen. Er glaubt endlich diese Einheit gefunden zu haben; [...] Ich kenne ihn, seit ich in Jena bin, durch Briefe.*[112]

---

[109] See REINHOLD's opening essay in *Beiträge vol. 2: Über den Unterscheid zwischen dem gesunden Verstande und der philosophierenden Vernunft in Rücksicht auf die Fundamente des durch beide möglichen Wissens* in: REINHOLD 2003, II 7-48. See also: HENRICH 1991, 242-4

[110] FINCHAM 2005, 309

[111] "*mit Reinhold namentlich knüpfte sich ein herzliches Freundschaftsverhältnis-, doch keinem seine Lage und Bedürfnisse vertrauend, fand er [i.e., Hülsen] die größte Schwierigkeit, durch Unterricht und kleine litterarische Arbeiten nur den notdürftigsten Unterhalt zu gewinnen.*" Cited in: KRÄMER 2001, 49

[112] FICHTE, GA, III-2, 428

The new basic systematic status that Reinhold conferred to the *plurality* of *Lemmata,* and the elimination of his previous synthetic *monistic* mode of deduction,[113] was unacceptable for Hülsen, whose main demand was original systematic unity. The "improved" systematic position of Fichte, with whom Hülsen, as the passage reveals, corresponded since 1794 also determined his decision.[114]

The same analytic shift can be found in Reinhold's own *Preisschrift: Was hat die Metaphysik seit Wolff und Leibniz gewonnen?*[115] In *Preisschrift,* Reinhold abandons his previous focus on the history of philosophy as the rational systematic explanation of all those evolutionary changes that philosophy underwent from its pre-critical institution until its exhaustive formulation.[116] Reinhold alternatively offers an unsystematic or atomized explanation of the historical progress of metaphysics. Reinhold explains this progress in many alternative ways by adopting the particular criteria of different philosophical schools. The following statements would have seriously increased Hülsen's disillusion with Reinhold:

Jede dieser streitenden Partheien hat ihren eigenthümlichen Gesichtspunkt, aus welchem sie den Sinn der Frage: Was die Metephysik seit Leibniz und Wolff für Fortschritte gethan habe? ins Auge fassen muss. Es sind daher auch genau so viele und so verschiedene Antworten auf dieselbe möglich, als Partheien wirklich und denkbar sind. [...] Die verschiedensten Lehrbegriffe älterer und neuer Metaphysiker wurden ohne Streit, aber auch ohne Eintracht, neben einander hingestellt.[117]

---

[113] See: STAMM 1995, 20-1

[114] Regretfully, the entire Hülsen-Fichte correspondence is lost.

[115] See: SCHWAB/REINHOLD/ABICHT 1971, 171-254. Reinhold finished this essay on May 1795, and published it after Hülsen left Kiel. However, during Hülsen's stay at the local university (1794/5 winter semester), Reinhold delivered some lessons on the history of philosophy [see: KRÄMER 2001, 65]. It could be assumed that Reinhold presented his *Preisschrift* approach in class. Although there are no records of Hülsen's attendance to these lessons, it could be speculated (because of the topic) that he took part of them.

[116] See: REINHOLD 1791, 21, 33

[117] SCHWAB/REINHOLD/ABICHT 1971, 174, 177

Still Rist's report, Fichte's letter to Voigt, and Hülsen's *Preisschrift* show that Hülsen remained a strong supporter of the synthetic character of Reinhold's early *Elementarphilosophie*. Rejecting Reinhold's new approach, Hülsen shifted his allegiance to Fichte's *Wissenschaftslehre*, the only contemporary system that preserved, dramatically modified, Reinhold's synthetic method. Nonetheless, in many important ways Hülsen remained throughout his short career as much a student of Reinhold as a disciple of Fichte.

2. Fichte

2.1 Fichte's Influence

Diez's objections caused Reinhold to modify his *Elementarphilosophie* in ways unacceptable to Hülsen. Fichte's position enabled Hülsen to reformulate Reinhold's system in his own way. The *Wissenschaftslehre* allowed Hülsen to embrace the new Fichtean paradigm: self-determining knowledge as a personal self-grounded expression of a *holistic* activity of the will, and not as a grounded form of *monadic subjectivism*.[1] Fichte's position provided Hülsen with a new synthetic alternative capable of fusing and re-grounding morality and epistemology. It paved the way for a critical monism capable of transforming and expanding Reinhold's systematic approach to the history of philosophy: the main missing feature of Fichte's "improved" *Elementarphilosophie* and Hülsen's own contribution. Fichte influenced Hülsen in many other ways. The adoption of a circular or self-reflecting method of derivation, the personal concept of infinite practical striving, its importance for the consolidation of a critical "moral order" within the sphere of a purposively coordinated community, the strict primacy of "spirit" on "letter", the articulating concept of inherent systematic coherence, the ethical model of the scholar, etc, are perhaps the most preeminent examples of such influence.

2.2 The *Rezension des Aenesidemus*: the Origins of the *Wissenschaftslehre*

1792 was a crucial year for the *Elementarphilosophie*. Apart from the objections raised by Diez, Arthur Schopenhauer's brilliant teacher, Gottlob Ernst Schulze (1761-1833), challenged Reinhold's system in an

---

[1] This paradigm was Fichte's critical alternative to the skeptically refutable paradigm of the monadic-subjectivist tradition, which saw philosophical knowledge as the result of contemplation or speculation. See: BEISER 2002, 259

anonymously published essay entitled *Aenesidemus oder über die Fundamente der von dem Herrn Professor Reinhold in Jena gelieferten Elementar-Philosphie: Nebst einer Vertheidigung des Skepticismus gegen die Anmaassungen der Vernunftkritik.* Schulze objected to the systematic value of Reinhold's first principle; Schulze's skeptical criticism was also aimed at questioning the status of the thing-in-itself and the grounded human capacity for philosophical knowledge. It invalidated the systematic possibility of affirming the correspondence of an empirically represented object and its noumenal correlate.[2]

By the time Schulze's essay appeared in print, Johann Gottlieb Fichte (1762–1814) was one of the prominent emerging figures of the critical movement. His *Versuch einer Kritik aller Offenbarung* (1792) made him one of the emergent hopes of the new generation of post-Kantian thinkers. Schulze's skeptical criticism of Reinhold forced Fichte to reconsider his early critical convictions and rethink his own philosophical premises.[3] Fichte reacted to Schulze's criticism in *Rezension des Aenesidemus* (1793), a short analytic review that appeared in the *Allgemeine Literatur-Zeitung*. Fichte's essay not only opened a new chapter in the history of German philosophy; its sketch of a critical solution to Schulze's criticism of Reinhold reinforced Hülsen's conviction that the early position of his first philosophy teacher was insufficiently grounded.

---

[2] See: SCHULZE 1911, 18. Dieter HENRICH (2003, 149) summarizes Schulze's criticism of Kant and Reinhold: "According to Schulze [...] transcendental philosophy shows, with sufficient evidence, that we cannot avoid thinking the idea of a cause of sensations or of what is given in our sensations. We also cannot avoid thinking some idea of an origin of our representations, concepts, and so forth. From these unavoidable thoughts, however, we may draw no legitimate conclusion about the existence of things-in-themselves, or a faculty of representation, or of reason — that is, some specific entity in terms of which we can understand why representation really exists. In particular, we may not say that our knowledge depends on the faculty of reason, nor attribute the content of our knowledge to external causes."

[3] See FICHTE's letter to J. F. Flatt from November or December 1793 in: KABITZ 1968, 30-1*

Reinhold's early *Elementarphilosophie* demands that philosophy's foundation be both materially (real) and formally (logical) valid. The proposition of consciousness is Reinhold's formal expression of the self-evidently existing fact of consciousness.[4] Fichte agrees with Reinhold on the need of grounding philosophy on a first self-evident principle. Fichte argued however, that Schulze's criticism of the early *Elementar-philosophie* finds a serious inconsistency in Reinhold's attempt to ground philosophy on a fact of consciousness.

Der Satz des Bewußtseins, an die Spitze der gesamten Philosophie gestellt, gründet sich demnach auf empirische Selbstbeobachtung, und sagt allerdings eine Abstraktion aus. Freilich fühlt jeder, der diesen Satz wohl versteht, einen innern Widerstand, demselben bloß empirische Gültigkeit beizumessen. Das Gegenteil desselben läßt sich auch nicht einmal denken. Aber eben das deutet darauf hin, daß er sich noch auf etwas anderes gründen müsse als auf eine bloße Tatsache.[5]

Fichte argued that Reinhold's principle of consciousness does not achieve the required criterion of a universal or unconditionally self-grounded synthetic principle. For according to Fichte, it is actually arrived at *a posteriori* through abstraction from objectively determined self-observation. Fichte accordingly claimed that Reinhold's principle is only an empirically valid and subordinated principle. It depends on the concrete representational conditions of consciousness. Fichte denied that Reinhold's principle be ascribed the self-evident status of a first principle of philosophy. If its establishment depends on a *mediating act of abstraction*, then its immediate and "transparent" self-certainty must be discounted. Fichte so undermined Reinhold's claims for the immediate *epistemic* and *semantic* self-grounding nature of the principle of consciousness. Also the subordinated character of Reinhold's principle allows for the possibility of skeptical objections. It is possible to question the validity of the presupposed or unjustified conditions from which this principle is derived.[6] Schulze claimed that the proposition of

---

[4] See: REINHOLD 1978, 109-10
[5] FICHTE, GA I-2, 46
[6] See: HARTMANN 1960, 46

consciousness is a subordinated proposition; it presupposes the highest rule of judgment, i.e., the logical principle of contradiction.[7] Consequently, Schulze concluded that the proposition of consciousness could not qualify as the first principle of philosophy.[8] Paul Franks pointed out the radical importance of Fichte's response to Schulze's criticism of Reinhold:

First, no universal and necessary principle can be justified through abstraction, so the Principle can be at best inductive and probable. Second, no absolutely unconditioned condition can be arrived at through mere negation of certain conditions. Such a procedure can yield at best a relatively unconditioned that is **homogeneous** with that which it is supposed to condition. Even if the Principle of Consciousness is not spatiotemporally conditioned, it will still turn out to share some conditions with the empirical acts or states from which it is abstracted, and so it will not be fit to serve as their absolutely unconditioned first principle, for it will be incapable of stopping the regress [i.e., the effect caused by the transformation of the principle into a part or a member subjected to the governing laws of the series from which it is abstracted]. […] His [i.e., Reinhold's] underlying conception of the first principle is itself ambiguous. On the one hand, he conceives it as a principle that is self-explanatory and therefore heterogeneous to what it conditions. On the other hand, he conceives it as a principle that is self-evident through "empirical self-observation" and therefore homogeneous with what it conditions. Moreover, this ambiguity must infect his conception of the entire system because it infects the character of his transcendental arguments. For if the first principle is heterogeneous with what it conditions, then systematic derivations from it should **progress** from ground to grounded. But if the first principle is homogeneous with what it conditions, then systematic derivations from it should **regress** from grounded to ground. Reinhold is — to use an apt phrase — **systematically ambiguous**.[9]

---

[7] According to Fichte (GA 1-2, 43), Reinhold may have accepted Schulze's criticism but have probably argued that "*der Satz des Bewustseyns freylich unter dem Princip des Widerspruchs stehe, aber nicht als unter einem Grundsatze, durch den er bestimmt werde, sondern als unter einem Gesetze, dem er nicht widersprechen dürfe; [...]*."

[8] See: Fichte, GA 1-2, 43

[9] Franks 2005, 234-5. For the bracketed clarification, see: Franks 2005, 226-7

Systematic ambiguity, Reinhold's failure to distinguish the transcendental and the empirical uses of representation, and the conditions which his strategy presupposed and which Schulze could legitimately question, led Fichte to the conclusion that philosophy cannot be grounded on a fact (*Thatsache*).[10]

According to Reinhold's own standards, Fichte argued, the principle of consciousness could only assure an *a priori* formal-logical certainty.[11] Reinhold conceded that the content of his principle is empirically given: that it only emerges *a posteriori* through the affecting action of a thing-in-itself. This dependence according to Fichte confirms that the principle of consciousness cannot fulfill the criteria of a first principle of philosophy; it is not a *universally self-determined* principle. Ontologically, Reinhold's principle is materially deficient.

Despite the systematic inconsistencies caused by the thing-in-itself, Fichte, as later Hülsen, demanded that the first principle of philosophy fulfill this material-ontological condition. Fichte pointed out that the principle of consciousness admits that in the act of representation two original simultaneous procedures of the human spirit are synthesized: distinction and relation. Schulze's objection was that in Reinhold's system these two procedures are vaguely defined and left open to ambiguous interpretations. Fichte, agreeing with Schulze, concluded that Reinhold did not entirely explain the necessary transcendental conditions of this original synthesis of the human spirit.[12]

Fichte was well aware of the skeptical implications of Schulze's criticism. The non-determined character of the transcendental conditions suggests that the principle of consciousness is not an exhaustive principle; it is not knowledge's superior instance. Since representation is (1) a transcendental *synthetic* act, Fichte reasoned, its grounding possibility must comprehend (2) a *thetic* ("subjective") and (3) an *antithetic* ("objective") constituting elements whereby the simultaneous acts of distinction and relation be accomplished. According to Fichte,

---

[10] See: FICHTE, GA, I, 2, 46

[11] FICHTE, GA, I, 2, 46

[12] See: FICHTE, GA, I, 2, 44

Reinhold conceded that a noumenal or original subject and object must be logically presupposed to enable the immediate possibility of representation. Both subject and object must be thought of as indirectly present in consciousness under the forms of the representing subject and a represented object. According to Reinhold, knowledge of these two noumenal elements could be claimed only after their representation. In addition, Fichte contended that the original acts of distinguishing and relating be understood as two simultaneous procedures that point to the *pre-* and *non-representational* way in which the human spirit must be thought to act to produce the transcendental possibility of representation. In *Versuch* Reinhold acknowledged, though only in passing, the systematic requirement of these four original proto-conscious elements, namely a pre-representational (1) subject and (2) objet, as well as their simultaneous acts of (3) distinction and (4) relation.[13] Fichte notwithstanding claimed, perhaps unfairly, that Reinhold reserved the discussion of this intrinsic issue for some future time.[14] What Reinhold argues, Fichte quoted in *Rezension*, is that

die bloße Vorstellung sei unmittelbar, Subjekt und Objekt aber nur vermittelst der Beziehung jener auf diese im Bewußtsein vorhanden; denn dasjenige, was im Bewußtsein auf Objekt und Subjekt bezogen werde, müsse zwar nicht der Zeit, aber seiner Natur nach vor den Handlungen des Bezogenwerdens da sein, inwiefern nichts bezogen werden könne, wenn nichts vorhanden sei, das sich beziehen lasse.[15]

For Fichte, the reinstitution of the critical status of philosophy demanded a systematic explanation of the transcendental possibilities of the three original elements comprehended in the act of representation [thesis, anti-thesis, and synthesis (of distinction and relation)].[16] Fichte

---

[13] See: REINHOLD 1963, 323-4
[14] See: FICHTE, GA, I, 2, 45-8
[15] FICHTE, GA, I, 2, 48
[16] In a letter from July 2, 1795, FICHTE [GA, III, 2, 345] gave Reinhold the following explanation: "*Kant fragt nach dem Grunde der Einheit des mannigfaltigen im Nicht-Ich. Wie vereinigt ihr A. B. C. u.s.w. die auch schon gegeben sind, zur Einheit des Bewußtseyns? und auch Sie scheinen mir die Philosophie bei diesem Punkte aufzunehmen. [...] Ich glaube es braucht nur gesagt zu werden [...], daß*

suggested, however, that the new original self-explanatory principle of philosophy should not be a *subjectivist monadic* principle, but a *holistic act* of the human spirit (*Thathandlung*). This act enables a critical monistic derivation of the exhaustive possibility of the subjectivist-monadic mechanism of representation, and secures it from all possible skeptical attacks.[17] Reinhold and Fichte's focus on the original subject also differ in another substantial aspect. As Frederick Neuhouser comments,

[...] Fichte starts with the world Tatsache but replaces Sache ("thing") with Handlung ("act"), thereby expressing what will become the central point of his theory of the subject: The I is not to be understood as a thing but as an activity. Furthermore, the subject is a "Tat"-Handlung, an activity that is at the same time a deed, or fact. The point of joining Tat with Handlung to coin a [...] term for the subject is to suggest that the existence of the I, its facticity, stands in some intimate relation to its activity and, further, that it is this relation that essentially distinguishes a subject from a thing.[18]

Fichte believed that through a holistic *Thathandlung* "act-grounding" of Reinhold's subjectivist-monadic fact of consciousness, philosophy is provided with a certain and unitary ground for all possible syntheses of the human spirit, including its concrete modes of representation. Through his criticism of Reinhold, Fichte sketches the foundations of a new synthetically grounded philosophy (in the sense of the early *Elementarphilosophie*) the building blocks of which seem to be outlined, at least to some extent, by Reinhold himself.[19] Among Reinhold's students,

---

jene Frage eine höhere voraussetzt, die: Wie kommt ihr denn erst zu A. und zu B. und zu C.? Sie werden gegeben; das heißt doch wohl auf gut Teutsch: ihr wißt es nicht – Wohl: so lange ihr es noch nicht wißt, nicht von Philosophie, als einer Wißenschaft."

[17] Fichte's strategy provides evidence of Schulze's criticism of critical philosophy. For as Dieter HENRICH (2003, 151) explains, "What Schulze is suggesting can be conceived as a variety of philosophical phenomenalism, a method of description of consciousness that does not have any hidden implications regarding the explanation of consciousness."

[18] NEUHOUSER 1990, 106-7

[19] See: FRANKS 2005, 229

Hülsen was one of the first enthusiastic receptors of Fichte's new paradigm.

For Fichte, the only possible way to keep the validity of Reinhold's theory is through an *a priori* subordination or derivation of its *Grundsatz* from a new original self-explanatory principle. Fichte focuses on Reinhold's early *Elementarphilosophie* as a propaedeutic that calls for critical re-grounding and correction. Fichte's attempt will be to incorporate Reinhold's system into a more encompassing system: the *Wissenschaftslehre*.[20] One of Fichte's efforts will be to disambiguate Reinhold's transcendental-empirical equivocation. As Paul Franks holds, Fichte's fundamental purpose will be to determine the *Thathandlung* as

a uniquely necessary, absolute first principle, heterogeneous with everything empirical, yet with demonstrable actuality; and to progressively derive from this principle, in uniquely necessary steps, the *a priori* conditions of experience and its objects, while demonstrating that these conditions have actuality within experience.[21]

According to Fichte, the progressive deduction of the subjectivist-monadic levels of the system of knowledge demands an inquiry about the original proto-conscious acts of the human spirit. Fichte will first discuss this issue systematically in his 1794-5 *Grundlage der gesammten Wissenschaftslehre*, an essay which will influence Hülsen crucially.

2.3 The *Grundlage der gesammten Wissenschaftslehre*: the Nodal
  Points of Fichte's Correction of Reinhold

The purpose of Fichte's 1794-5 *Grundlage der gesammten Wissenschaftslehre* is to lay down the entire foundations of the Science of Knowledge. For Hülsen it paved the way for his expansion and rearticulating of Reinhold's approach to the history of philosophy. As during the last decades Fichte's *Grundlage* was the object of many

---

[20] See: FICHTE, GA, I, 2, 149, and BREAZEALE 1982, 812
[21] FRANKS 2005, 259

Anglo-Saxon and German scholarly studies, I will here discuss only those results of Fichte's correction of Reinhold which are relevant for the understanding of Hülsen's achievement.[22]

Fichte's holistic monism is committed to a first absolute principle: the *Thathandlung*. The self-reflectively grounded character thereof determines an immediate self-complementary fusion of the real and the ideal activities of the human spirit.[23] Thus, an original pattern is established for all that that will emerge as the immanently self-posited system of knowledge: no practical grounding element can exist without

---

[22] Scholars of Fichte do not agree on the nature of the foundations of the *Grundlage*. Although a full discussion of this topic transcends the limits of this monograph, a brief discussion is necessary for the understanding of Hülsen's logical-historical project. Some commentaries of Fichte's work such as those of Frederick Beiser and Alain Perrinjaquet ascribe to Fichte a moral foundational position. [See: BEISER 1992 and PERRINJAQUET 1994]. Others such as Tom Rockmore focus on Fichte's approach as a theoretically ungrounded system the foundations of which attain at best only a regulative status. [See: ROCKMORE 1994, 96-112]. I myself am in agreement with Paul Franks. This commentator characterizes Fichte's self-grounded standpoint as a practical-theoretical or rather real-ideal "holistic monism", which explains why Fichte strongly recommended the study of *Preisschrift* for understanding his own *Wissenschaftslehre*. Franks' position is that "holistic monism" should fulfill the following criteria: "*The Holistic requirement is that, in an adequate philosophical system, empirical items must be such that all their properties are determinable only within the context of a totality composed of other items and their properties. The Monistic requirement is that, in an adequate philosophical system, the absolute first principle must be immanent within the aforementioned totality, as its principle of unity. The two requirements together entail, first, that the absolute first principle both necessitates its derivatives and is impossible without them and, second, that between the principle and its derivatives, there can be no real distinctions.*" Franks 2005, 85-6

[23] According to Paul Franks, the separated presentation of the theoretical and the practical divisions of the *Grundlage* encourages a misreading of their self-complementary condition. [See: Franks 2005, 317]. Fichte characterizes these divisions only as "*logically distinguished, or rather reciprocally presupposing moments of the same single positing activity of the I.*" [See: FICHTE, GA, I, 2, 286]. For Fichte's later clarification of this aspect of the *Grundlage*, see: FICHTE, GA, IV, 2, 16-7

its theoretical derivatives and *vice versa*. This necessary nexus prevents real ensuing distinctions between grounding and grounded elements.

[1] The deduction of the *Grundsatz* or the *Thathandlung* proposition "I=I" or "I am", has a significant role in overcoming three major failings of Reinhold's early *Elementarphilosophie*: (1) the material deficiency of the principle of consciousness, (2) the idea of a noumenal subject presupposed by all representation, and (3) the concept of an immediately given certainty.

(1) Fichte argues that according to Reinhold's own standards the principle of consciousness can only assure an *a priori* formal-logical certainty. The *Thathandlung* is Fichte's holistic way to overcome this uncritical inconsistency. As an original onto-epistemic act, the *Thathandlung* establishes immediately and exhaustively the necessary proto-conscious material and formal features demanded by a true first principle of philosophy. According to Fichte, Reinhold unsuccessfully tried to have provided these universal features through the ambiguous dualistic interrelation of the formal *a priori* principle of consciousness, and the *a posteriori* evident factual materiality enabled by the thing-in-itself.

(2) Fichte's position plays an intrinsic role in the overcoming of Reinhold's uncritical argument about the presupposition of a noumenal subject as a necessary logical condition for all representation. Fichte refutes and develops Reinhold's thesis by showing that the Absolute I is not a transcendent entity. The concept "Absolute I" conceptualizes a holistic activity of immediate "self-awareness" that exists exclusively for, in and by itself. The Absolute I is not a *noumenal entity* or a *"thing"* at all; it is nothing but an *unconditional act of self-positing* in the sense explained earlier. What follows is that philosophy should be idealistic. For even the most elemental condition demanded by a critical epistemology, namely an unconditionally self-posited I, can only exist for itself.

(3) Through the *Thathandlung*, a necessary logical coincidence is established between the *universal-formal-factor-I* and the *universal-content-factor-I*. The original proto-conscious possibility of all certainty is thus established as an immediate act of connection of all possible

form and matter of cognition.[24] So the proposition expressing the form, the matter, and the necessary reciprocal presupposition of these two, namely the *Thathandlung* proposition "I = I" is an absolutely valid proposition.

Fichte and Reinhold's concept of immediate certainty differ in a significant way. Certainty in Fichte's *Wissenschaftslehre* is not *immediately given* as in Reinhold's early *Elementarphilosophie*. Instead, it is *immediately self-produced* or *self-derived* by the I as something exclusively valid for itself. In this way, Fichte gives a critical answer to one of his implicit *Programmschrift* objections to Reinhold, namely: how the certainty of the first principle of philosophy is itself established.[25] Immediate self-grounding frees Fichte's concept of certainty from previous logical determinations such as the law of contradiction (Schulze's objection to Reinhold); it secures the concept *Thathandlung* from possible skeptical objections.[26]

As *Preisschrift* shows, Fichte's original monistic act enabled Hülsen, who sought original unity of thought or presumably the holistic possibility of original systematic certainty, to not only distance himself from the objectionable position of Reinhold's principle of consciousness, but also to approach the disambiguated self-grounded standpoint of the *Wissenschaftslehre*.

[2] The three foundational acts of the *Wissenschaftslehre* (thesis, antithesis, and synthesis) provide the holistic grounds for all that that will emerge as the subjectivist-monadic system of knowledge.[27] Fichte's system, as Wayne Martin points out, abandons Reinhold's ideal of a

---

[24] See: FICHTE, GA, I, 2, 120-2

[25] See: FICHTE, GA, I, 2, 116

[26] See: PIPIN 2000, 149. According to Rolf-Peter HORSTMANN (2000, 120), Fichte "[...] wants to overcome skepticism by showing that most of the judgments that are subject to skeptical attacks have the status of indisputable truths because they all have in common the characteristic of certainty. Thus, what has to be done in order to refute skepticism is to dispute not skepticism's material claims but rather its assumption that there is a basis for doubt about the propositions it challenges."

[27] See: FICHTE, GA, I, 2, 272

single and self-evident starting point. Fichte's *Wissenschaftslehre* is not founded on a universal "transparent" principle such as the fact of consciousness. Instead, it is self-grounded on a set of three original acts of the Absolute I, namely self-positing (thesis), counter-positing (antithesis), and quantified limitation (synthesis). Nonetheless, these appear as three correlative moments of an original synthetic principle.[28] So Fichte's reformulation enables, though in an entirely new way adherence to the ideal of the first principle of Reinhold's early system.

Fichte's reformulation, as *Preisschrift* shows, enabled Hülsen, a persistent supporter of the synthetic character of Reinhold's early *Elementarphilosophie*, to find a *pure systematic Archimedean point* to reground and expand Reinhold's logical-historical insights.[29]

[3] For Fichte the quantified formal-subjective and material-objective agents involved in the foundational act of all finite knowledge are transcendental products of the self-reflecting activity of the imagination spontaneously, immanently, and synthetically counter-posited. Both this self-positing activity and its immanently self-posited products are opposed aspects of the same single practical-theoretical activity of the Absolute I. The self-reflective act of the imagination provides the transcendental ground of representation.[30] It emerges as (1) a synthetic act of the Absolute I whereby (2) an objective-material agent, a quantified Not-I, is counter-posited to (3) a subjective-formal agent, a quantified I. In this way, the possibility of the acts of distinction and relation that Reinhold presupposed in the act of representation is determined systematically. The quantified subject and object furnish the basic ground for the emergence of the representing subject and a represented object. The faculty of imagination lays down the transcendental foundation for a parallel spontaneous (active) and receptive (passive) activity of the subjective agent, another feature that Reinhold attributed to the faculty of representation. Through it, the principle of all individuation is furthermore established systematically.

---

[28] See: Martin 1997, 96
[29] On this point, I am partially indebt to Franz G. Nauen.
[30] FICHTE, GA, I, 2, 306-8, 311-4, 325-6, 330-8

The rational being emerges as a pure-empirical spiritual being, the holistic foundational moment of whom is absolute rationality.

Fichte's theory of the imagination enabled Hülsen to distance himself from Reinhold on two other questionable issues. (1) Fichte's theory lays down the foundations for an innovative transformation of reason into logical-historical self-reflecting agent embodied in the real-ideal figure of the subject. This is the systematic ground of Hülsen's holistically self-grounded alternative to Reinhold's vague concept of philosophizing reason. (2) Hülsen's transformation of the activity of the imagination also furnishes the ground for a historical self-reflecting capacity of the subject to strive after a regulative reconciliation of the pure (holistic) and the empirical (monadic) characters of the Absolute I. For Hülsen, the subject's spontaneous ability to self-determine himself autonomously is a necessary *constitutive feature* of his spiritual nature. For Reinhold self-determination was only the result of an *unexplained causal coincidence* between the personal independent theoretical account of the self-thinker and the true *a priori* system of knowledge.

The importance of all this for understanding Hülsen must be stressed. Hülsen's original contribution is his interpretative transformation of reason into a logical-historical imaginative agent. Regarding all the antecedent acts that integrate the system of all knowledge, Fichte and Hülsen are in complete agreement.

2.4 The Spiritual-Imaginative Dimension of the *Wissenschaftslehre*

The self-reflective activity demanded for the systematic articulation of the *Wissenschaftslehre* is personal. The only way possible to uncover the *timelessly accomplished* acts of the Absolute I is by repeating them personally through a *temporal-actualizing* series of correlative representing acts of the imagination. Philosophizing or rather the self-reflecting articulation of the system of all knowledge, is an activity that each single individual must *exclusively* do for himself.[31] Fichte wrote

---

[31] See: FICHTE, GA, II, 3, 325. Notice in addition the following passage from the Programschrift: "*Nun aber ist ja die Wissenschaftslehre selbst die Wissenschaft*

this in *Ueber den Unterschied des Geistes und Buchstabens in der Philosophie,* a series of lectures delivered in Jena on 1794.[32] These lectures were published only on 1800. It is more than probable that owing to his close friendship with Fichte, Hülsen was acquainted with their content when he wrote *Preisschrift.* Some specific aspects of these lectures demand a short discussion. They may have furnished the ground of one of Hülsen's central arguments: critical knowledge cannot be expressed through the printed letter.

In the opening section of *Ueber den Unterschied,* Fichte identifies the faculty of imagination, the spontaneous capability of self-reflection responsible for creating all epistemic contents, with the human spirit.[33] No philosophizing is possible without spirit, for

Diese Vorstellungen aber, über welche die Philosophie reflektiert werden soll, sind durch, u. vermittelst der bloßen abstraction noch nicht da; sie müßen erst, wenigstens zum Theil d.i. insofern in ihnen eine Anschauung enthalten ist, durch Einbildungskraft hervorgebracht werden. Dieses Vermögen der Einbildungskraft aber, besonders insofer es höhere, u. in der gewöhnlichen Erfahrung nicht vorkommende Bilder zum Bewußtseyn erhebt, heißt Geist. Ohne Geist ist demnach nicht einmal der Stoff der Philosophie möglich.[34]

No epistemic outcome can be divorced from the personal activity that brings it about. Such a hypothetic divorce causes what Fichte calls "philosophy by formula", namely a philosophy in which imaginative intuition or spirit is absent.[35] Fichte concludes:

Diese Gesinung, M. H. ist Philosophie, und sie ist die einige Philosophie. Nicht das, was in unserem Gedächtniße schwebt, nicht das, was in unsern Büchern gedruckt zu lesen ist, ist Philosphie; sondern das, was unsern Geist

---

von etwas; nicht aber dieses Etwas selbst. Mithin wäre dieselbe überhaupt mit allen ihren Sätzen Form eines gewissen vor derselben vorhandenen Gehaltes. [...] Das Object der Wissenschaftslehre ist nach allem das System des menschlichen Wissens. Dieses ist unabhängig von der Wissenschaft desselben vorhanden, wird aber durch sie in systematischer Form aufgestellt." FICHTE, GA, I, 2, 140

[32] See also Fichte's *Grundlage* statement in: FICHTE, GA, I, 2, 414-5
[33] See: FICHTE, GA, II, 3, 309
[34] FICHTE, GA, II, 3, 334
[35] See: FICHTE, GA, II, 3, 329-30

ergriffen, und umgeschaffen, u. in eine höhere geistige Ordnung der Dinge eingeführt hat, ist Philosphie. In uns, in uns muß die Philosophie seyn [...].[36]

Fichte develops this idea in a letter to Reinhold from July 2, 1795. According to Fichte, what the *Wissenschaftslehre* tries to communicate cannot be said nor grasped through discursive thought alone, but it demands personal intuition. The printed word only guides the reader to bring about the required inherent successive series of imaginative intuitions so that he can personally self-reflect on them and portray the system of all knowledge.[37] Accordingly, the exhaustive possibility of this system can be proved only through its actual spiritual articulation.[38] The *Wissenschaftslehre* demands that one "let words be words" and try instead to awake a series of necessary intuitions.[39] All philosophizing demands a spiritual activity without which any critical thought is possible. No text can convey this activity. Each single reader must supply it for himself while reading the text.[40] The standpoint of philosophy therefore is as it will be in Hülsen's *Preisschrift* a personal standpoint.

According to Fichte, the system of all knowledge emerges as a "pragmatic history of the human spirit" (*pragmatische Geschichte des menschlichen Geistes*).[41] Fichte employs this term as a synonymous of "transcendental deduction". It designates a *personal* systematic account of the transcendental acts whereby the human spirit produced the sys-

---

[36] FICHTE, GA, II, 3, 332-3

[37] As Steven Hoeltzel (2001, 44) reminds us, "[...] the philosopher begins by intending representations of the protodiscursive activities of the I. These are one and all representations of a spontaneous dynamism, but the acts of the mind invariably occur in determinate, law-governed ways, and therefore "present a system for any observer". Thus the reflecting philosopher should find that one representation — one represented act of the mind — necessarily gives way to a certain new representations, and no other, until the highest level of determinacy is reached: reflection grasps a representation of representational consciousness, structured as Reinhold's principle describes it."

[38] See: FICHTE, GA, I, 2, 119, 126

[39] See: FICHTE, GA, III, 2, 344

[40] See: FRANKS 1997, 312

[41] See: FICHTE, GA, I, 2, 146-7, 365

tem of knowledge.[42] Or rather, a *genetic* systematization of reason's *a priori* or timeless course of production of the different transcendental levels of this system to be exclusively self-determined *a posteriori* by personal self-conscious reflection (imagination/spirit).[43] Hülsen will fuse Fichte's bi-dimensional position in his own temporal-imaginative concept of rationality.[44]

2.5   The Systematic Fusion of Method and System of Knowledge

In Hülsen's *Preisschrift*, the logical-historical deduction of system re-produces the self-reflective steps taken by reason throughout its course of development. This fusion of deductive method and system of knowledge is another aspect of Fichte's overcoming of Reinhold adopted and augmented by Hülsen.

The object of inquiry of Fichte's *Wissenschaftslehre* is knowledge itself or rather its actual self-grounded possibility. Philosophizing demands that one proceed self-reflectively. The system of knowledge should be articulated in a *progressing circular* manner starting from its *Grundsatz*. Its deduction demands gradual ascension in thinking and self-reflection on the transcendental possibility of each performed thought. For Fichte and Hülsen the circularity of this method does not entail either an obstacle or an error as for Reinhold, for whom deduction is essentially linear. Since a circular method of deduction is unavoidable, Fichte argues, it should be openly acknowledged.[45]

---

[42]   See: BREAZEALE 2001, 23

[43]   See: BREAZEALE 2001b, 687, 693, 699

[44]   Fichte's distinction between spirit and letter in *Ueber den Unterschied* differs from the distinction made by Kant, Reinhold, and Fichte himself in the 1798 *Zweite Einleitung in die Wissenschaftslehre*. For in this early text Fichte focuses neither on the interconnected reading of philosophical texts according to the idea of the whole, nor on the "spirit" and the intention that individual passages may display. See: FICHTE, GA, I, 4, 231-2

[45]   See: FICHTE, GA, I, 2, 132-3

The intuitional self-reflection, first enabled by the faculty of imagination, emerges as the necessary ensuing part of the original analytic-synthetic method of deduction brought about by the self-excluding I and Not-I. With it, reflection ceases to be mainly inferential. The philosopher appears as a spectator of the imaginative products that he has gradually self-deduced for himself as well as of the self-positing I behind them. As Daniel Breazeale points out, the derivative method of Fichte's *Wissenschaftslehre* is a "mixed" method. For it combines analytic-synthetic logical inference, imaginative production, and self-reflective or rather pragmatic descriptive observation.[46]

Fichte's "mixed" method is crucial for the overcoming of another problem posed by Reinhold's standpoint. Fichte in the *Programm-schrift* objected to the syllogistic method of deduction of Reinhold's early *Elementarphilosophie*. Fichte criticized Reinhold for (1) omitting the discussion of the key systematic relation of the *Grundsatz* to it's *a priori* method of inference, as well as (2) for the spurious authority (*Befugniß*) of this method to derive the subordinated propositions of philosophy.[47] Fichte suggested that Reinhold used the syllogistic rule of logic in an arbitrary and thereby uncritical way. Fichte's "mixed" method provided a solution to these two major inconsistencies derived necessarily from the original proto-conscious set of acts of the Absolute I. Its unavoidable circular or self-reflective character enables that the system of all knowledge be articulated by reproducing the same genetic (correlative) acts accomplished by the Absolute I. Fichte's method is connected therefore transcendentally to its *Grundsatz*. The system of all knowledge can only be articulated by following a "mixed" method; only this disarms the objections of a possible skeptic opponent. What distinguishes Fichte's *Wissenschaftslehre,* and by extension, Hülsen's historically enlarged version from Reinhold's *Elementarphilosophie,* is its fusion of method and system of knowledge. Only by a "mixed" method can philosophy's propositions be determined critically.

---

[46] See: Breazeale 2001, 29
[47] See: Fichte, GA, I, 2, 116

2.6 The Qualitative Completeness of the *Wissenschaftslehre*

Hülsen holds that the *qualitative* logical-historical evolution of the system of knowledge, and of its inherently contained history of philosophy, is exhausted with the emergence of philosophy's distinctive self-conscious insight. This self-reflective act is *regressive.* Reason (or the Absolute I) reemerges through it as one's own original articulating point of departure. Self-consciousness reveals the impossibility of deriving additional transcendental or qualitative *progressive* instances of cognition from *The Grundsatz.* What for Fichte and Hülsen remains is for the rational being to achieve striving after a *quantitative* expansion of these exhaustive instances. For Fichte morality demands self-determination of all possible reality (Not-I); quantitative progress is the rational being's practical means to reach reason's *originally* and absolutely self-posited being. For Hülsen, the inexhaustible character of this being also compels an unending *logical-historical process of self-determining approximation.* Hülsen's position is therefore that the pragmatic portrayal of philosophy, the systematic articulating thereof, will yield full *qualitative completeness.* Hülsen's logically-historically augmented position tallies in this theoretical aspect with Fichte's own moral position, which Hülsen shared. Fichte's insight enabled Hülsen to complete his own critical reformulation of Reinhold's skeptically objectionable logical-historical views, provide them with a new inherent systematic coherence, and develop a history of philosophy to augment Fichte's *Wissenschaftslehre.*

In section "Four" of the *Programmschrift*, Fichte discusses the articulating criteria, which the *Wissenschaftslehre*, the pragmatic portrayal of the *a priori* system of all knowledge, has to fulfill. These criteria were of significant importance for enriching and consolidating Hülsen's historically expanded concept of systematic articulation. Fichte distinguishes between (1) negative and (2) positive criteria.

*Ein Grundsatz ist erschöpft, wenn ein vollständiges System auf demselben aufgebaut ist, d.i. wenn der Grundsatz nothwendig auf **alle** aufgestellten Sätze führt, und **alle** aufgestellten Sätze nothwendig wieder auf ihn* *zurückführen. Wenn kein Satz im ganzen System vorkommt, welcher wahr seyn kann, wenn der Grundsatz falsch ist — oder falsch, wenn der Grundsatz wahr ist, so ist dies der negative Beweis, dass kein Satz **zuviel** in das System aufgenommen worden; denn derjenige, der nicht in das System gehörte, würde wahr seyn können, wenn der Grundsatz falsch, — oder falsch, wenn auch der Grundsatz wahr wäre. Ist der Grundsatz gegeben, so müssen **alle** Sätze gegeben seyn; in ihm und durch ihn ist jeder einzelne gegeben. Es ist aus dem, was wir oben über die Verkettung der einzelnen Sätze in der Wissenschaftslehre gesagt haben, klar, dass diese Wissenschaft den angezeigten negativen Beweis unmittelbar in sich selbst und durch sich selbst führe. Durch ihn wird erwiesen, dass die Wissenschaft überhaupt **systematisch** sei, dass alle ihre Theile in einem einzigen Grundsatze zusammenhängen.*[48]

Fichte's method of deduction fulfils the negative logical proof demanded to ground the *Wissenschaftslehre* systematically. Its pragmatic (self-subsuming) condition assures (1) the rigorous necessary character, as well as (2) the exclusive gradual inclusion of each derived proposition. This conclusion applies to *Preisschrift*. Fichte's method is one of Hülsen's main sources. As to the required positive criteria, a point about which there is much confusion in scholarly literature Fichte writes that

*— Die Wissenschaft ist ein System, oder sie ist vollendet, wenn weiter kein Satz gefolgert werden kann: und dies giebt den positiven Beweis, dass kein Satz zu wenig in das System aufgenommen worden. Die Frage ist nur die: wann und unter welchen Bedingungen kann ein Satz weiter gefolgert werden; denn es ist klar, dass das bloss relative und negative Merkmal: **ich** sehe nicht was weiter folgen könne, nichts beweist. Es könnte wohl nach mir ein anderer kommen, welcher da, wo ich nichts sah, etwas sähe. Wir bedürfen eines positiven Merkmals zum Beweise, dass schlechthin und unbedingt nichts weiter gefolgert werden könne; und das konnte kein anderes seyn, als das, dass der Grundsatz selbst, von welchem wir ausgegangen wären, zugleich auch das letzte Resultat sey. Dann wäre klar, dass wir nicht weiter gehen könnten, ohne den Weg, den wir schon einmal gemacht, noch einmal zu machen. — Es wird sich bei einstiger Aufstellung der Wissenschaft zeigen, dass sie diesen Kreislauf wirklich vollendet, und den Forscher gerade bei dem*

---

[48] FICHTE, GA, I, 2, 130

Puncte verlässt, von welchem sie mit ihm ausging; dass sie also gleichfalls den zweiten positiven Beweis in sich selbst und durch sich selbst führt.[49]

Fichte's positive criterion is to exhaust the theoretical grounding of the system of knowledge by preventing *unconditionally* the possibility of further transcendental deduction. The closing of the deductive circle is not meant to determine the definitive logical certainty of the first principle of the *Wissenschaftslehre*.[50] Its *raison-d'être* is rather to provide a rigorous logical proof of the *inherent systematic coherence* or *consistency* of the system of philosophy, to establish an *inherent systematic identity* between its starting and concluding point. This identity assures the *deductive correctness* of system. Fichte claimed that the articulation of the *Wissenschaftslehre* closes the circle and provides the required positive proof. The *Wissenschaftslehre* has the ability to yield full qualitative theoretical completeness. By expanding this strategy, Hülsen derived from Fichte systematic benefits for his own historically augmented concerns.

The purpose of the theoretical division of the *Wissenschaftslehre* is to deduce the *transcendental possibility* behind the Absolute I's self-limiting of itself through a counter-posited quantified Not-I. The deduction of the faculty of imagination furnishes the ground of the first sensually represented object. The full discursive self-determination of this object demands an ascending self-subsuming series of imaginative self-reflections. This series is a pragmatic disclosure and portrayal of

---

[49] FICHTE, GA, I, 2, 130-1

[50] As Daniel BREAZEALE (1994, 51) comments, "one should not […] be misled by Fichte's remarks […] and […] conclude that, for all of his insistence upon the need for a self-evidently certain starting point, he actually anticipated the familiar Hegelian view that criticizes all claims to immediate certainty and that treats the truth of the starting point as something that can be established **only** as a "result" of the system. However attractive one may find such a position to be, it is not Fichte's." [my bold]. *The Grundsatz* is a postulate, namely the propositional expression of a principle that is not susceptible to logical proof. *The Grundsatz* represents a meta-logical principle, the exclusive establishment of which demands the actual accomplishment of a pure or immediate act of self-positing. See: FICHTE, GA, I, 2, 255

the remaining levels of the *a priori* system of all knowledge. Each one of these deductive steps represents a higher degree of transcendental self-determination of *the same single empirically represented object* posited by the faculty of imagination. In other words, the emerging content of these concatenated self-reflections is the *transcendental* and therefore *qualitatively* "evolving" structure of an actual fixed *quantity*.[51] This self-subsuming series ends with the emergence of finite self-consciousness, a self-referential abstracting capability founded on the faculty of reason. Reason's deduction, the topic that closes the theoretical division of the *Grundlage,* may be the key to Fichte's claim that his approach provides the positive articulating proof demanded to establish the required inherent logical coherence. The pragmatic series unveils the transcendental "evolution" of a fixed quantity. Hence, the *scope* of the resulting logical coherence will be only qualitative. The self-determination of reason's possibility is the pragmatic "event" that ends *unconditionally* the deduction of the system of all knowledge. From its self-conscious regressive angle, the Absolute I emerges as a *non-transcendent* and therefore *exhaustive* instance of deduction. This explains Fichte's claim that reason's deduction constitutes that theoretical instance from which the *Wissenschaftslehre* cannot advance any further.[52] Self-consciousness proves that reason or the Absolute I is the universal and hence exhaustive *qualitative* agent behind the actual self-positing of the aforementioned *quantity*. The pragmatic procedure enables the systematic self-determination of the *universal a priori conditions* whereby the Absolute I self-limits itself through a counter-posited quantified Not-I; it enables the systematic deduction *in concreto* of the transcendental ground of all theory. Fichte therefore concludes that

---

[51] As Tom Rockmore (2001, 66) alternatively puts it, "[...] Fichte does not focus on the a priori analysis of the conditions of the possibility of experience in general, but rather on the conditions of real experience. He takes experience [...] and argues [...] form conditioned to condition thereof in order to explain how experience is really possible. He never attempts to deduce conditions of abstract possibility, or possibility whatsoever. He consistently describes real conditions of actual experience."

[52] See: FICHTE, GA, I, 2, 384

Die Wissenschaftslehre hat also absolute Totalität [i. e., logical totality]. In ihr führt Eins zu Allem, und Alles zu Einem. Sie ist aber die einzige Wissenschaft, welche vollendet werden kann; Vollendung ist demnach ihr auszeichnender Charakter. Alle andere Wissenschaften sind unendlich, und können nie vollendet werden; denn sie laufen nicht wieder in ihren Grundsatz zurück. Die Wissenschaftslehre hat dies für alle zu beweisen und den Grund davon anzugeben.[53]

The consolidation of a critical "moral order" compels a regulative striving after an exhaustive quantitative expansion of philosophy's transcendental conditions. All these *systematic* aspects of Fichte's *Wissenschaftslehre* apply to Hülsen's *Preisschrift*. Fichte's position enabled Hülsen to complete his critical reformulation of Reinhold's unjustified logical-historical views, and provide them with a new inherent systematic coherence.

---

[53] FICHTE, GA, I, 2, 131. Some passages of the *Programmschrift* (particularly in section "Seven") question the possibility of establishing this inherent logical coherence. Fichte held that there ought to be something that could not be demonstrated strictly, something that ought to be assumed to be probable only, namely the fact that systematic coherence could have been established accidentally through incorrect deduction. [See: FICHTE, GA, I, 2, 146-7, 149] Nevertheless, in the 1798 reediting of the *Programmschrift*, Fichte acknowledged that these doubts were concerned with his own early deductions. See: FICHTE, GA, I, 2, 146

2.7 The *Wissenschaftslehre* and its Systematic Connection with the History of Philosophy

Still, Fichte did not neglect entirely the history of philosophy.[54] Fichte's exhaustive reconstruction of Reinhold's system impelled a reconstruction of its introductory part. Although Fichte never reconstructed Reinhold's history of philosophy systematically, his writings on the *Wissenschaftslehre* contain many passages in which different aspects of Reinhold's insight are restated in passing. Most of these passages can be found in the *Programmschrift*, the 1794 essay in which Fichte outlined the program of his forthcoming system. Due to their incidental character, most of Fichte's statements are not justified systematically.

My modest purpose here is to show ways in which Fichte may have intended to develop a history of philosophy on the foundations of the *Wissenschaftslehre*. This discussion will uncover another reason for Fichte's 1797 enthusiastic identification of Hülsen's *Preisschrift* with the *Wissenschaftslehre*. Since Reinhold's early *Elementarphilosophie* is the historical source of this key aspect of Hülsen's approach, I will limit myself to showing the Reinholdian origins of Fichte's own fragmentarily developed position.

It would be a mistake however to confuse Fichte's occasional remarks which connect the *Wissenschaftslehre* with the history of philosophy with his description of his system as a pragmatic history of the human spirit. *Pragmatische Geschichte des menschlichen Geistes* designates reason's timeless course of production of the different levels of the *a priori* system of all knowledge, which are exclusively uncovered and portrayed genetically by personal self-conscious reflection. *History of philosophy* on the other hand refers to the gradual systematic process

---

[54] Both German and Anglo-Saxon studies of Fichte do not pay sufficient attention to the fragmentary allusions in the *Wissenschaftslehre* to the history of philosophy. Scholars overlook this issue because they fail to notice the systematic connection of Reinhold's early *Elmentarphilosophie* with the history of philosophy.

of development whereby the necessary philosophizing activity of many different finite rational beings results in the historical discovery of the self-conscious pragmatic capability to articulate the *a priori* system of all knowledge.

Fichte following Reinhold focuses on the history of philosophy as a necessary accumulative process. As in Reinhold's early *Elementarphilosophie*, a transcendental agent carries out this process: the reflecting or philosophizing faculty of judgment (*reflectierende* or *philosophirende Urtheilskraft*). Fichte shares Reinhold's focus on philosophy's historicity as the ascendant product of a logical-historical activity of reason. Fichte's scattered remarks are causal restatements of some of Reinhold's arguments. The scope of the task of the exhaustive articulation of the *Wissenschaftslehre* is too great for a single human lifetime.[55] Every ascending step taken to reach philosophy has to be first climbed before a higher step is reached.[56] All past efforts made throughout the history of philosophy appear as necessary *partial attempts* of the philosophizing faculty of judgment at an articulation of a *Wissenschaftslehre*.[57] The articulation of philosophy depends on all previous logical-historical steps. Philosophers emerge as necessary historical moments of this general process. Through their philosophizing activity, the philosophizing faculty of judgment gradually uncovers the *a priori* system of all knowledge.[58]

According to Fichte, the articulation of the *Wissenschaftslehre* demands that concrete rational beings spontaneously turn their rational activity in a specific direction: self-conscious reflection. Fichte's argument that *personal* articulation is an indispensable condition to establish

---

[55] See: FICHTE, GA, I, 2, 118
[56] See: FICHTE, GA, I, 2, 111
[57] Note the following statement from *Ueber den Unterschied*: "*Alle, die jemals Erfinder in der Philosophie wurden, alle welche neue Systeme aufgestellt haben, die wenn sie sich auch nicht behaupteten, doch immer einer von den nothwendigen Versuchen des menschl. Geistes zur Hervorbringung einer Wißenschaftslehre waren* [...]." FICHTE, GA, II, 3, 337
[58] See: FICHTE, GA, I, 2, 110-1

the possibility of the Science of Knowledge,[59] can be connected to a *general* logical-historical process of development, the carrying out of which might be the result of the ascending degree of self-conscious activity (philosophizing) of different historically situated philosophers.[60] This fusion of the *general* and the *personal* spheres of logical-historical development is also a distinctive feature of Reinhold's standpoint. In the third book of the *Grundlage*, Fichte however implies the practical grounding of this possibility. The self-reflecting nature of the rational being is a holistically individuated striving nature. Fichte implies in this way the possibility for a general-personal logical-historical activity by the philosophizing faculty of judgment.[61]

Fichte also shares Reinhold's idea that all philosophers shared the same logical-historical goal: the attainment of critical knowledge. According to him, they all tried to use reflection to separate the human spirit's necessary mode of acting from its contingent conditions. By attempting to achieve this, the philosophizing faculty of judgment progressed historically and approached its inherent goal: the *Wissenschaftslehre*.[62] Reinhold and Fichte do not only agree as to the necessary

---

[59] See: FICHTE, GA, I, 2, 119

[60] The following statement from *Ueber die Bestimmung* des *Gelehrten* provides additional evidence of this point. In his discussion of rational coordination, Fichte (GA, I, 3, 49) argues: "*Wenn wir die entwickelte Idee auch nur ohne alle Beziehung auf uns selbst betrachten, so erblicken wir doch wenigstens ausser uns eine Verbindung, in der keiner für sich selbst arbeiten kann, ohne für alle anderen zu arbeiten, oder für den anderen arbeiten, ohne zugleich für sich selbst zu arbeiten — indem der glückliche Fortgang Eines Mitgliedes glücklicher Fortgang für Alle, und der Verlust des Einen Verlust für alle ist [...].*"

[61] Jürgen Stolzenberg discusses the personal possibility of such a practically grounded historical capability. He however does not enlighten it as the philosophizing faculty of judgment's ground of logical-historical striving. Nor does he connect this point to any of the Reinholdian influences that I attribute to Fichte. See: STOLZENBERG 2002, 93-106

[62] See: FICHTE, GA, I, 2, 143. In the preface to the first edition of the *Programmschrift*, Fichte describes Kant as someone who drove philosophizing judgment from the standpoint at which he found it toward its final goal. See: FICHTE, GA, I, 2, 110

teleological character of all logical-historical philosophizing activity. They additionally concur on the empirically reachable character of reason's goal.

Fichte argues that it was reserved for critical philosophy to take the final developing step of the philosophical history of reason and uncover the true concept of philosophy.[63] The following seems to be an adaptation of Reinhold's claim that philosophy's necessary emergence enables a universal reconciliation of all possible systematic positions. Fichte argues that the conclusive step taken by the philosophizing faculty of judgment enables a universal reconciliation of the conflicting claims of the only two possible systems of thought, namely dogmatism and criticism.[64]

The main purpose of Fichte's approach is to ground Reinhold's ungrounded concept of representation. In his *Vergleichung des vom Herrn Prof. Schmid aufgestellten Systems mit der Wissenschaftslehre*,[65] Fichte states this unambiguously

Meines Erachtens — dies ist eine historische Behauptung, und ich appellire über diesen Punct an die besseren unter den jetzt lebenden philosophischen Schriftstellern, und an die gesammte Geschichte der Philosophie — meines Erachtens ist die Frage, welche die Philosophie zu beantworten hat, folgende: wie hangen unsere Vorstellungen mit ihren Objecten zusammen; inwiefern kann man sagen, dass denselben etwas, unabhängig von ihnen, und überhaupt von uns, ausser uns entspreche? […] Alle Philosophie, von Anbeginn an bis jetzt, hat die Beantwortung dieser Frage zu ihrem letzten Zwecke gehabt.[66]

Fichte shared Reinhold's view that what is crucial is to give an exhaustive grounding answer to the question about the transcendental possibility representation. An asking mechanism also characterizes philosophizing judgment's logical-historical *modus operandi*.

---

[63] See: FICHTE, GA, I, 2, 282

[64] See: FICHTE, GA, I, 2, 109

[65] Fichte's essay dates from 1796, a year after Hülsen wrote *Preisschrift*. I however include it here for it provides additional evidence of Fichte's incidental interest in a rational history of philosophy prior to his sympathetic rating of Hülsen's *Preisschrift* in 1797.

[66] See: FICHTE, GA, I, 3, 247

Es versteht sich, dass die philosophirende Urtheilskraft in der Beantwortung dieser Frage, oder in den Versuchen sie zu beantworten, systematisch zu Werke geht.[67]

According to Fichte, the philosophizing faculty of judgment progresses historically by giving systematic answers to the question about the transcendental possibility of representation. All systematic attempts therefore are necessary developing stages of an exclusive historically secured philosophy the possibility of which may finally emerge as an exhaustive accumulative answer to this question. All such attempts constitute a single historically extended systematic attempt of reason at an articulation of philosophy. The correlative emergence of these developing stages is an ascending series of rectifying or actualizing perspectives whereby the philosophizing faculty of judgment uncovers the supra-historical system of all knowledge. The logical-historical process of development that culminates in the critical concept of philosophy, in the personal self-conscious ability to portray the pragmatic history of the human spirit, should be understood as the history of reason climbing systematically to a full awareness of itself as an *a priori* system of knowledge.[68] All these arguments, as one could once again confirm, may have been inspired by Reinhold's approach to the history of philosophy.

For Fichte the *Wissenschaftslehre* enables an increasing display of reason's practical potential (expanding self-determination). Fichte should be committed to Reinhold's claim that the logical-historical emergence of philosophy establishes the possibility of a moral improvement of the human species.

---

[67] See: FICHTE, GA, I, 3, 247. The following passage from *Ueber den Begriff* provides a negative evidence of the teleologically progressing character of the philosophizing faculty of judgment: "*Diese Handlungsart überhaupt* [i.e., the human spirit's necessary way of acting], *soll nach dem obigen durch eine reflectirende Abstraction von allem, was nicht sie ist, abgesondert werden. Diese Abstraction geschieht durch Freiheit, und die philosophirende Urtheilskraft wird in ihr gar nicht durch blinden Zwang geleitet.*" FICHTE, GA, I, 2, 143

[68] See: BUBNER 2003, 110

Fichte should also be committed to the following conclusion: as in Reinhold's early *Elementarphilosophie*, neither the recognition of reason's systematic process of teleological production, nor the articulation of the introductory history of philosophy is possible prior to the logical-historical attainment of critical knowledge. Earlier it is impossible to identify either the striving direction of the philosophizing faculty of judgment, or the possibility of articulation. This follows from Fichte's discussion of pure philosophical and philosophical-historical (logical-historical) knowledge in *Ueber die Bestimmung des Gelehrten.*

Die Kenntniß der ersten Art gründet sich auf reine Vernunftsätze, und ist philosophisch; die von der zweiten zum Theil auf Erfahrung, und ist insofern philosophisch-historisch; (nicht bloß historisch; denn ich muß ja die Zwecke, die sich nur philosophisch erkennen lassen, auf die in der Erfahrung gegebenen Gegenstände beziehen, um die leztern als Mittel zur Erreichung der ersten beurtheilen zu können).[69]

A similar view follows from Fichte's brief discussion in *Programmschrift* of the ongoing, though partially self-aware attempts made throughout the history of philosophy to reach the standpoint of the *Wissenschaftslehre.* Prior to the *Wissenschaftslehre's* insight, the philosophizing faculty of judgment can only strive unconsciously after its logical-historical goal. It cannot recognize the inherent correlative character of its own logical-historical course of systematic production.[70]

Der menschliche Geist macht mancherlei Versuche; er kommt durch blindes Herumtappen zur Dämmerung, und geht erst aus dieser zum hellen Tage

---

[69] FICHTE, GA, I, 3, 53. The following passage from the late 1796 *Philosophische Wissenschaft des Rechts von Professor Fichte [Nachschrift Lossius. Fragment]* provides further evidence of this point. "*Die Geschichte dieser Wissenschaft* [i.e., the science of law] *kann man, wie die einer jeden andern, nicht eher verstehen, bis man die Wissenschaft selbst hat: denn Geschichte eines Dinges, das nicht ist, ist nichts. So war die bis herige Geschichte der Philosophie immer nur Geschichte der Philosophen.*" FICHTE, GA, IV, 3, 59

[70] As in Reinhold's system, Fichte ought to be committed to the view that during the epoch of pre-critical thought, all products of the philosophizing faculty of judgment appear to the observer as atomic facts.

über. Er wird Anfangs durch dunkle Gefühle (deren Ursprung und Wirklich-
keit die Wissenschaflslehre darzulegen hat) geleitet; und wir hätten noch
heute keinen deutlichen Begriff, und wären noch immer der Erdkloss, der
sich dem Boden entwand, wenn wir nicht angefangen hätten, dunkel zu füh-
len, was wir erst später deutlich erkannten. — Dies bestätiget denn auch die
Geschichte der Philosophie; und wir haben jetzt den eigentlichen Grund
angegeben, warum dasjenige, was doch in jedem menschlichen Geiste offen
da liegt, und was jeder mit Händen greifen kann, wenn es ihm deutlich dar-
gelegt wird, erst nach mannigfaltigem Herumirren zum Bewusstseyn einiger
wenigen gelangte.[71]

According to Fichte, the *Wissenschaftslehre* provides an explanation of
why so much wandering was necessary to enable the final grasping of
the ever-existing system of knowledge. Still, apart from implying the
systematic possibility of this logical-historical striving task fragmentarily, Fichte did not develop this topic during the years that concern
us here. One of the issues that Fichte's "improved" *Elementar-*
philosophie fails to develop is the systematic grounding of its historical
standpoint.[72]

Though Fichte did not develop fully Reinhold's concept of a history of
philosophy, his systematic introduction to the *Wissenschaftslehre* agrees
with Reinhold's position in a number of central points. (1) The history
of philosophy is a logical-historical ascending process. (2) Historical

---

[71] See: FICHTE, GA, I, 2, 143

[72] Peter Baumanns (1974, 119) is right in objecting to Fichte that *"Wenn die*
Wissenschaftslehre "Naturlage" und das Prinzip der Wissenschaftslehre durch
Evidenz ausgezeichnet soll, warum bedurfte es dann eines so langen Prozesses
der Wegräumung von Evidenzhindernissen? Welcher art waren die Evidenz-
hindernisse, daß sie einen so langen und mühseligen Prozeß ihrer Hinweg-
räumung bedingten? Auf dieser Frage aber gibt die „Programmschrift" keine
antwort. Sie will zwar „den eigentlichen Grund angegeben" haben, warum alle
bisherigen Philosophen die philosphierende Urteilskraft immer nur ein Stück
vorrücken konnten; in Wahrheit aber wird bloß behauptet, daß es so sein mußte.
Das, was zu erklären wäre: das herumtappen zur Dämmerung mittels dunkler
Gefühle (eines „Wahrheitssinnes") und das schließliche Übergehen zum „hellen
Tage", wird nicht erklärt, sondern in tautologischer Weise selbst als Erklärungs-
grund ausgegeben."

progress is accomplished teleologically through the self-reflecting activity of a transcendental agent (philosophizing reason or the philosophizing faculty of judgment). (3) The articulation of philosophy depends on all previous logical-historical steps taken by this agent. (4) Critical knowledge emerges as the ultimate rational outcome of philosophy's history. (5) It is the empirical result of reason's reaching of a non-regulative inherent goal. (6) Teleological progression is carried out through a systematic and ongoing answer attempt of the question about the transcendental possibility of representation. (7) All the systematic attempts made throughout the history of philosophy appear as necessary developing stages of a single systematic attempt of reason at a definitive articulation of philosophy. (8) The correlative systematic emergence of all developing stages appears as an ascending sequence of rectifying or actualizing perspectives that reason attains of the *a priori* system of all knowledge. (9) The necessary emergence of philosophy enables a universal reconciliation of all philosophical positions. (10) It furthermore makes possible a moral improvement of the human species. (11) Neither the necessary process of logical-historical development, nor the articulation of the introductory history of philosophy is possible prior to the attainment of critical knowledge. (12) Philosophers emerge as necessary historical moments of the rational history of philosophy. Through their ascending general-personal efforts, reason uncovers the system of all knowledge.

These coincidences provide sufficient evidence that the re-articulation of most of Reinhold's introductory approach to the history of philosophy was an idea that Fichte originally had in mind but did not develop.

As to the intriguing question of why Fichte did not re-articulate this aspect of Reinhold's approach, two different answers are plausible. (1) During the period of 1794-1799, Fichte's interests were mainly focused on the development of the foundational epistemic principles of the *Wissenschaftslehre*, as well as on the formulation of its *Rechts-* and *Sittenlehre* parts. (2) Fichte lost interest in this historical dimension. Friedrich Schlegel's correspondence provides evidence that already in August 1796, a few months after writing *Vergleichung des vom Herrn*

Prof. Schmid,[73] Fichte told him that he was not interested in history.[74] Notwithstanding Schlegel's report, another possible reason for Fichte's desistence was that he relegated this task to Hülsen.

2.8   The Practical Vocation of the Scholar

While as theorist, Hülsen was as much a student of Reinhold as a disciple of Fichte, as a moral philosopher Hülsen's dependence on Fichte is unambiguous. There is no evidence that Hülsen was affected by either Reinhold's writings on the first principle of morals in *Beiträge vol. II*[75] or by the practical philosophy at the close of the *Versuchsschrift*. Fichte's *Wissenschaftslehre* explains and insures an infinite moral improvement of the human species. The spontaneous or unconditioned activity of the self-positing I, enables an ongoing self-determination of the human will. According to Fichte in *Ueber die Bestimmung des Gelehrten*, a series of public and non-systematic lectures delivered in Jena in 1794, the scholar, as the true expert on philosophy, the "heir" of the Reinholdian *Selbstdenker*, should be the most outstanding ethical person of his time. He is responsible for the advancement and supervision of the ethical improvement of the human species. Hülsen integrated Fichte's scholar with Reinhold's *Selbstdenker* in his own ethical model of *Selbstdenker*; the critical philosopher responsible for turning humanity's attention to the logical-historical path of philosophizing reason leading to a moral perfection via the historically enlarged *Wissenschaftslehre. Ueber die Bestimmung* discusses two key features that Hülsen will embrace. (1) It introduces the idealistic concept of a purposive coordinated community, a stance that opened the road for Hülsen's further understanding of a joint

---

[73]   Fichte's essay appeared in print in the 12th issue of the *Philosophisches Journal*. It was officially announced on May 25, 1796 in the *Allgemeine Literatur Zeitung*. See: FICHTE, GA, I, 3, 231

[74]   See Schlegel's letters to Körner from September 21 and 30, 1796 in: SCHLEGEL (KA), XXIII, 333

[75]   See: *Über das vollständige Fundament der Moral* in: REINHOLD 2003, II, 131-81

"rational fate" of the human species. (2) It reformulates the Kantian concepts of the "categorical imperative" and "the highest good", and links their expanding possibilities, the critical consolidation of a universal "moral order", with personal regulative striving.

According to Fichte, the scholar is a human being. The disclosure of his practical vocation demands a previous inquiry into the vocation of the rational being as such, a strategy that Hülsen will apply. In the theoretical *Wissenschaftslehre*, the knowing subject cannot achieve exhaustive self-determination. As a finite rational being, he cannot attain absolute self-conscious knowledge. The subject attains consciousness of itself only as an empirically determined self-reflecting agent.[76] Empirical self-consciousness presupposes a quantitatively undetermined, and hence conditioning Not-I. This Not-I emerges infinitely as an extra-reflective aspect of self-determining reflection. It appears to the knowing subject as an insurmountable quantitative dependence, the alleged origin of which is "external" and "foreign". Moral improvement impels a regulative striving for the overcoming of this empirically restricted freedom. As Hülsen learns from Fichte, the subject should subordinate under or harmonize this quantitative "foreign" indeterminacy of the Not-I with the holistic (thetic) self-positing activity of the pure or Absolute I.[77] The result of this should be absolute self-identity or self-agreement, for the absolutely self-posited I is indivisible and non-contradictable.

Das Resultat aus allem Gesagten ist folgendes: Die vollkommene Uebereinstimmung des Menschen mit sich selbst, und — damit er mit sich selbst übereinstimmen könne — die Uebereinstimmung aller Dinge ausser ihm mit seinen nothwendigen praktischen Begriffen von ihnen, — den Begriffen, welche bestimmen, wie sie seyn sollen, — ist das letzte höchste Ziel des Menschen.[78]

The subject's higher ethical goal is for Fichte as later for Hülsen in *Preisschrift*, absolute being or rationality, namely the quantitative self-

---

[76] See: FICHTE, GA, I, 3, 28
[77] See: FICHTE, GA, I, 3, 30-1
[78] FICHTE, GA, I, 3, 31

conscious subsuming of all possible experience. Fichte formulates this in a practical command: "*Der Mensch soll seyn, was er ist, schlechthin darum, weil er ist*".[79] Exhaustive self-determination compels the subject to strive personally and accomplish empirically the full practical potentiality of reason. The subject ought to grasp himself as the unconditional agent behind his own infinitely expanding empirical existence. Ongoing practical striving is his way to bring about a critically intensifying "moral order" and improve himself existentially: the coincidence between Fichte and Hülsen on this point is irrefutable.

Fichte's concept of self-determination results in an innovative reformulation of Kant's "categorical imperative", a reformulation that Hülsen will incorporate. According to Fichte, a manifold of *quantitative* empirical determinations contradict the original *proto-quantifiable* identity of the absolute I. That is the reason why *reason* and *sensibility*, the *pure* and the *empirical* spheres of the human spirit, are at first not in harmony. Nonetheless, this harmony should be brought about. Moral perfection, the "categorical imperative", demands their ultimate self-subsuming identity. While the Kantian concept of the "highest good", ethical virtue combined with happiness, is twofold, for Fichte the "highest good" is a unitary concept. In Fichte's *Wissenschaftslehre*, the "highest good" is rational harmony of the rational being with himself, a self-determining identification of all Not-I as his own self-posited product, thus no happiness without moral acting. Only that which is good makes us happy and not conversely.[80] The "highest good" is, as Fichte will persuade Hülsen, an unavoidable by-product of the critically emerging "moral order".

Nonetheless, for Fichte his finite character prevents the subject from reaching absolute identity or harmony. Our practical vocation (*Bestimmung*) is not for Fichte or Hülsen to reach this goal. Qua finite rational being, the subject's vocation lies in an unending approximation to absolute self-harmony.

---

[79] FICHTE, GA, I, 3, 29
[80] See: FICHTE, GA: I, 3, 31-2

*Nennt man nun jene völlige Uebereinstimmung mit sich selbst Vollkommen-
heit, in der höchsten Bedeutung des Wortes, wie man sie allerdings nennen
kann: so ist Vollkommenheit das höchste unerreichbare Ziel des Menschen;
Vervollkommnung ins unendliche aber ist seine Bestimmung. Er ist da, um
selbst immer sittlich besser zu werden, und alles rund um sich herum sinnlich,
und wenn er in der Gesellschaft betrachtet wird, auch sittlich besser, und
dadurch sich selbst immer glückseliger zu machen.*[81]

According to Fichte, the rational being is not an isolated being. He is
destined to live in society, to interact with other autonomous beings.
After discussing the ontological existence of other free acting agents
outside oneself, Fichte employs Kant's terminology and defines society
as a purposeful coordinated community of self-determined rational
beings. Fichte's insight will be Hülsen's way to expand Reinhold's
concept of self-determined consensus. Such a coordinated society is
characterized by the mutual respect of the self-determined nature of its
interacting members. To restrict someone's freedom is tantamount as
to master or subordinate him by not taking into account his rational
nature. Such acting is immoral, as it does not consider one's own
fellowmen as practical ends. So acting would interfere with one's own
ability and by extension, with the ability of one's fellowmen to achieve
self-determined harmony. For Fichte, coordination demands the
cultivation of the practical skills of autonomous giving and receiving.
As Hülsen will learn from him, reason is in complete agreement with
itself regarding humanity's ultimate goal: universal moral perfection.[82]

*Die Vollkommenheit ist nur auf eine Art bestimmt: — sie ist sich selbst völlig
gleich; könnten alle Menschen vollkommen werden, könnten sie ihr höchstes
und letztes Ziel erreichen, so wären sie alle einander völlig gleich; sie wären
nur Eins; ein einziges Subject.*[83]

Fichte argued that in a coordinated society the activity of each rational
being is characterized by an ongoing striving for exhaustive improvement of his own moral quality as well as of that of his fellowmen.

---

[81] FICHTE, GA, I, 3, 32
[82] See: FICHTE, GA, I, 3, 36-8, 40-1
[83] FICHTE, GA, I, 3, 40

Each rational being accomplishes this by attempting to raise himself and his fellowmen to his own moral ideal of man. The ultimate moral goal of society is a complete unanimous unity of all its members. The achievement of this goal presupposes the achievement of the human vocation as such. Nonetheless, this social goal remains unachievable; the complete unity of all members of society is the final ideal goal of all rational coordinated beings but not their achievable vocation. Moral perfection therefore compels an infinite striving approximation to this social goal.[84] Fichte writes:

Dieses Annähern zur völligen Einigkeit und Einmüthigkeit mit allen Individuen können wir Vereinigung nennen. Also Vereinigung, die der Innigkeit nach stets fester, dem Umfange nach stets ausgebreiteter werde, ist die wahre Bestimmung des Menschen in der Gesellschaft: diese Vereinigung aber ist, da nur über ihre letzte Bestimmung die Menschen einig sind und einig werden können — nur durch Vervollkommnung möglich. Wir können demnach eben so gut sagen: gemeinschaftliche Vervollkommnung, Vervollkommnung seiner selbst durch die frei benutzte Einwirkung anderer auf uns: und Vervollkommnung anderer durch Rückwirkung auf sie, als auf freie Wesen, ist unsere Bestimmung in der Gesellschaft.[85]

Hülsen learned from Fichte that all coordinated beings resort to the same rational means to strive after the same single moral perfection. That is the reason their personal strivings interrelate.[86] The ability to affect and let others affect oneself demands the cultivation of two practical skills. (1) The trait of giving, namely the moral ability to affect or cultivate the personality of other free rational beings precisely in those aspects of one's own personality in which one is strong and they are weak. (2) The trait of receiving, namely the moral ability to let others affect or cultivate one's own personality in those precise aspects in which one is weak and they are strong.[87] Hülsen will apply this idea

---

[84] See: FICHTE, GA, I, 3, 40-1

[85] FICHTE, GA, I, 3, 40

[86] As Wilhelm Weischedel (1973, 17) clarifies, "*Wenn nun die Erfahrung anderer notwendig zum Menschsein gehört, dann gehört auch ihre unabtrennbare Voraussetzung, die Gemeinschaft mit den anderen, notwendig dazu.*"

[87] See: FICHTE, GA, I, 3, 43-5

to the history of philosophy, and justify thereby the personal self-determined ability to contribute to and to incorporate someone else's systematic degree of practical progress. Hülsen will share Fichte's conclusion that

Wenn wir die entwickelte Idee auch nur ohne alle Beziehung auf uns selbst betrachten, so erblicken wir doch wenigstens ausser uns eine Verbindung, in der keiner für sich selbst arbeiten kann, ohne für alle andere zu arbeiten, oder für den anderen arbeiten, ohne zugleich für sich selbst zu arbeiten — indem der glückliche Fortgang Eines Mitgliedes glücklicher Fortgang für Alle, und der Verlust des Einen Verlust für Alle ist: ein Anblick, der schon durch die Harmonie, die wir in dem allermannigfaltigsten erblicken, uns innig wohlthut und unseren Geist mächtig emporhebt.[88]

According to Fichte, a certain kind of knowledge is required to enable the moral progress of the human species. Philosophical knowledge of moral perfection alone is insufficient for making moral progress possible. Moral progress demands knowledge of the particular cultural level of historical development of one's own society. The philosopher must also be acquainted with the subsequent purposive level to be reached as well as with the means required for achieving this. This demands that the philosopher know the means whereby the moral aptitudes of the rational being develop. The moral improvement of the human species requires a joint application of (1) philosophical, (2) historical, and (3) philosophical-historical (logical-historical) knowledge.[89] Taken together, these three types of knowledge constitute what Fichte calls learning (*Gelehrsamkeit*). The scholar is the person that dedicates his life to the attainment of this knowledge. Learning makes the scholar the ethically best man of his time. Only the scholar is acquainted with the means required to improve the moral performances of man. Fichte therefore argues that the scholar should be the educator of humanity. His knowledge should be applied for the benefit of society. The scholar is required to turn the attention of his fellow-men upon their true needs, and make them acquainted with the means

---

[88] FICHTE, GA, I, 3, 49
[89] See: FICHTE, GA, I, 3, 52-4, and FICHTE, GA, II, 3, 357

demanded for their satisfaction. This pedagogic task compels the scholar to act according to the moral law, to employ ethical means to influence society.[90] Thus, the vocation of the scholar is to promote and to supervise unceasingly the moral progress of the human species.[91] The pedagogical task of the Fichtean scholar does not really differ from that of the Reinholdian *Selbstdenker*. What distinguishes these two figures is the level of post-critical impact that the labour of the Fichtean scholar has on communal life. This higher degree of communal commitment, a key moral concern of the Hülsenian *Selbstdenker*, is another source of *Preisschrift*.

Self-determination compels the scholar not to yield his will to any academic authority. Fichte encourages the scholar to rigorously autonomous and independent scholarship. It could be claimed that Fichte's position will inspire Hülsen's ideas about a true academy of sciences. Fichte discusses this in the *1ste Vorlesung. Im Winter-Halbjahr. [von der Bestimmung der Gelehrten.]*[92] not included among the five published lectures of *Ueber die Bestimmung*.

[...] *alle Geisteskultur ist nichts, u. hilft nichts, ohne Characterbildung; u. ich erinnere abermals, was ich schon mehrmals erinnert habe, daß man irrt, wenn man in einer Akademie bloß eine Schule der Wissenschaften zu erbliken glaubt. Sie soll zugleich seyn eine **Schule des Handelns**. Bilden Sie dahero zuförderst Ihren Character zum festen entschloßen Halten an Wahrheit, u. an Recht. Thun Sie nichts gegen Ihre Ueberzeugung; suchen Sie aber beständig Ihren Geist der beßeren Ueberzeugung offen zu erhalten. Unterlaßen Sie alles, wodurch Sie auf irgend eine Art abhängig, wodurch Sie zum Instrumente eines fremden Willens werden; oder wodurch Sie gehindert*

---

[90] As Liang Zhixue (1991, 229) reminds us: "*Wenn der Gelehrte im moralischen Leben zurückbleibt oder sogar durch eine entscheidende Handlung seinen eigenen Lehren widerspricht, so werden die anderen seinen Lehren nicht folgen. Fichte lieh sich an dieser Stelle die Worte, die der Stifter der christlichen Religion an seine Schüler richtete, um die Gelehrten zu ermahnen: „Ihr seyd das Salz der Erde; wenn das Salz seine Kraft verliert, womit soll man salzen?" wenn die Auswahl unter den Menschen verdorben ist, wo soll man noch sittliche Güte suchen?*"

[91] See: FICHTE, GA, I, 3, 54-8

[92] For this lesson see: FICHTE, GA, II, 3, 357-67

werden, frei jedem unter die Augen zu treten. Erhalten sie sich diese Freiheit, die Ihnen die Gesetze geben.[93]

The primordial significance that Fichte attributes to the personal labour of the scholar confirms that the *Wissenschaftslehre* plays an existential role in the moral improvement of the human species. As Klaus Vieweg points out,

[...] *die Bestimmung des Gelehrten als des höchsten wahren Menschen ist somit die letzte Aufgabe für philosophisches Forschen. Bei Fichte ist ebendiese Wissenschaft auf die Humanität verpflichtet, er hält ausdrücklich alle Philosophie und Wissenschaft für nichtig, die nicht auf das Ziel der Förderung der Kultur und der Erhöhung der Humanität ausgeht.*[94]

A joint application of philosophical, historical, and logical-historical knowledge is required to enable the moral progress of humanity. Nonetheless, Fichte suggests that in this triad logical-historical knowledge plays a preponderant role. In *Ueber die Bestimmung*, moral progress is described as depending directly upon the progress of philosophy.[95] A similar statement is found in the *1ste Vorlesung*, in which Fichte claims that

Nichts in der ganzen Geschichte seiner Zeit liegt dem Gelehrten näher, als der Zustand der Wissenschaften selbst; der Hoffnungen, oder Befürchtungen, die er vernünftiger weise über den Fortgang oder Rückgang derselben zu faßen hat.[96]

Peter Baumanns' studies reveal that for Fichte true philosophy is ethical anthropology, a foundation of personal critical knowledge according to the idea of the practical vocation of man, or rather a

---

[93] FICHTE, GA, II, 3, 366 [my bold]

[94] VIEWEG 1995, 180. In a letter to Friedrich Heinrich Jacoby from August 30, 1795 Fichte writes: "*Wozu ist denn nun der spekulative Gesichtspunkt und mit ihm die ganze Phlosophie, wenn sie nicht für's Leben ist? [...] Wir fingen an zu philosophieren aus Uebermuth, und brachten uns dadurch um unsere Unschuld; wir erblickten unsere Nacktheit, und philosophieren seitdem aus Noth für unsere Erlösung.*" FICHTE, GA, III, 2, 392-3

[95] In FICHTE's (GA, I, 3, 54) own words: "*Von dem Fortgange der Wissenschaften hängt unmmitelbar der ganze Fortgang des Menschengeschlechts ab.*"

[96] FICHTE, GA, II, 3, 357

simultaneous foundation of metaphysics of experience and metaphysics of man.[97] Fichte's claim about the preponderance of logical-historical knowledge suggests that an exhaustive formulation of the *Wissenschaftslehre* demands a systematic discussion of the relationship of the rational history of philosophy and the personal pre- and post-critical labour of the scholar (the self-determining subject). Fichte however does not discuss this issue. All he seems to imply is, as we saw earlier, that the reaching of the standpoint of the *Wissenschaftslehre* depends on a general, ongoing, and ascending logical-historical process of development the exclusive rational architects of which are concrete self-reflecting philosophers. Fichte's writings of 1794-5 leave this question open. Hülsen's *Preisschrift* characterization of all rational activity as general-personal logical-historical activity appears in the history of German idealism as the first attempt to fuse these two apparent stems of Fichte's approach systematically.

2.9 The Spiritual-Normative Character of the *Wissenschaftslehre*

The main difference between Fichte's *Wissenschaftslehre* and Hülsen's *Preisschrift* is Hülsen's inclusion of a constitutive temporal dimension to Fichte's *a priori* concept of rationality. This divergence did not prevent Fichte from identifying Hülsen's position with his own standpoint. Fichte recommended *Preisschrift* strongly as a work which facilitated the study of the *Wissenschaftslehre*.

   Both Fichte and Hülsen agree that the concept of the *Wissenschaftslehre* is a "*spiritual*" as opposed to "*literal*" concept, that it demands an *independent explanation,* or rather a *self-adaptable normative completion*. This explains Fichte and Hülsen's identification of their not entirely concordant systematic positions and Fichte's motives for recognizing Hülsen as a partner in the completion of his system.
Reinhold was the first post-Kantian thinker to refer to the possibility of reformulating a philosophical standpoint and keep its "spirit" intact.

---

[97] See: BAUMANNS 1974, 107

The reassertion of critical philosophy appears in Reinhold's early *Ele-mentarphilosophie* as an attempt to step back from the "printed letter" of the *Kritik* and complete it *normatively* with a *Grundsatz*.[98] The objections of Schulze-Aenesidemus and Fichte's determination not to award victory to the skeptic led him to develop Reinhold's distinction between "spirit" and "letter".[99] Fichte's insistence that the *Wissen-schaftslehre* is the "*spiritual-normative*" critical complement to Kant's propaedeutic is well known.[100] A nuance of Fichte's stance is the *self-adaptable* character of the normative task of "spiritual" completion.[101] Fichte attributes to the critical philosopher (or the scholar) a promi-nent role in the achievement of this "spiritualizing" task. In *Rezension des Aenesidemus* Fichte writes that

Er [i.e., the reviewer—Fichte] *wünscht nichts lebhafter, als dass seine Be-urtheilung dazu beitragen möge, recht viele* **Selbstdenker** *zu überzeugen, dass diese Philosophie* [i.e., the critical philosophy] *an sich, und ihrem innern Gehalte nach, noch so fest stehe, als je, dass es aber noch vieler Arbeit be-dürfe, um die Materialien in ein wohl verbundenes und unerschütterliches Ganze zu ordnen. Möchten sie dann durch diese Ueberzeugung selbst auf-gemuntert werden, jeder an seinem Orte, so viel in seinen Kräften steht, zu diesem erhabenen Zwecke beizutragen!*[102]

Fichte acknowledges that the self-thinker, an *independent* philoso-phizing figure, is responsible for the restitution of the critical status of philosophy. Fichte makes a similar statement in *Grundlage*, though in this text the term "self-thinker" is omitted. Fichte holds that the

---

[98] See: HORSTMANN 1991, 47-8

[99] See: BREAZEALE 1981, 548-9

[100] Take for instance the following passage from the *Grundlage*: "*Die hier aufgestellten und aufzustellenden Principien liegen offenbar den seinigen [i.e., Kant's] zum Grunde, wie jeder sich überzeugen kann, der sich mit dem* **Geiste** *seiner Philosophie (die doch wohl Geist haben dürfte) vertraut machen will. Dass er in seinen Kritiken die Wissenschaft nicht, sondern nur die Propädeutik der-selben aufstellen wolle, hat er einige Mal gesagt; und es ist schwer zu begreifen, warum seine Nachbeter nur dieses ihm nicht haben glauben wollen.*" FICHTE, GA, I, 2, 335

[101] As far as I know, this topic was neglected in scholarly literature.

[102] FICHTE, GA, I, 2, 67 [my bold]

normative philosophizing activity whereby the "spirit" of critical philosophy should be completed demands independence (*Selbstständigkeit*), a position, which according to Fichte each philosopher can only confer on himself.[103] This independence is a not explicitly clarified *extension* of self-determining autonomy, the expression of which might be a *normative* degree of *personal appropriation* or *self-adapting completion* of a given standpoint. The following passage in the 1797 *Zweite Einleitung*, an essay that Hülsen of course could have not known while writing *Preisschrift*, is perhaps where Fichte formulates this already apparent early "spiritualizing" conviction most clearly.

Es ist nicht die Art der Wissenschaftslehre, noch ihres Verfassers, unter irgend einer Autorität Schutz zu suchen. Wer erst sehen muss, ob diese Lehre mit der Lehre irgend eines anderen Mannes übereinstimme, ehe er sich von ihr überzeugen will, anstatt zu sehen, ob sie mit **den Aussprüchen seiner eigenen Vernunft** *übereinstimme, auf den rechnet sie überhaupt nicht, weil ihm die absolute Selbstthätigkeit,* **der ganz unabhängige Glaube an sich selbst,** *fehlt, die durch jene Lehre vorausgesetzt werden. Aus einem ganz anderen Grunde sonach, als aus dem, seine Lehre zu empfehlen, ist der Verfasser der Wissenschaftslehre mit der Vorerinnerung angetreten, dass dieselbe mit der Kanntischen Lehre vollkommen übereinstimme, und keine andere sey, als die wohlverstandene Kantische.*[104]

The standpoint of the *Wissenschaftslehre* presupposes (1) personal independent observance of and (2) conformation to the practical demands of *one's own* reason. Fichte implies that a *particularizing* and therefore *distinguishing self-adapting procedure of analysis* ought to *condition* the "spiritual" self-determined adoption of his standpoint.[105] Hülsen will

---

[103] See: FICHTE, GA, I, 2, 326. FICHTE (GA, I, 4, 184) makes the same statement in the 1797 *Erste Einleitung*. There he claims that "[…] *mein System kein anderes sei als das Kantische, d.h.: Es enthält dieselbe Ansicht der Sache, ist aber in seinem Verfahren* **ganz unabhängig** *von der Kantischen Darstellung.*" [my bold]

[104] FICHTE, GA, I, 4, 221 [my bold]

[105] In a letter to Niethammer from December 6, 1793, FICHTE (GA, III, 2, 21) seems to argue the same about Kant's *Kritik*. He writes: "*Noch keiner hat ihn verstanden; die es am meisten glauben, am wenigsten; keiner wird ihn verstehen, der nicht auf* **seinem Wege** *zu Kants Resultaten kommen wird, […].*" [my bold]

deepen this point and hold that the autonomous adoption of a philo-sophical standpoint conforms, inevitably, to a particular degree of logical-historical development. Originally, for Reinhold the notion of "spiritual" reformulation presupposed the possibility of *normative completion*. Regarding the *Wissenschaftslehre*, this option is assured by Fichte's own claims about the incompleteness of his system. This may have persuaded Hülsen to introduce significant changes, and still call his modified system *Wissenschaftslehre*.

An immediate consequence of this is Fichte's recognition of the right of other philosophical authors to develop the concept of the *Wissen-schaftslehre* into *normative* and hence *not entirely concordant syste-matic positions*. This is implied in the *Ersten Einleitung*, where Fichte recommends Jakob Sigismund Beck's 1796 *Einzigmöglicher Ständ-punkt, aus welchem die kritische Philosophie beurtheilt werden muss* as the best philosophical preparation for "those who whish to study the *Wissenschaftslehre* from my writings".[106] This may explain Fichte's 1797 identification of Hülsen's *Preisschrift* with his own standpoint. It also explains his 1795 identification of Schelling's *Vom Ich als Princip der Philosophie* with the *Wissenschaftslehre*,[107] a statement, which seems to reconfirm the implicit existence of this "spiritualizing" trend prior to the writing of the *Ersten* and *Zweite Einleitung*. It even could be held that Fichte's claims that (1) his account is not complete, that (2) he wants his reader to develop his own thought, that (3) he encourages independent thought, that (4) his system is subjected to revision, that (5) the *Grundlage* is a plan for how to erect further systematic cons-truction upon its foundations, and (6) that he welcomed suggestions from other philosophers,[108] are encouragements to "*read*" and *develop* the "spirit" of the *Wissenschaftslehre* as Hülsen did: probably another reason why Fichte recommended *Preisschrift* so strongly.

---

[106] In FICHTE's (GA, I, 4, 203) own words: "*Ich halte die angeführte Schrift* [i.e., Beck's essay] *für das zweckmässigste Geschenk, das dem Zeitalter gemacht wer-den konnte, und empfehle sie denen, welche aus meinen Schriften die Wissen-schaftslehre studiren wollen, als die beste Vorbereitung.*"

[107] See Fichte's letter to Reinhold from July 2, 1795 in: FICHTE, GA, III, 2, 347-8

[108] See: FICHTE, GA, I, 2, 252-4

3. Hülsen

3.1 Hülsen's *Preisschrift*

Hülsen took advantage of the 1795 prize-question of the Berlin Academy of Sciences on the progress of metaphysics since Leibniz and Wolf to present his own historically augmented *Wissenschaftslehre* and also supplement Fichte's "improved" version of Reinhold's *Elementarphilosophie*. Hülsen conceded some preliminarily importance to the academic contest, as it was an attempt at establishing universal consensus in philosophy.[1]

The "spirit" of Fichte's idealism taught that a critical or "scientific" solution to the prize-question must include self-consciousness and not contain unjustified premises. Hülsen therefore demanded that it be preceded by an inquiry into the transcendental possibility of its *grounding* and *solving*; an insight that the Academy of Sciences overlooked.

Die Preisfrage der Akademie ist durch Zeitumstände veranlasst. Diesen zu Folge enthält sie eine bestimmte Forderung, welcher irgend eine Antwort, und eine Antwort zwar, eben so bestimmt entsprechen soll. Es ist aber einleuchtend, dass zwischen der Aufgabe und der möglichen Antwort ein bestimmtes Verhältniss Statt finden müsse, ein Verhältniss, nach welchem es nicht gleichgültig seyn kann, wie die letztere der Forderung der ersten entsprechen, und wie diese wieder für jene solche Forderung aufstellen könne. Die wharheit und richtigkeit dieses Verhältniss aber lässt sich gar nicht schon mit der wirklich ergangenen Aufgabe, und der hierdurch als möglich gedachten Antwort voraussetzen; sondern erfordert, um bestimmt darüber urtheilen zu können, eine eigene Untersuchung, und so wird daher die Aufgabe der Akademie, um ihrer Rechfertigung willen, erst selbst eine Aufgabe.[2]

Hülsen began by posing the following two tasks: (A) how the prize-question, in its given form, relates to itself and to its possible answer,

---

[1] See: HÜLSEN 1796, 37
[2] HÜLSEN 1796, 40

namely whether and how it can really fulfill our philosophical demands. (B) How the prize-question independently of any accidental
circumstances relates to itself and to its possible answer, namely whether and how it constitutes a necessary logical-historical task of reason.
In task (A), Hülsen discusses the *ungrounded* character of the prize-
question. In task (B), he addresses its possibility by offering his reader
a systematic grounding and solving of the academy's question.[3] Hülsen
held such a critical evaluation necessary. The uncovering of the prize-
question's imperfect character serves reason's common knowledge
(*Gemeingute*). It was his duty to communicate it openly.[4]

Hülsen's inquiry into the transcendental possibility of grounding
and solving the prize-question pushes the topic intended by the academy into the background. Hülsen's historically augmented *Wissenschaftslehre* is the central topic of *Preisschrift*. I will therefore first
discuss Hülsen's system by abstracting from most of the accidental
circumstances of the academic contest. Hülsen does not always follow
a rigorous correlative order of discussion. He assumes that his reader is
familiar with Fichte's thought.[5] This enables him to begin his exposition in *medias res*. I however will reconstruct Hülsen's arguments and
exposit them in systematic order.

Historical circumstances forced Reinhold and Fichte to concentrate
mainly on the discussion of their own innovative insights. Both Reinhold and Fichte discussed only partially the connection of their
systems with the history of philosophy. According to Hülsen, Fichte's
rearticulating of Reinhold's early *Elementarphilosophie* forced this
issue to be raised. Hülsen's efforts were therefore directed at rearticulating and expanding the *"spiritual"* (as opposed to *"literal"*)
connection of Fichte's concept of philosophy with the history of philosophy. Hülsen's innovation was to deduce reason's logical-historical
ability to progress purposively. Hülsen grounded the historical standpoint of Fichte's *Wissenschaftslehre*, and established a new critical

---

[3] See: HÜLSEN 1796, 41-2
[4] See: HÜLSEN 1796, 40
[5] See: LANGEWAND 1991, 112

paradigm as to the possibility of formulating a systematic approach to the history of philosophy. Hülsen's achievement prompted Fichte to recommend *Preisschrift* as a work facilitating the study of his own system. Fichte's statement presents Hülsen as a partner in the foundation of German idealism.

Hülsen begins his discussion with a number of introductory remarks. All theoretical knowledge presupposes the existence of a transcendental system of knowledge. This system conditions the emergence of all objects of cognition. Hülsen like Kant, Reinhold, and Fichte claimed that knowledge should relate to a *real* or *concrete* object. Philosophy must critically determine its concrete object of cognition: the transcendental system of knowledge. Conversely, philosophy's actual capability to determine its object implies its being already a critical discipline. Hülsen therefore claims that there is no way possible to determine or to know the true object of philosophy prior to philosophy's transformation into a critical discipline and vice versa.[6]

Hülsen also argued that the *Wissenschaftslehre* could not be dissociated from its history. Its object, the developing system of all knowledge, is a previously existing, though systematically undetermined condition of all pre-critical thought. All systematic efforts made to transform philosophy into a universal discipline are, Hülsen claims, *real* and *necessary* attempts of reason, a holistic self-reflecting *Geist*, to determine the true object of philosophy.[7] Hülsen's opening remark develops a thought raised by Reinhold: the *logical* character of philosophy's history.

Hülsen claims that insight into the history of philosophy confirms that humanity strives after one determined universal goal (*bestimmten Zweck*): philosophy's transformation into a critical discipline. The historical securing of critical philosophy, Hülsen argues after Reinhold, enables an exhaustive consensus (*Einverständnis*) on the true object of philosophical knowledge. A state of disputes among partisan or non-universally determined philosophical standpoints is all that can be found

---

[6]   See: HÜLSEN 1796, III-IV
[7]   See: HÜLSEN 1796, V

in the epoch of pre-critical thought. The true concept of philosophy is, as Hülsen learned from Reinhold, the object of these disputes.[8]

Hülsen claims that the establishment of philosophical consensus demands determination of its systematic possibility, of the transcendental condition of its historical attainment (*Erreichbarkeit*). Hülsen's purpose is a preliminary grounding of Reinhold's vague concept of logical-historical progress. Hülsen argued that a practical self-reflecting capability enables reason's historical development. Reason achieves an ascending positing of different experimental systems of philosophy. Its goal is to attain critical knowledge, to reach the standpoint of the *Wissenschaftslehre,* and self-determine the exhaustive concept of philosophy. Critical knowledge is reason's ultimate reconciling outcome. According to Hülsen, critical knowledge enables a *universal self-conscious unification* of reason's entire practical course of production. Hülsen developed Reinhold's thesis that reason's history is a necessary material condition to the emergence of critical philosophy, which subsumes reason's non-universally determined partisan standpoints under the universal form of an exhaustively self-determined object of thought.[9]

Hülsen emphasizes the individual nature of reason's historical production. Reason's practical activity is a self-limiting activity; it hence manifests itself *exclusively* through personal positions. Philosophers, finite rational beings, push reason forward through their striving. Reason's progress is simultaneously a *general-personal* or rather a *holistically individuated* progress. According to Hülsen, the striving of a reduced number of avant-garde philosophers opens up the road for a general progress of the human species. Their personalized activity is the condition to reason's historical development. Hülsen holds that the attainment of progress demands a *personal reproduction* of this leading activity. In their gradual personal strivings, all rational beings meet the same general "spirit" (as opposed to "letter") of reason's historically developing positions.[10] "Spiritualization" is determined by the fact that

---

[8] See: HÜLSEN 1796, V
[9] See: HÜLSEN 1796, VI
[10] See: HÜLSEN 1796, 128-30

reproduction of a philosophical standpoint conforms, ultimately, to a *determining* subjective degree of logical-historical development. The intellectual history of the human species and the personal history of the rational being can develop in parallel.

Personal production assures that the attainment of critical knowledge be equivalent to self-determination. Philosophy's standpoint is a personal standpoint; its securing is the *necessary result* of individual reflection. Hülsen holds that when an "unscientifically" cultivated rational being philosophizes, whether he knows it or not, he necessarily approximates universal self-determined consensus (critical insight). This proves for Hülsen the impossibility of resorting to the "objective" authority of a *forum externus*. All philosophical objectivity implies a subjective degree of practical self-referential (self-reflective) development. Hülsen concludes that, inevitably, each philosopher must remain the judge of his own progressive production.[11] Hülsen evinces an *Aufklärung* concern shared by Reinhold and Fichte: autonomous or independent inquiry.

Hülsen's opening remarks show a strong interest in rearticulating and expanding the underdeveloped logical-historical side of Fichte's "improved" *Elementarphilosophie*. One of Hülsen's innovations was to develop and to fuse two vaguely, albeit explicitly integrated stems of Reinhold's system: (1) reason's philosophical history and (2) the personal philosophizing labour of the self-determining philosopher (*Selbstdenker*), a combination that Fichte implies in the *Grundlage* and in *Ueber die Bestimmung des Gelehrten*. Hülsen so enriched the connection of the theoretical and the practical divisions of the *Wissen-*

---

[11] See: HÜLSEN 1796, VII. Regarding his own essay, HÜLSEN (1796, VIII-IX) argues that "*Habe ich geirrt, und bald dieses oder jenes nicht verstanden, so wird dennoch meine Absicht dieselbe bleiben, denn die möglichen Irrthümer galten mir als Wahrheit, und ich selbst werde sie darum gewiss auch zurücknehmen, sobald ich etwas besseres an ihre Stelle zu setzen weiss. [...] Wer in diesem Geständniss den Beweis von einem noch schwankenden Systeme findet, der mag für sich Recht haben. Für mich indess hätte er nicht geurtheilt, [...] und ich selbst, das bin ich mir bewusst, werde immerfort streben, mich in meinem ganzen Wesen, und also auch in meinem Wissen zu veredeln und zu vervollkommnen.*"

schaftslehre, and provided a solution to another pending aspect of Fichte's reworking of Reinhold's early *Elementarphilosophie.*

3.2 The Morally Adverse Situation of Man

Hülsen continues with a discussion of humanity's historical situation. He claims that resistance to moral perfection, self-determination, has been a characteristic feature of the history of the human species.

[...] *die Menschen sich von jeher gegen nichts so sehr gesträubt haben, und gegen nichts so sehr noch fortfahren, sich auch gegenwärtig zu sträuben, als gegen ihre eigene, in ihnen gelegene Bestimmung: gegen das Fortschreiten zum Vollkommnern.*[12]

Humanity's history has been so far the history of *heteronomy.* Moral imperfectability is determined by a historically persisting self-contradiction of reason. This is the condition of the rational being throughout the non-self-aware epoch of pre-critical thought. Reason's self-contradiction prevents the rational being from achieving his true moral vocation (*Bestimmung*): *autonomy* or self-determining expansion of all heteronomically given natural relations. This rational handicap manifested itself historically in all personal philosophical positions. Although reason already attained critical knowledge in the *Wissenschaftslehre,* most philosophers ignore it. Neither peace, nor happiness, Hülsen claims, will be established on earth before all rational beings gain a true self-conscious insight into reason's self-contradiction and seek its overcoming.[13]

According to Hülsen, careful analysis shows that rational beings cannot give up their *natural disposition* to moral perfection.[14] Their

---

[12] HÜLSEN 1796, 3

[13] See: HÜLSEN 1796, 3

[14] Hülsen's statement evinces the universal "spirit" of critical philosophy. For as HÜLSEN (1796, 4) holds, "*Nicht der Träge und Verirrte, nicht der Schwache und Gedrückte, nicht der Sklave und Gebiether, Nein — der Mensch überhaupt kann seiner Bestimmung nicht entgehen.*" Hülsen's position can be aligned with Fichte's moral-political position. Compare Hülsen's statement with FICHTE's (GA, III, 2,

true moral vocation, he argues with Fichte, consists in a *necessary* striving after reason's original self-identity. The rational being's apparent historical counter-striving against his true vocation is only an unaware striving after it.[15] Hülsen's sources clarify this point. (1) Hülsen following Reinhold identifies ignorance of critical philosophy with a logical-historical epoch of moral imperfectability. (2) Hülsen shares Fichte's identification of practical striving after self-consciousness, self-determined identity or self-harmony, with the "categorical imperative", moral perfection. He also shares Fichte's identification of self-harmony with the "highest good", a necessary combination of moral virtue and happiness.[16] This explains Hülsen's position that for the human species, the historical inability to self-determine philosophy's true concept is morally detrimental. Hülsen therefore claims that

Darum heisst uns nun: die Quelle alles menschlichen Elends ableiten, und der Vernunft den Frieden mit ihr selber zuführen, auch notwendig nichts anders als: den Menschen über seine wahre Bestimmung belehren. Er kann ihr nicht entgehen, denn es ist seine, in seiner eignen Vernunft d.i. in ihm selbst gegründete, Bestimmung, und nur darum bedarf er über sie der blossen Belehrung, um ihr auch nicht mehr entgehen zu wollen.[17]

Accordingly, the rational being should look for moral improvement within himself. He should uncover the transcendental structure of his spirit. Moral maturity demands self-knowledge. Expanding self-conscious insight should be the key to subsume reason's heteronomic self-contradiction and approach moral perfectibility (self-identity).

---

298) statement in his letter to Bagessen from April/May, 1795: "*Mein System ist das erste System der Freiheit; wie jene Nation* [i.e., France] *von der aüßerer Ketten den Menschen lostreis't, reis't mein System ihn von den Feßeln der Dinge an sich* [...] *Indem ich über ihre Revolution schrieb, kamen mir gleichsam zur Belohnung die ersten ›Winke‹ u. Ahndungen dieses Systems.*" Following Fichte, Hülsen expands the right to revolution (political freedom) into a moral duty to revolution. See: Buhr 1965, 65 [Hülsen not mentioned].

[15] See: HÜLSEN 1796, 4, 6
[16] See: HÜLSEN 1796, 206-9
[17] HÜLSEN 1796, 5

Historical ignorance of his true vocation is the cause behind the rational being's persisting incapacity to overcome the contradictory state of disputes and reach exhaustive philosophical consensus. Hülsen follows Reinhold by stressing that philosophical consensus presupposes the personal possibility of spiritual self-agreement (self-consciousness in Hülsen's case). Hülsen however expands Reinhold's position through Fichte's thought. He argues that as the historical era of *philosophical discrepancy,* the state of disputes worsens the rational being's moral situation. For it prevents *integrative coordination,* a key feature of critical morality.[18]

Hülsen argued that the purpose of his book is to turn the rational being's attention on his true spiritual vocation, and enable a speeding up of moral perfection (philosophical truth), a pedagogic task reminiscent of the Fichtean scholar and the Reinholdian *Selbstdenker.* Hülsen holds that it is fruitless to expect that the epoch of moral improvement will come by itself. To overcome his adverse situation, the rational being should strive personally and develop a self-determining ability. Only in this way, Hülsen concludes, will rational beings finally become "true sons of freedom".[19] According to Hülsen, Fichte's *Wissenschaftslehre* is a factual "external sign" that critical knowledge can emerge in the course of our practical strivings.[20]

For Hülsen the rational being cannot give up his moral vocation. Reason is in a constant self-struggle for self-determined consensus. Humanity is destined to pursue one single necessary objective. The rational being is determined, spiritually, to solve one single task (*Aufgabe*). All struggle for the same single moral improvement. Critical philosophy, the means required to achieve improvement, must emerge at a determined stage of rational progression. Hülsen concludes from that that humanity is destined, inevitably, to an unprecedented moral order, to an infinitely progressing epoch of "highest good".[21] For

---

[18] See: FLITNER 1913, 32 [Reinhold and Fichte not mentioned]
[19] See: HÜLSEN 1796, 6-7, VI-VII
[20] See: HÜLSEN 1796, 156
[21] See: HÜLSEN 1796, 5, 7

Hülsen the attainment of critical knowledge is messianic event. Critical philosophy is a personal freeing tool. The following enthusiastic statement reveals Hülsen's immediate expectations of this morally mature epoch of humanity.

Das werde doch geredet von allen Zungen, die da lehren, von allen Lippen, die sich aufthun, und auf den Strassen und von den Dächern! Dass der Geist der Verfolgung, der Arglist und Bezüchtigung endlich immer mehr vertilgt werde, und Menschlichkeit und Milde in den Herzen erwache. [...] So wandelte lange der Irrthum im Dunkeln, und schirmte seine Wege mi den Schrekken der Nacht. Erst im Lichte des Tages erschien die Wahrheit mit dem Sonnenblikke des Friedens, und die Schrekken flohen, und die Frucht und der Widerstreit. Diesen endlich einsehen war das Gelingen des Mannes, und ihn einsehen und aufheben eine Handlung: ein Augenblick der Vernunft für alle Vernunft überhaupt. O ein segenvoller Augenblick, von welchem an die Tage des Friedens in der lichten Ferne der Zukunft leicht und schön wie ein Nachhall der Harmonien unsrer Geister nun in ewig froher Folge sich dahin reihen müssen.[22]

Hülsen's book is a pedagogic book. For Hülsen philosophy is an applicable discipline. As the genuine system of moral truth, the object of which is rational activity, critical knowledge should be a supreme law for the will. It should provide the epistemic means necessary to approach the higher moral ideal: absolute autonomy. Philosophy, Hülsen

---

[22] HÜLSEN 1796, 5, 7. On this point, Hülsen diverges from Fichte. As Willy FLITNER (1913, 31-2) comments, "[...] *hier geht Hülsen ganz seinen eigenen Weg. Für Fichte wäre es sinnlos, den idealen Zustand inhaltlich zu beschreiben, denn als unerreichbar hat er ebenso kein Interesse, als er überhaupt unfaßbar ist. Hat der Mensch nach Fichte die Idee der Wissenschaft konzipiert, so erfüllt er sich mit sittlichem Geiste, und sein ganzes Leben wird ein harter Kampf, diesen Geist auch nur zu behaupten. Das Wesen des Menschen ist Streben, erst recht das Wesen des in sich geeinten Menschen; denn jede Einigung ist nur momentan und unterliegt ständiger Anfechtung.*" Christoph JAMME (1990, 90) following Flitner adds that "*Im Unterschied zu Fichte, der es für sinnlos hielt, den Idealen Zustand inhatlich zu beschreiben, definiert Hülsen das Ziel seiner und aller philosophischen Bemühungen als völligen Sieg des „Lichts" der Aufklärung über die „Schrekken der Nacht" des Obskurantismus.*"

concludes, should enable an infinite expansion of self-determining activity.[23]

According to Hülsen, critical philosophy is reason's historically developed outcome. Its achievement involved the learning of reason's history.

Die Wissenschaft also muss den Gemüthern zugeführt werden, und zu dieser Einführung, sag ich, wird ihre Geschichte – die Geschichte des werdenden Menschen- wo nicht das einzige, doch gewiss das zuverlässigste Mittel seyn.[24]

The history of philosophy should provide the reader with the personal means necessary to attain self-determination. The first step is a deduction of reason's logical-historical ability to progress. Hülsen's augmented *Wissenschaftslehre* is the final developing outcome of a purposive history of reason. Reason's non-universally determined efforts at a definitive establishment of critical philosophy are necessary developing stages of a single historically self-posited discipline. All its developing stages are subsumed under reason's universal perspective. Articulated, the history of philosophy enabled a "harmonic" reconciliation of all disputing standpoints. Hülsen's approach provides a holistically self-grounded explanation of (1) the historical manifestation and (2) the definitive self-determined consensual solution to humanity's adverse moral situation.[25] Hülsen so reformulated and developed what was only implicit in Reinhold's logical-historical approach to the history of philosophy. Hülsen targets, expands, and regrounds undeveloped aspects of Reinhold's unproven or skeptically objectionable remarks regarding the history of philosophy. Hülsen's chief purpose is to reformulate Reinhold's claim that self-determination demands personal understanding of philosophy's historical relation to its evolutionary stages.

---

[23] See: HÜLSEN 1796, 28-9
[24] HÜLSEN 1796, 29
[25] See: FLITNER 1913, 32

3.3 The Genesis of Consciousness

According to Hülsen, philosophy is not a product of pure chance; it is the result of rational freedom and self-active thinking. As a *produced* discipline, Hülsen holds, philosophy must have had a *beginning in time*. Rational historicity begins with the historical effort of reason to attain philosophical knowledge. For Hülsen the holistic foundations of philosophy are supra historical. The necessary emergence of a *concretely determined* capability of intuitional representation characterizes reason's first spatiotemporally or historically developed outcome. All succeeding stages develop in time. The rational history of philosophy is preceded by a self-grounded, though not entirely exhausted history of the possibility of consciousness. When rational beings achieve a judging capacity to represent experience in systematic terms, these two rational histories fuse and develop together.

Reason's history should focus on the simultaneous perspectives of (1) its real historical development, and (2) its philosophical reconstruction. Historical development focuses on a purely self-grounded process, the subsequent part of which is a purposively ascending production of the *temporally developing* possibility of consciousness. Philosophical reconstruction produces a *retrospective self-conscious portrayal* of all pre-critically taken steps. The exhaustive rational condition for each one of these steps can be uncovered and portrayed systematically only by self-conscious reconstruction.

Reason's first historical achievement is a concretely determined act of intuitional representation. From the reconstructive perspective of the inquirer, Hülsen holds, this act should first appear as a fact of consciousness. Hülsen, following Fichte's criticism of Reinhold, argues that this act, intuitional representation, should not be confused with the foundational act of knowledge.[26] The articulation of reason's history demands analysis of its transcendental possibility. Uncovering this possibility should be tantamount to ground this act. The opening

---

[26] See: HÜLSEN 1796, 8, 203-4

"chapter" of reason's history is on the genesis of consciousness. One of Hülsen's purposes is to show that reason's ability to produce the transcendental ground of intuitional representation enables its immediate transformation into a logical-historical purposive agent.

Analysis of the factual act of representation leads Hülsen, a strong supporter of the *Grundsatz* tradition, to Fichte's holistic point of departure. Pure reason, the equivalent of Fichte's unconditional I, is for Hülsen an absolute ground or first principle. Hülsen argues that pure reason, or in his own words, reason as reason (*Vernunft als Vernunft*), is originally a self-identical agent ("I=I" or "I am"). Through spontaneous or unconditioned self-activity, pure reason posits all possible being immediately and exclusively in, for and by itself. As in Fichte's *Wissenschaftslehre*, immediate self-sustainability exempts this *meta-logical* principle from any subsequent logical proof.[27] Pure reason's absolutely undeterminable character prevents its objective conditioning or limitation, a necessary requirement for consciousness' emergence. Consequently, pure reason neither can recognize, nor attain knowledge of itself as an absolutely self-determined agent; it cannot identify itself as the holistic agent behind the immediate self-positing of its being as absolutely identical to itself. This cognitive inability, Hülsen like Fichte claimed, compels pure reason to leave its absolute realm, self-posit in, for, and by itself an *actual* realm of experience, and develop through it a system of knowledge.[28] For Hülsen unlike Fichte, this process is intrinsically historical.

---

[27] Hülsen employs Fichte's terminology and rejects the possibility of grounding critical knowledge on an absolute object [see: HÜLSEN 1796, 84-7]. According to HÜLSEN (1796, 86), "*Aber ist das Nicht-Ich das Absolute und Unbedingte; so ist es auch – nicht weil etwas anderes ist, dadurch es ist – denn alles andere ist das Bedingte – sondern weil und in so fern es durch nicht anderes, mithin: weil es SELBST ist. Sein völlig bestimmter Charakter, als eines Absoluten, ist also Selbs-tseyn d.i. ein SELBST seyn, folglich – ein ICH seyn. [...] alles absolute Seyn d.i. alles Selbst-Seyn, schlechterdings nur ein Ich seyn kann.*" A similar insight can be found in section II of Schelling's 1795 *Vom Ich als Princip der Philosophie oder über das Unbedingte in menschlichen Wissen* [See: SCHELLING 1985: 1, 53-6], an essay that Hülsen knew.
[28] See: HÜLSEN 1796, 25, 191, 203

Die Vernunft überhaupt ging also dadurch von sich aus, dass sie in die Welt der Erscheinungen eintrat. Folglich war sie schon Vernunft, noch ehe es für sie eine Vorstellung und durch Vorstellung eine Erfahrung und Natur gab. Aber sie war sich selbst nicht diese Vernunft, diese von aller Erfahrung unabhängige Vernunft. Dennoch sollte sie es seyn. Sie sollte wissen und erkennen, dass sie Vernunft sey, sich selbst also wissen als das selbstthätige Seyn, dessen Wesen [...] Freiheit und höchste Einheit ist. Darum ging sie aus in das Gebiet des Bewusstseyns, um zu sich selbst wieder zurück zu kommen, und sich selbst Vernunft zu seyn.[29]

The inherent self-positing of experience's realm transforms pure reason into a concretely or spatiotemporally conditioned agent. Reason develops most of knowledge's system *in concreto*, that is, through an objectively determined *historical* process of self-subsuming reflection. Philosophy's emergence represents for Hülsen the historical stage in which reason performs its first *discursive self-conscious* reflection on itself. This self-reflective condition determines the entire *teleological* self-pursuing character of reason's *circular* development. Philosophy's emergence enables that reason start striving after an infinite *self-conscious* accomplishment of a *mediated* self-positing of itself as reason. Critical insight is its way to attempt to obtain exhaustive knowledge of its pure, unlimited, and timeless being, to seek rigorous self-determination.[30]

For Hülsen, pure reason is an absolutely undeterminable agent. As such, it cannot carry out the historical development of the system of knowledge. According to Hülsen, reason divides itself into two concomitant agents: (1) pure reason and (2) empirical or progressing reason (*empirische* or *fortschreitende Vernunft*). Progressing reason is in charge of the historically extended development of the system of knowledge. Through it, pure reason attempts to attain exhaustive philosophical knowledge of its original or supra-historical being.[31]

---

[29] HÜLSEN 1796, 25

[30] See: HÜLSEN 1796, 25-6

[31] See: HÜLSEN 1796, 25-6. Dieter KLAWON (1977, 189) sums up this point: "*Die Vernunft vor aller Empirie ist zwar rein sie selbst, doch hat sie in ihrer Reinheit kein Bewußtsein ihrer selbst. Um zu einem Bewußtsein von sich selbst zu kommen,*

According to Hülsen, pure reason determines the logical-empirical *modus operandi* of progressing reason. Its absolute determining primacy prevents progressing reason's unconditional self-determinability.[32] Hülsen's discussion of reason's twofold role reveals the transcendental causes for reason's transformation into a logical-historical striving agent.[33] Hülsen thus goes a step beyond Reinhold who does not discuss the possibility of rational historicity. Hülsen reformulates the key question of critical philosophy, namely how critical knowledge *is* possible. His question is rather how this knowledge *has become* possible.[34]

3.4 The Deduction of Intuitional Representation: Rational Historicity

According to Hülsen, critical insight reveals that a transcendental capacity for concrete objective limitation is necessary if reason is to leave its pure realm and posit an inherent realm of space and time. In its first deductive steps, this capacity represents only a *logical* or *momentary* "development". This determines the *pure conditions* for the subsequent emergence of intuitional representation: reason's first *logical-historical* outcome. The question is how an absolutely self-posited agent such as pure reason, or the Absolute I, can be limited through a spatiotemporal object. Hülsen's account drives heavily on Fichte's presentation of his *Wissenschaftslehre* in *Grundlage*, especially its early sections.

---

muß sie sich ihres „reinen" Zustandes begeben und sich auf Welt, Natur, Erfahrung einlassen. Dadurch wird sie zeitlich faßbar, wird geschichtlich, kann demzufolge fortschreiten und in diesem ihrem Fortschreiten erkannt werden. Sie durchläuft die Geschichte, arbeitet sich durch die Empirie wieder zu ihrem reinen Zustand hoch, in dem sie eine neue Qualität, ihr Selbstbewußtsein, gewonnen hat."

[32] See: HÜLSEN 1796, 26

[33] Hülsen refers in passing to all human striving activity as a drive activity [see: HÜLSEN 1796, 48]. However, Hülsen did not connect this activity with Fichte's drive theory in book III of the *Grundlage*.

[34] See: FREYER/STAHL 1984, 118

Originally, the Absolute I is a purely self-acting agent. The possibility of its actual limitation is, Hülsen holds, an immediate result of its logical capability to *quantify* itself into a divisible and synthetically counter-posited I and Not-I. Quantification takes place through two *simultaneous acts*: (1) *counter-positing* and (2) *synthesis*. It is one of the *logical* steps the Absolute I takes to enable the *logical-historical* grounding of intuitional representation. Hülsen deduces the ground of synthetic quantified counter-position by refuting in parallel the possibility of a limiting/determining affection caused by a hypothetic absolute objective entity.

Reconstructive insight reveals that the Absolute I must attain the character of a knowing or limited agent. In its original supra-historical moment, the Absolute I posits all Being (*Seyn*) immediately and exclusively in, for, and by itself. Idealism demands that this Absolute Being should not to be absolutely negated. Therefore, the ensuing act of limitation or determination, Not-Being (*Nicht-Seyn*) for Hülsen, should not be in itself the affecting product of Absolute Not-Being (*absolute Nicht-Seyn*). All possible Not-Being should be a self-limiting act of the Absolute I, a conditioned product of its Self-Being (*Selbst-Seyn*).[35]

Sind demnach die beide Sphären: Seyn und Nicht-Seyn ursprünglich als Absoluta sich entegengesetzt; so soll, um des Seyns willen, auch notwendig das absolute Nicht-Seyn nicht seyn, sondern alles = Ich seyn. So gewiss das Ich also ein Selbst ist; so gewiss muss durch dasselbe auch die Sphäre des absoluten Nicht-Seyn realisiert werden, und alle Negation also aufhören, dadurch das sie = Ich wird und überall nichts als absolute Realität ist.[36]

All Not-Being should be a self-limiting product of the Absolute I. At this stage, Hülsen claims, the Absolute I determines all Not-Being by counter-positing it to itself as "something as such", as a still specifically undetermined objective world. As a self-limiting posited product of the Absolute I, all *Not-Being* attains the status of a *Not-I*. In this way, Hülsen argues, the spontaneous self-activity (*Selbstthätigkeit*) of the

---

[35] See: HÜLSEN 1796, 86-7
[36] HÜLSEN 1796, 87-8

Absolute I is not abolished absolutely. Instead, it is simultaneously abolished and not abolished. It emerges as an unconditioned-conditioning self-reflecting activity.[37]

Die absolute Thätigkeit des Ich ist aufgehoben, in wie fern das Ich sich ein Nicht-Ich entgegensetzt. Aber sie ist eine Thätigkeit des Ich, also auch nicht vernichtet, sondern durch die Gegensetzung nun reflektiert. Mithin ist die beschränkte Thätigkeit des Ich eine reflektierte Thätigkeit überhaupt.[38]

The counter-positing activity of the Absolute I is simultaneously (1) pure or absolute and (2) self-reflective or self-limited. According to Hülsen, counter-positing is the first logical self-reflective step the Absolute I takes to establish the logical-historical ground of spatio-temporal objectivity. Still, Hülsen holds that the Absolute I is not yet aware of the inherently counter-posited character of the Not-I. From its perspective, the Not-I remains an absolutely coercive entity, that is, Absolute Not-Being. This compels the Absolute I to strive forward in order not to lose its absoluteness. According to Hülsen, the Absolute I

[...] kann aber offenbar das Absolute nur bleiben, in wie fern es seine reflektierte Thätigkeit zur Selbstthätigkeit wieder herzustellen strebt, folglich in wie fern es dieselbe als seine Thätigkeit betrachtet, und über sie also reflektiert. Um demnach seine absolute Selbstthätigkeit zu erhalten, muss das Ich über seine reflektierte Thätigkeit selbstthätig reflektieren, durch Reflexion dieselbe sich beilegen, und dadurch Intelligenz werden.[39]

This self-reflection constitutes the first possible discursive act of knowledge. Through it, the Absolute I uncovers that the Not-I is its own posited product; it self-determines for itself the transcendental character of its antecedent act of counter-positing. It appears at this stage as one of the systematic conditions of intuitional representation. Hülsen also refers to this self-determining act as the procedure whereby the Absolute I becomes an intelligent agent. An exhaustive establishment of the transcendental ground of intuitional representation

---

[37] See: HÜLSEN 1796, 88-9
[38] HÜLSEN 1796, 89
[39] HÜLSEN 1796, 90

demands, however, a further determination of the act of counter-positing.[40]

Turning the act of counter-positing into a self-reflected object, enables recognition of the following two inherent constituents: (1) the Absolute-I, and (2) the Not-I, or what amounts the same thing, (1) the pure self-activity of the Absolute I, and (2) its own being-reflected (*Reflektiertseyn*) through a counter-posited Not-I. According to Hülsen, the Absolute I realizes that a Not-I conditions its original activity, which now gets the self-determined form of counter-positing. The Absolute I ceases to be an indivisible agent. It transforms itself into a *divisible* or *quantifiable I/Not-I substance*. Both the subjective and objective products of quantification, the quantified I and Not-I inherently counter-posited (or inter-determined), share now the Absolute I's original sphere of being. Self-reflection enables that the Absolute I self-determine its two quantified products as constituting parts of the act of counter-positing. For Hülsen this means in addition that counter-positing synthesizes the quantified I and Not-I. Synthesis is a concomitant *moment* of counter-positing.[41] Hülsen's concludes that

Da ursprünglich nichts als das Ich ist, und durch das Ich erst schlechthin dem Ich entgegengesetzt wird; da mithin die reflektierte Thätigkeit nur dadurch eine solche ist, dass eine Thätigkeit des Ich reflektiert worden ist; so ist auch nothwendig aller Gehalt der synthetischen Handlung Thätigkeit des Ich: und alle Form derselben Thätigkeit des Nicht-Ich, beides als innere und nothwendige Bestandtheile der Handlung. Hieruas aber folgt, dass da Ich und Nicht-Ich = Ich die absolute Sphäre alles Seyns befassen, auch keiner synthetischen Handlung, welche sie immer auch seyn möge, je ein anderer Stoff als Thätigkeit des Ich d.i. Selbstthätigkeit, und je eine andere Form als Thätigkeit des Nicht-Ich d.i. Einschränkung der Selbstthätigkeit – vorkommen könne.[42]

---

[40] See: HÜLSEN 1796, 90
[41] See: HÜLSEN 1796, 91
[42] HÜLSEN 1796, 91-2

As in Fichte's *Wissenschaftslehre*, the I appears under three different forms. (1) It first is an absolutely indivisible agent responsible for all subsequent holistic acts of positing. (2) It then is transformed into a divisible or quantifiable I/Not-I substance. (3) It finally emerges as a concomitant *moment* of the act of substantiation. Its form, is the form of a quantified accident synthetically counter-posited to a quantified Not-I.

According to Hülsen, self-reflection shows that the Absolute I self-determines the synthetic act of counter-positing as the procedure responsible for the original concurrence of all form and content of cognition. Through it, the self-reflecting I gains insight into the ability of its inherently posited quantified I and Not-I to distinguish and relate. These transcendental features are indispensable conditions for the establishment of reason's first logical-historical product: intuitional representation. Hülsen's next step is to develop the possibility of this act fully.

Self-reflection enables the Absolute I to uncover synthetic quantified counter-positing as its means to self-reflect on its own absolutely self-posited Being (*Seyn*). In this way, the Absolute I gains insight into its own transcendental form (*Form*) of unending self-limitation. It also realizes that its purely self-posited being is the only possible self-determined content (*Stoff*) of its unending self-reflective act of synthetic counter-positing. This same being also emerges for the I as the unending material condition behind this self-determining act.[43]

Hülsen agrees with Fichte that quantification provides the transcendental ground for (1) the original concurrence of all possible form and content, as well as (2) for the simultaneous distinction and relation of the inherently posited quantified I and Not-I. In Fichte's *Wissenschaftslehre*, however, the deduction of the categories, the faculty of imagination, intuition, and the reproductive imagination precede the exhaustive deduction of representation. These transcendental instances appear in Fichte's system as *simultaneous moments* of the act of quantification. According to Fichte, the imagination assures the spontaneous

---

[43] See: HÜLSEN 1796, 92

transference of reality from the substance I to the accident Not-I. The quantified Not-I attains thereby the status of real affecting object as such. The imagination enables actual spontaneous self-determination (or self-limitation) of the Absolute I. The positing of a passive quantified I is its means. Parallel activity and passivity are indispensable requisites for the systematic establishment of the ground of distinction and relation comprehended in the act of representation. Imaginative activity enables the sensing of an actual, though specifically undetermined object. Intuition's deduction demands an additional imaginative step capable of reproducing sensed objects. Through it, the reproductive imagination is established. A simultaneous engagement of all these transcendental moments comprehended in the act of quantification is mandatory to represent an object as such. Only their combination enables exhaustive transformation of the synthetically counter-posited quantified I and Not-I into two intuitional agents, into a representing subject and object. In Hülsen's thought, however, apart from completing quantification and determining the ground of intuitional representation, these acts enable a transformation of pure reason (or the Absolute I) into *empirical* or *progressing reason.*

Hülsen does not discuss any of the transcendental instances discussed by Fichte. Without disagreeing with Fichte, quantification for Hülsen is that definitive act whereby the Absolute I self-determines for itself the synthetic counter-positing of an *actual* or *real* object as such. For Hülsen quantification should be ascribed the status of an exhaustive imaginative act of intuitional representation. For Hülsen, all acts that succeed quantification are simply logical-*temporal* acts accomplished through the faculty of imagination.[44] Hülsen omitted the deduction of these transcendental instances as he simply assumed his reader's familiarity with Fichte's thought.

According to Hülsen, two modes of action of the Absolute I ought to be distinguished: (1) the *free* or the *absolute* one, and (2) the *necessary* or the *self-reflected* one. The Absolute I is an unconditional agent; it furnishes the ultimate ground of all ensuing epistemic acts.

---

[44] See: HÜLSEN 1796, 203-4

Freedom, according to Hülsen following Fichte, is the principle behind all possible subsequent necessity. Spontaneous self-reflection on itself is the Absolute I's way to become aware of and regulate its own innate freedom. It self-determines itself to be its own necessary spatiotemporal mode of intuitional representation, its actual mode of synthetic quantified counter-position.[45] According to Hülsen,

Das Ich ist alsdann frei, in Rücksicht dass überhaupt gehandelt wird, aber bedingt und nothwendig, in wie ferne so und nicht anders d.h. auf eine bestimmte Art und Weise gehandelt wird. Hierdurch entsteht also eine dritte und neue Handlungsart des Ich, eine Handlungsart, die ihren Grund weder allein in der absoluten Selbstthätigkeit noch in der blossen reflektierten Handlung, sondern in beiden zugleich hat. Da sie nun als Handlung schlechthin unbedingt und frei ist, und durch die Regel, die sie annimmt, in jede nothwendige Handlung unsers Geistes eingreift, folglich durch dieses Eingreifen auch Kausalität auf die objektive Welt hat; so könenn wir sie mit Recht transcendentale Freiheit nennen.[46]

Transcendental freedom according to Hülsen is the Absolute I's way to enter the spatiotemporal realm of historical development. Through it, the Absolute I attains the form of an actual *undetermined-determining* or rather *pure-empirical* agent. As in Fichte's *Wissenschaftslehre*, the system of all knowledge is for Hülsen a realism-idealism. Transcendental freedom is pure reason's (the Absolute I's) logical way to determine progressing reason's empirical *modus operandi*. It furthermore furnishes the possibility of objective causality as such. Hülsen implicitly characterizes transcendental freedom as the cause to exhaustive intuitional representation. Transcendental freedom enables a transformation of the Absolute I into a logical-*historical* agent.

Consciousness, however, cannot grasp the Absolute I itself. This would demand an absolute identification of the limited or real product of the Absolute I, the object it grasps through its own self-determining form of synthetic quantified counter-position, with the unlimited condition behind its own self-reflective activity, that is, its pure or

---

[45] See: HÜLSEN 1796, 93-4
[46] HÜLSEN 1796, 94

undetermined being. Such identification requires an unending process
of teleological approximation. The Absolute I strives infinitely to
achieve its highest ideal: the elevation of all synthetically counter-
posited reality to its original sphere of absolute being; progressing
reason is its self-reflecting means.[47]

> [...] *der freien und absoluten Selbstthätigkeit des Ich ist die reflektierte
> entgegengesetzt. Beide verhalten sich also wie Thesis und Antithesis. Sie
> sollen mithin gleich gesetzt werden. Sind sie wirklich gleich gesetzt, d.h. ist
> die Reflexion durch das Nicht-Ich gleich der absoluten Selbstthätigkeit des
> Ich, mithin Nicht-Ich = Ich; so ist auch Alles in Einem, folglich das Ideal alles
> unsers Nachstrebens realisiert, und es bleibt nichts weiter denkbar als:
> absolute Selbstthätigkeit in Rückwirkung auf sich selbst. Wird die Gleich-
> setzung der reflektierten Thätigkeit mit der unbedingten und absoluten,
> durch transcendentale Freiheit nun vermittelt: so ist diese also der Punkt,
> worin beide zusammen treffen sollen, und die Sphäre aller Thätigkeit ist
> dadurch völlig beschrieben.*[48]

Logical-historical striving is the absolute I's way to combine its thetic
and anti-thetic activities. Absolute synthesis is its teleological ideal.
According to Hülsen, this striving works itself out through an ascending series of theoretical objects, of imaginative syntheses. Although the
Absolute I is not aware of its own teleological activity, striving is
behind the methodical-regulative development of a system of knowledge. Manfred Frank's commentary illuminates Hülsen's position:

> *Hülsen deutet nun die Synthesis als dasjenige, welches die [...] Reflexion als
> Ziel ins Auge faßt, um ihre eigentliche Aufgabe, das Nicht-Ich, Schritt für
> Schritt dem absoluten Ich zu ›vergleichen‹, also – wie er sagt – gleich oder
> identisch zu machen. Dabei setzt er durchgängig die Begriffe ›Synthesis‹ und
> ›Identität‹ gleich, womit er heutige analytische Standards schnöde verletzt.
> [...] Diese Gleichsetzung scheint, [...] Identität für eine subalterne Form der
> (absoluten) Thesis zu halten. Da ihre Realität nicht schon zu Anfang besteht,
> sondern als Ziel des ganzen Prozesses verstanden wird, kann man sagen, daß
> Hülsen die Synthesis für die Kreation des idealen Ziels verantwortlich macht.
> Dann wäre die Synthesis gerade zu die Produzentin der Idee, als die das—*

---

[47] See: HÜLSEN 1796, 92-3
[48] HÜLSEN 1796, 94-5

vom Nicht-Ich um seine Dichte gebrachte—Ur-Ich nunmehr dem Bewußt-sein erscheinen kann [...] [also] als Ziel einer unendlichen Aufgabe (>un-endlich< darum, weil kein Zeitpunkt abgesehen werden kann, zu dem das Nicht-Ich, die Totalität aller Prädikate, die Extension des in der Ur-Thesis Enthaltenen erschöpft haben könnte; das war schon Fichtes Konzeption).[49]

Transcendental freedom, or rather an original set of non-historical procedures, provides the system of all knowledge with a sound synthetic foundation. Apart from enabling progressing reason's emergence through self-limiting acts, Hülsen holds, transcendental freedom determines the possibility of concrete intuitional representation. Pure reason's transformation into a *pure-empirical* or rather *general-particular* agent must be understood in conjunction with the appearance in history of a *universal-personal* progressing agent. In this way, the holistic ground of individuation is established. Progressing reason's logical-historical ability to produce a system of knowledge should be identified with the finite rational being's concrete teleological ability to strive after self-determination and conversely.[50]

For Hülsen the rational being first appears in history as a pure representing being (*bloss vorstellendes Wesen*). As such, it can only intuit. At this logical-historical stage, the rational being can neither self-reflect on his acts of objective representation, nor self-determine them as self-reflective products of transcendental freedom (or the imagination). For the rational being at this stage, this representational state emerges as an ongoing series of spatiotemporally determined units.[51] Hülsen concludes that

Als bloss vorstellendes Wesen ist der Mensch demnach nicht frei, folglich der Freiheit entgegengesetzt. Mithin als Wesen betrachtet, ein blosses Natur-wesen. Er stehet daher, als vorstellend, auch unter objektiven Bestimmungen, und ist völlig bedingt und nothwendig. In jedem gegenwärtigen Augenblick

---

[49] Frank 1998, 918-9
[50] This shows, as Karl Obenauer (1910, 3) comments, that "*Da aber das höchste Ziel der Vernunft das Wissen ihrer selbst, die Selbsterkenntnis sei, so könne es gleichgültig sein, ob man Fichte als Urheber der Wissenschaftslehre bezeichne. Jeder sei ihr Urheber, der nach Selbsterkenntnis strebe.*"
[51] See: Hülsen 1796, 8-9

tritt er nur durch den vorgehenden, und sein ganzes Daseyn ist — ein ewiger Wechsel in der Zeit: ein Entstehen und Vergehen, beides zugleich in einem Momente.[52]

According to Hülsen, the inability of progressing reason to self-determine its representing condition prevents the rational being from synthetically grasping his actual; though still undetermined objects of intuitional representation. The logical-historical nature of progressing reason and its striving after self-determination overcomes this blindness. The rational being resorts to the spontaneous activity of the imagination. He self-reflects on his representational acts and self-determines them. So, the rational being can know the transcendental condition of his representational acts. This self-determining ability is the logical-historical act which enables progressing reason to judge. Judgment is for Hülsen the act whereby reason self-determines the possibility of intuitional representation and so attains the status of an intelligent agent.[53]

In Fichte's *Wissenschaftslehre*, the ability to judge is preceded by the deduction of the understanding. The understanding enables a discursive self-determining fixation or reification of the posited product of the reproductive imagination. The object of the understanding is in Fichte's *Wissenschaftslehre* a conceptualized real object of thought. In Fichte's presentation, this procedure enables the propositional determination of objects by the different modes of judgment. The understanding is not deduced in *Preisschrift*. Hülsen probably omitted this deduction assuming his reader's familiarity with Fichte's thought. Crucial for Hülsen is however a deduction of the faculty of judgment.

---

[52] HÜLSEN 1796, 9
[53] HÜLSEN 1796, 9, 12-3

3.5 The Deduction of the Faculty of Judgment

As a pure representing being, the rational being cannot self-determine his own acts of intuitional representation. They do not appear to him at this stage as personal self-reflective products of transcendental freedom. Rather, pure reason's original sphere of freedom and the rational being's sphere of intuitional representation seem to be two mutually exclusive spheres. Original freedom is exclusively a sphere of *immediate identity*. No spatiotemporal succession or alteration is yet possible. Intuitional representation is a sphere of conditioning. Its exclusive feature is permanent spatiotemporal alternation, i.e., disunity and *non-identity*.[54]

Reason now reflects on its own actual acts of intuitional representation. Through reflection, each in turn attains the logical-temporal form of discursive identity, of a qualitatively unified temporal existence (*Daseyn*). This self-reflecting act emerges as the first possible *judgment*, which Hülsen, agreeing with Reinhold and Fichte, understands as a spontaneous *representation of representation*. Judgment is the systematic ground of the first possible *discursive knowledge*. It also enables the first historical attempt to philosophize, the first real intellectual effort to construct a system of knowledge.[55]

The first knowledge attained by judgment is that *something is absolutely (dass etwas absolut sey)*. This judgment is thetic.[56] As Hülsen explains,

[...] *bemerken wir den Zeitpunkt, da alles Reflektieren noch ein Vorstellen überhaupt, noch blosse Bestimmung durch Objekt ist. Soll die Freiheit nun jetzt in den Wechsel eingreifen, und selbstthätig reflektieren, mithin das Urtheil fällen dass etwas sey; so nimmt sie nothwendig in diesem Momente die blosse, durch Objekt bestimmte, Vorstellung in sich auf. Sie reflektieren also durch die Vorstellung, aber durch die vom Objekt bestimmte Vorstellung. Mithin*

---

[54] HÜLSEN 1796, 12-3
[55] See: HÜLSEN 1796, 12-3
[56] See: HÜLSEN 1796, 16

reflektiert sie durch die Vorstellung das Objekt der Vorstellung. Reflektiert die Freiheit aber durch die Vorstellung, so ist diese ihr selbst auch das Gesetz der Reflexion. Die vorstellung ist selbst aber bestimmt vom Objekte, und nur durch dasselbe Vorstellung. Reflektiert daher die Freiheit durch Vorstellung das Objekt der Vorstellung, d.h. urtheilt sie von diesem Objekt zu folge der Vorstellung, dass es sey; so urtheilt sie auch nothwendig, dass es absolut sey. Denn die Freiheit bestimmt durch die vom Objekt bestimmte Vorstellung das Daseyn dieses Objekts. Folglich hat das Gesetz der Reflexion, oder die Reflexion als solche, auch nur Gültigkeit durch dasselbe, und das Urtheil von ihm ist darum nothwendig kein anderes, als A=A d.h. A ist, weil es ist.[57]

This self-determined object of the first possible judgment is a previously represented intuitional object ("A"). Through it, Hülsen claims, the rational being recognizes both the self-active and the self-reflective character of his own representing capability.[58] The determined content of the first possible judgment is unspecified. The capacity for particularity, and hence plural discursive determination, will be established with ensuing anti-thetic and synthetic judgments. Unspecified discursive determinacy, judging's inability at this stage to disjoin and conjoin, is for Hülsen the logical-historical cause behind transcendental freedom's unconditional-conditioning assertion that the object of the first possible judgment is or exists absolutely.[59] Thetic judgment furnishes the ground of this first discursive knowledge. What it unconditionally asserts is that the reality of the intuitional object "A" is identical to its intuiting subject. This object should not be thought of as being opposed to anything else, nor as being like anything else.[60]

For Hülsen following Fichte, thetic judgment enables propositional formulation of the representational ground of all theory: "A=A", which should not be mistaken with the higher thetic judgment possible, namely the *Grundsatz* proposition "I=I" or "I am". Thetic judgment emerges for the first time at a determined stage of consciousness'

---

[57] HÜLSEN 1796, 13-4
[58] See: HÜLSEN 1796, 163
[59] See: LANGEWAND 1991, 110
[60] Hülsen's position is inconsistent, for what he now implies is that "synthesis" and "identity" ought not to be equated.

history. That is why the logical validity of its self-determined rule (*Gesetz der Reflexion* in the passage) should not be dissociated from the historical context in which it takes place. Thetic judgment is in this case not a mere formal-logical act. As progressing reason's first discursive product, it is the first theoretical dictum (*Philosophem*), for Hülsen, a determined representational form of that which is or should be.[61]

Hülsen claims that philosophical reflection shows that from a logical-historical perspective thetic judgment emerges for the first time as an unconditional and complete knowledge (*vollendetes Wissen*). As the first discursive step possible, it determines progressing reason's ensuing self-determining activity.[62]

Thetic judgments are the imaginative products of progressing reason. Their content, their material conditions, are previously intuited objects of representation.[63] According to Hülsen, progressing reason's ascending repetition of the imaginative procedure behind thetic judgments enables (1) gradual logical-historical production and (2) ensuing self-determination of all qualitatively evolving levels of the concretely emerging system of knowledge.

Reflektieren wir hierüber als einen Punkt in der Zeit, da alles Wissen noch unmöglich ist, weil das Ich noch nicht das wissende ist, und setzen nun die Wissenschaften als bloss problematisch [i.e., as not yet actual]; so müssen wir unter ihnen auch nothwendig eine denken, die der Ausdruck von demjenigen sey, wodurch das Ich zum Wissen gelangt, wodurch es also ein wissendes wird, und folglich: eine Wissenschaft von der Möglichkeit alles Wissens. [...] so ist nothwendig diese Möglichkeit nur dadurch erklärbar, dass die Wissenschaft von ihr, als die eine unter den möglichen, wirklich sey. [...] Darum konnte auch die Wissenschaft von der Möglichkeit alles Wissens, oder die Wissenschaft schlechthin, nur allein durch einen vollendeten Versuch, und dadurch nur wirklich werden, dass ihre Möglichkeit durch die Wirklichkeit gegeben wurde.[64]

---

[61] See: HÜLSEN 1796, 15
[62] See: HÜLSEN 1796, 14-5
[63] See: HÜLSEN 1796, 15
[64] HÜLSEN 1796, 9-10, 10, 11

According to Hülsen, a series of imaginative self-reflections enable gradual self-determination of the transcendental possibility of the logical-historical system of knowledge. To attain the status of transcendental possibility, each practically produced stage of this system must be concretely self-reflected. Otherwise, the last produced stage remains a theoretically undetermined presupposition. In other words, systematic development compels progressing reason's transformation of each one of its produced stages –say intuitional representations– into the object of an ensuing self-determining act. What follows, Hülsen claims, is a logical-historical process of *practical production* and ensuing *theoretical deduction*, the *real* developing outcome of which is the self-conscious possibility of critical philosophy. Progressing reason's ongoing effort towards the articulation of a system of knowledge is what Hülsen calls in the passage a complete attempt (*vollendeten Versuch*). A characteristic of pre-critical development is progressing reason's striving, by following necessary though not exhaustively self-determined teleological laws. Only the attainment of critical knowledge, as the passage indicates, enables real deduction of the logical-historical possibility of the system of knowledge. That is the reason Hülsen holds, the transcendental possibility of an augmented *Wissenschaftslehre* can be established exclusively through its reality;[65] a logical-historical position inspired but not articulated by Fichte.

Hülsen's conclusion involves the history of reason as an amendment of Reinhold and Fichte's standpoints. Neither Reinhold, nor Fichte understands philosophy as a true logical-historical product. Neither focuses on reason as a *temporally developing* agent. What develops in time is a general-personal series of rectifying or actualizing perspectives of a *a priori* or supra-historical system of knowledge.[66]

---

[65] See: HÜLSEN 1796, 163

[66] Reinhold and Fichte's positions are typical of those philosophical essays on the history of philosophy of the early 1790's, which according to Willy FLITNER (1913, 27) "[...] *suchen nun neben den „empirischen" die „reinen" Bestandteile herauszuarbeiten und damit der Philosophiegeschichte ein im Kantischen Sinne wissenschaftliches Gepräge zu geben. Hier steht also zunächst gar nicht der Sinn der Geschichte und der Modus ihres Verlaufs in Frage, sondern die Verbindung*

Fichte reflects on his *Wissenschaftslehre* in two *simultaneous* ways. (1) It can be understood as a universal process, as a logical or timeless production. The *Wissenschaftslehre* contains the eternal transcendental conditions necessary to determine the general possibility of experience. (2) Fichte also refers to it as a logical-historical process in which the concrete philosophizing activity of many different thinkers enables the gradual uncovering of the ever-existing system of knowledge. Pragmatic history, an insight obtained through joint effort, records the personal self-conscious articulation in time of this timelessly produced system of knowledge. Fichte understands his *Wissenschaftslehre* in both (1) an abstract logical-non-historical, and in (2) a concrete logical-historical way. The conceptual agreement between the eternal system of knowledge and its concrete historical presentation demands that the *Wissenschaftslehre* be presupposed, though not as a self-determined object.

Hülsen, however, disagreed with Fichte insisting that an inconsistency arises if these two positions are simultaneously held. In his discussion of the impossibility of founding the system of knowledge on Absolute Not-Being or Nothingness (*Nichts*), Hülsen argued that

[…] *weil Nichts das Entgegengesetzte ist, und absolut es ist, so trifft auch die Selbstthätigkeit auf einen Stoff, der dem ihrigen, dem absoluten Seyn, schlechthin widerstrebt. Dennoch muss sie, so gewiss sie Selbstthätigkeit ist, selbstthätig seyn d.i. ein Selbst hervorbringen; also das entgegengesetzte Nicht-Seyn, durch ihr absolutes Seyn nothwendig einschränken d.i. bedingen und demnach ein bestimmtes Etwas als ein **Werden** zum Seyn setzen.*[67]

For Hülsen the *concrete* establishment of intuitional representation's possibility determines reason's entering into a self-posited realm of *conditioning* spatiotemporal limitation. Reason has the *constitutive* character of a personally embodied logical-historical agent, the emerging self-reflecting product of which is the system of knowledge. It is not enough to distinguish between the concepts of simply general *a*

---

    der Tatsachenstücke [i.e., developing systems]; *die Zugehörigkeit der Tatsachen*
    zu dieser und keiner anderen Disziplin; das Prinzip ihrer Verknüpfung."
[67] HÜLSEN 1796, 64-5 [my bold]

priori productivity embodied in the activity of the Absolute I and personal *a posteriori articulation* (self-determination) embodied in the philosophizing activity of the finite rational being. From a certain stage all rational activity is general-personal or pure-empirical activity. Both (1) the realization and (2) the production of a system of knowledge are *simultaneous aspects* of progressing reason's logical-historical activity. According to Hülsen, whenever the transcendental possibility of a cognitive instance is self-determined, a new instance emerges, whose transcendental possibility can, in turn, be deduced in ensuing self-reflecting thought, so revising Fichte's theory of an impersonal or general production of the absolute I only subsequently to be un-covered and articulated by the philosophizing activity of individuals. Hülsen's insight so reconciles two incompatible positions of Fichte's *Wissenschaftslehre*; the system of knowledge is the logical-historical result of a simultaneous *productive-deductive* activity of reason. Hül-sen so reinterprets Fichte's thesis that the transcendental possibility of this system should be given exclusively by its reality.

Through this normative "spiritual" modification, Hülsen also solved a problem posed by Reinhold's history of philosophy: progressing reason's *logical-historical* ability to progress teleologically.[68]

An interpretation according to the "spirit" of Fichte's system is the cause of Hülsen's revolutionary and innovative turn to rational con-

---

[68] Although ignorant of Reinhold's virtually forgotten approach to the history of philosophy, and of how Hülsen's insight into intuitional representation enabled reason's transformation into a historically striving agent, Klaus FREYER and Jürgen STAHL (1984, 118-9) in a three page article characterize Hülsen's innova-tion as follows: "*Die Menschliche Erkenntnisfähigkeit, die Fichte nur logisch-systematisch faßte, sah er [i.e., Hülsen] als real-historisch geworden an und forderte deshalb die [...] Einheit von logischer und historischer Methode im Prozeß der theoretisch-philosophischen Wirklichkeitseinigung. [...] Zudem wei-tete Hülsen die objektiv-idealistische Tendenz des Fichteschen Ich-Begriffes auf eine Philosophie der Geschichte aus. Das Verhältnis von absolutem und empiri-schem Ich wurde bei ihm methodisch wirksam: wissenschaftliche Geschichts-schreibung könne das Allgemeine nur am Konkreten darstellen, weil die reale Geschichte sich so vollziehe.*"

stitutive historicity.[69] Hülsen does not claim that this "spiritual" modification was a step forward beyond what could be found in Fichte's
writings. Nor did it seem such to Fichte, for whom Hülsen's position
supplemented his own *Wissenschaftslehre*.

Hülsen employs an alternative Fichtean term to refer to his logical-
historical agent: the reflecting faculty of judgment (*reflectierende
Urtheilskraft*). Thetic judgment enables the discursive self-determination of intuitional objects. This intuitional distinction allows that
a spatiotemporal series of intuitional objects or *absoluta* (say, "A",
"B", "C", etc.) be given to the emerging rational being within his
original sphere of representation.[70] Hülsen's position is that

*Nie würde aber die Urtheilskraft einen weiteren Fortschritt haben können,
wenn nicht dennoch eine ursprüngliche Mannichfaltigkeit der Objekte vorhanden gewesen wäre. So wie daher das Vemögen, etwas schlechthin zu
setzen, an den Gegenständen A, B als einem X überhaupt, einigermassen entwikkelt war, wurden diese nicht mehr als ein blosses X –als Daseyn
überhaupt- sondern als Ax und Bx, und folglich mit Unterscheidung des
einen vom andern gesetzt. [...] Ursprünglich sind A und B bloss und
schlechthin gesetz. Aber ihr blosses Gesetztseyn als ein x schliest das A=A und
das B=B, folglich die Merkmale A und B in x darum nicht aus. Dies wenigstens nicht für eine Intelligenz ausser dem Urtheilenden. Mit der grössern
Fertigkeit im thetischen Urtheilen wurde aber die Urtheilskraft eben diese
Intelligenz. Sie setzte also A=A und B=B; folglich A-B und B-A. Aber B
sowol als A waren schchthin gesetzt, mithin, insofern A gesetzt war, B dem A
schchthin entgegen gesetz.[71]*

Judgment in its logical-historical determination enabled further thetic
predications (objective existences "as such" or "X"). Thetically judged
objects (say, "A" and "B") are self-reflected and posited with their

---

[69] Although there is no direct evidence that Hülsen influenced Schelling and Hegel
on this point, the history of ideas could still record HÜLSEN's *Preisschrift* as a
predecessor of Schelling's *System des transcendentalen Idealismus* and of
HEGEL's *Phänomenologie des Geistes*. The discussion of this interesting topic,
however, transcends the limits of this monograph.
[70] See: HÜLSEN 1796, 16
[71] HÜLSEN 1796, 16-7

implicitly produced, though still not discursively deduced predicate of distinction (say, "Ax" and "Bx"). This subsequently enables judgment on the simultaneous self-identity and distinction of two objects of thought. The more "A" and "B" are determined as self-identical, the more they are distinguished and counter-posited. This judging procedure furnishes the preliminary ground of discursive quantification. Judgment so enables a second logical-historical epoch: anti-thetic thought.[72]

Quantification reveals that no anti-thesis is possible without synthesis and vice versa. Synthetic thought is the faculty of judgment's third logical-historical epoch. According to Hülsen, synthetic thought does not constitute a moment of anti-thetic thought. The faculty of judgment produces synthetic thought in exactly the same way it produces the ability to judge anti-thetically, i.e., through a logical-historical self-reflection. In its third epoch, the faculty of judgment uncovers its own implicit production of the ground of synthetic judgment in its previous anti-thetic epoch. Hülsen holds that no judgement can refer to the real discursive distinction or counter-positing of two specifically self-determined objects (say, "A" and "B") without presupposing the possibility of their synthetic unification.[73]

Gradual self-reflecting progression, Hülsen claims, is the faculty of judgment's way to self-determine for itself its previous acts and enhance its sphere of freedom. The logical-historical epoch of synthetic thought closes its transcendental evolution.[74] For as Hülsen states,

[...] *es wird geurtheilt, dass etwas sey, dass etwas nicht sey, und dass etwas nur irgend etwas nicht sey, folglich dass es etwas sey. Oder mit andern Worten: es wird gesetzt, entgegengesetzt und gleichgesetzt. Ist alles Entgegengesetzte gleichgesetzt; so ist nothwendig wiederum nichts als Thesis. Durch Synthesis kommt daher die Reflexion wieder auf die Thesis zurück, folglich auf dasjenige zurück, wovon sie ausgegangen war, und mit ihr ist demnach die ganze Sphäre der Urtheile erschöpft und beschrieben.*[75]

---

[72] See: HÜLSEN 1796, 16-7
[73] See: HÜLSEN 1796, 17-8
[74] See: HÜLSEN 1796, 18
[75] HÜLSEN 1796, 18-9

The faculty of judgment is spontaneously self-posited. This means that in its three logical-historical epochs its self-reflecting mechanism is determined unconditionally. From the developing perspective of the judging subject, the knowledge obtained in each one of these epochs emerges as a complete knowledge (*vollendetes Wissen*). In this way, the faculty of judgment is established exhaustively and absolutely.[76]

Thetic judgment ("A=A") enables unconditional self-determination of a concrete intuitional object. This first discursive effort to construct a system of knowledge enables the unconditionally self-posited reality of an intuited object to be identified with its intuiting subject; the reality of "A" is asserted, immediately, as a representing I. In addition, thetic judgment enables the judging subject to uncover the personally self-posited character of his intuitional objects. Hülsen concludes that at this logical-historical stage the subject mistakes his individual uncon-ditionally self-positing self for a transcendent Absolute I. The positing structure of the Absolute I is transferred immediately and unconsciously to the sphere of discursive representation.[77] Such personifying procedure is for Hülsen characteristic of all early human thought. Thetic judgment is the distinctive form of antiquity's consciousness exemplified by Greek mythology.[78]

Das Wandelbare im Raume und in der Zeit konnte kein letzter Grund des Wissens seyn. Man erkannte bald hieran nichts als Accidenzen, die im Strome der Zeit entstehen, und im Entstehen gegen einander verschwinden. Ursprüng-lich zwar setzte man [...], alle Sinnenerscheinungen absolut. Aber mit der Wahrnehmung des Veränderlichen, setzte man nothwendig auch ein Heer absoluten Ursachen, und subordinierte auch diese wieder unter eine höchste. Daher die Gottheiten der Griechen. Jede Quelle hat ihre Nymphe, jeder Hayn seinen Sylfen. Man suchte also etwas von dem Wechsel der dinge Unabhängi-ges, und in der bildlichen sowol als abstrakten Vorstellungsart daher ein Seyn an Sich Selbst. Hierbei war man, auf dem Wege des empirischen Fortschreitens der Vernunft zu ihr selber, nothwendiger Weise nur in der objektiven Welt.[79]

---

[76] See: HÜLSEN 1796, 18
[77] See: LANGEWAND 1991, 104
[78] See: HÜLSEN 1796, 19-20
[79] HÜLSEN 1796, 144. HÜLSEN (1796, 20) additionally argues that "*Der Sprach- und*

Unconscious transference determined the finite rational being's positing of himself in Greek mythology as the absolute source of experience; as a subordinating I-in-itself. After Greek mythology, all human intellectual achievements are logical-historical products of reason. Hülsen's interest in the history of culture transcends the sphere of the history of philosophy proper. His interest in mythology as a "prelude" to the history of philosophy transforms philosophy's history into a rational history of the human species.[80]

Hülsen claimed that through a process of transference the logical-historical epochs of anti-thetic and synthetic thought affected and structured the history of culture. They enabled the establishment of the family and other such human relations.[81] For Hülsen, the history of philosophy and the philosophy of history are identical.[82]

Philosophical reconstruction shows that thetic, anti-thetic, and synthetic thought are the three logical-historical stages whereby the self-reflecting faculty of judgment is established. According to Hülsen, the first possible discursive synthesis results in a higher discursive thesis (unification). The self-reflecting faculty of judgment impels progressing reason forward methodically by an ascending repetition of the judging acts of thesis, anti-thesis and synthesis. In this way, reason progresses. From the developing historical perspective of the judging subject, this evolutionary mechanism is not yet self-consciously reflected. This requires that progressing reason strive and self-determine for itself the transcendental possibility of the faculty of judgment. Only the logical-historical emergence of critical philosophy enables this

---

Alterthumsforscher wird eine geistlose Untersuchung anstellen, wenn er nicht nach diesem nothwendigen Gesetze unsers Geistes beobachtet."

[80] See: FLITNER 1913, 34. Hülsen's standpoint is an original position within German idealism. Although there is no direct evidence that Hülsen influenced Hegel on this point, the history of ideas could still record Hülsen's *Preisschrift* as a predecessor of the Hegelian Phenomenology of Spirit. See: FREYER/STAHL 1984, 118. For coincidences between Hülsen and Hegel, see: GIRNDT 1965, 157

[81] See: HÜLSEN 1796, 20

[82] See: KLAWON 1977, 194

through an ascending series of self-posited systems of thought, i.e., the entire history of philosophy.

3.6 The Asking-Answering Mechanism of Judgment

Imaginative activity is the Absolute I's way to attain the constitutive character of a logical-historical agent. Progressing reason produces a system of knowledge through an ascending self-subsuming series of imaginative syntheses, the emerging object of which are new developing theses and anti-theses. According to Hülsen, critical philosophy, the *Wissenschaftslehre*, is an empirically reachable goal of reason; its teleological function is to provide striving activity with a progressing direction. With judgment's emergence, it ceases to be progressing reason's exclusive means. For Hülsen discursive knowledge is more than the self-posited result of logical-historical judgment. It is also the *concomitant* product of an *asking-answering* mechanism. All discursively developing stages of the system of knowledge attain the simultaneous character of *self-posited answers* that progressing reason gives to previously formulated *self-posited questions*. Deduction of this concomitant mechanism of judgment enables determination of the transcendental possibility of what is assumed in Reinhold's early *Elementarphilosophie*: philosophizing reason's ability to progress historically by answering questions.

Hülsen anticipates Heidegger. Hülsen begins by assuming the factual existence of questions. Like Heidegger, Hülsen discusses the essential nature (*Wesen*) of a question as such. The uncovering of this essence will reveal the existence of a transcendental asking-answering mechanism of judgment.[83] Hülsen's assumption is that

Jede Frage überhaupt nun ist nothwendig dadurch nur möglich, und nur dadurch eine Frage: dass sie ihrem ganzen Wesen nach auf ein WISSEN gerichtet seyn muss. Es ist unmöglich, je zu fragen, ohne etwas wissen zu

---

[83] See: HÜLSEN 1796, 83

wollen, und alles wirkliche Wissen, oder die Allwissenheit überhaupt, schliesst nothwendig daher alles Fragen aus.[84]

This preliminary definition has the status of an uncritically established fact of consciousness (*Thatsache des Bewusstseyns*). The fact that the attainment of discursive knowledge is the essence of a question as such, suggests that this essence should be a transcendentally conditioned product of reason.[85] Hülsen's assumption is that the *discursive* procedures of *asking* and *answering* are *judging* procedures of the human spirit, the necessary systematic location of which should be deduced from its developing nature. Hülsen will thus uncover the ground of a key, though critically dodged procedure of all philosophizing activity: the transcendental mechanism whereby questions are formulated and replied.[86]

Hülsen assumes that asking and answering are procedures of the human spirit. If so, their regulation by transcendental freedom's self-reflecting activity (or the imagination) follows. Insight into thetic judgment reveals the constitutive existence of two concomitant or *momentary* procedures, which Hülsen will later characterize as (1) question (*Frage*) and (2) answer (*Antwort*). Asking and answering are not temporally separated, but complementary aspects of one single logical-historical act of reason.[87] Hülsen argues that

Bei dieser Reflexion [i.e., thetic judgment] *nun aüsseren sich zwei Momente. Einmal: dass die Freiheit über den ganzen Akt als bloss möglich reflektiere, d.i. ihn als Handlung aufgebe; und Zweitens: dass sie über ihn in actu, d.i. als*

---

[84] HÜLSEN 1796, 83

[85] Hülsen applies the same circular deductive method applied by Fichte to determine the original character of the *Thathandlung*.

[86] See: HÜLSEN 1796, 84, 93

[87] Hülsen does not call this discursive activity thetic judgment, but reflected activity (*reflektierte Thätigkeit*). It represents the same activity whereby the I self-reflects on its synthetically counter-posited object of intuition and becomes an intelligent agent [See: HÜLSEN 1796, 96]. This is precisely the function that Hülsen attributes to the imaginative procedure that furnishes the ground of thetic judgment.

135

geschehend reflektiere, und folglich als eine nothwendige Handlung pragma-tisch darstelle.[88]

According to Hülsen, these *moments* constitute the (1) *content* and (2) the *form* of thetic judgment. The first moment represents that rational act whereby the ground of intuitional representation is brought about *in concreto*; the second, that ensuing act whereby reason *self-deter-mines for itself* intuitional representation's *transcendental possibility*. Pragmatic portrayal is reason's only self-reflective means to *deduce* the necessary character of its antecedent act of intuitional representation. Thetic judgment endows intuitional representation with an additional *qualitative* status, which transforms it into a systematically self-deter-mined *content*. This content condition is *exclusively* a *simultaneous* result of thetic judgment's *formal* self-reflective act. That is why intuitional representation appears from this logical-historical angle as a transcendental *moment* of thetic thought. Hülsen calls thetic judg-ment's first moment the problem (*Problem*) and the second moment the result (*Resultat*) of reflection. Both moments will later emerge as equivalents of (1) question and (2) answer, respectively.[89]

According to Hülsen, the *problem of reflection* refers to that self-reflective act whereby reason brings about the ground of intuitional representation, while the *result of reflection* refers to reason's ensuing pragmatic self-determination of intuitional representation. Only thetic judgment allows problem and result to be characterized as simul-taneous moments of the *discursive* act of asking-answering. For Hülsen, this condition cannot be established by *intuitional* represen-tation, but by what he alternatively calls *reflection as such (Reflexion überhaupt)*. Asking-answering, he claims, is the outcome of *free reflection (Reflexion aus Freiheit)*, of reason's first *discursive* self-determining act, and not of intuitional representation or reflection as such.[90]

---

[88] HÜLSEN 1796, 96
[89] See: HÜLSEN 1796, 96-7
[90] See: HÜLSEN 1796, 98

Critical insight shows that the outcome of *reflection as such* is a synthesized counter-positing of an intuitively representing subject (thesis) and an intuitively represented object (anti-thesis). At the logical-historical stage of intuitional representation, Hülsen claims, the intuiting subject is not aware of the synthetic character of its intuition. Only *free reflection* enables discursive self-determination of this intuition. According to Hülsen, this procedure, thetic judgment, takes place through two *momentary* stages. At first, for the thetically judging subject intuitional representation is a *problem*. The thetic reality of the representing subject (quantified I), and the anti-thetic negation caused by the represented object (quantified Not-I), appear as reciprocally excluding principles. Subsequently, the judging subject apprehends the synthetic character of its act of intuitional representation. This second moment is the *result* of reflection. Thetic judgment's two concomitant moments enable self-determining insight into the synthetically counter-posited character of the two agents of representation.[91] Hülsen's next identifies *problem* and *result of reflection* with the constitutive procedures of *question* and *answer*.

Wir haben im Systeme des menschlichen Geistes jetzt den Ort bestimmt, wo die Frage, als Handlung der freien Selbstthätigkeit, durch die Bedingung der Reflexion inhren festen und unveränderlichen Sitz hat. Ihr Begriff ergiebt sich aus der Erörterung nun leicht. Sie ist nehmlich nicht anders, als: die durch Thesis und Antithesis völlig bestimmte aufgabe zu einer Synthesis. Durch die Antwort soll diese Synthesis wirklich gegeben, und die Antithesis der Thesis also gleich gesetzt werden. Beide Frage und Antwort, machen daher den ganzen Umfang der freien Reflexion aus, und hier ergiebt sich nun bestimmt, wie ganz unmöglich es ist, irgend eine Aufgabe richtig aufzustellen und zu lösen, wenn das höchste Problem: das Nicht-Ich = Ich, nicht schön richtig gefast und durch die Idee gelöst ist.[92]

For Hülsen, thetic judgment provides the ground for an ensuing qualitative development of judgment as a simultaneous act of asking-

---

[91] See: HÜLSEN 1796, 98-9
[92] HÜLSEN 1796, 99-100

answering.[93] Thetic judgment sets up a logical-historical mechanism that regulates all ensuing questions and answers. For Hülsen, progressing reason's discursive production-deduction of the system of all knowledge represents a universally extended act of asking-answering.[94]

Asking-answering is a product of the logically-historically developed faculty of judgment. Its essence is the attainment of discursive knowledge. Hülsen proves his point by discussing a supplementary aspect of the moment of asking. Hülsen intends to provide additional evidence of the coincidences of judging and asking-answering. Hülsen claims that insight into thetic judgment reveals that the moment of asking is itself constituted by two additional moments: (1) something (*etwas*) which one whishes to know, a potentially self-reflected object, and (2) something from which (*wovon*) or rather whereby this object can be known, a self-reflecting subject.[95]

Die Frage überhaupt nehmlich ist, als Handlung der freien Reflexion, die aufgabe zu einem Wissen; oder, in wie fern durch die Frage die Freiheit sich zum wirklichen [i.e., discursive] Reflektieren erst bestimmt — ein Wissen-Wollen. Wer also frägt, will irgend etwas wissen, und in jeder Frage muss daher nothwendig vorkommen: 1) etwas, das man wissen will; und 2) etwas, wovon man es wissen will. Ausser diesen Bedingungen kann schlechthin keine Frage Statt finden, denn sie gehören zu ihrem innern Wesen, und die Frage is daher durch sie auch völlig erschöpft.[96]

Every possible question contains something that one wishes to know, something whereupon (*wonach*) one asks, namely a potential object. Hülsen assigns this object the preliminary status of a *determinative* (*Zubestimmendes*) moment. In any question an intuitional I and Not-I appear to the thetically judging subject as two mutually excluding thesis and anti-thesis. Only ensuing self-determination of this self-annulling object reveals its subsequent synthetically *determinable* (*Bestimmbares*) moment condition. Each object emerges as a potential

---

[93] See: HÜLSEN 1796, 97-8
[94] See: HÜLSEN 1796, 104
[95] See: HÜLSEN 1796, 100
[96] HÜLSEN 1796, 100-1

determinative-determinable (*Zubestimmend-Bestimmbares*) posited product. Every possible question presupposes *something original* from which (*wovon*) or rather whereby all asking is possible, a pure subject or reason. This pure agent must not be identified with that whereupon one asks, with that one wishes to know, namely with a potential synthetically self-determined object. These two principles are opposites. The pure subject is for Hülsen the original foundation of the question, that which enables that all questions be self-posited. The unconditional character of this original agent precludes asking about it; no answer can self-determine it synthetically. This original subject is a *non-determinative-determinable* agent, which should be presupposed meta-logically as a purely self-determined agent.[97] The asking-answering mechanism coincides with progressing reason's self-determining judging mechanism.

Ist dies nun die Natur der beiden Bestandtheile der Frage; so bestimmt sich aus ihnen selbst auch ihr Verhältniss zu einander. Das Zubestimmend-Bestimmbare soll nehmlich durch die Antwort dem schlechthin und bestimmt Gesetzten gleich gesetzt werden. Dies geschieht demnach durch Synthesis. Mithin verhält sich in der Frage das Zubestimmend-Bestimmbare zu dem schlechtin Bestimmten: wie das Bedingte zu seiner Bedingung als Unbedingten.[98]

Whenever the transcendental possibility of a systematic instance is self-determined, progressing reason creates an additional instance, the transcendental possibility of which is deduced with ensuing self-reflection. The same, Hülsen next claims, holds true for the act of asking-answering. Every *deduced answer* (synthesis) brings about the logical-historical ground for an ensuing *question* (thesis/anti-thesis).

---

[97] See: HÜLSEN 1796, 102-4. As HÜLSEN (1796, 169) alternatively puts it: "*Es ist für die Vernunft, in so fern sie philosophiert, eine nothwendige Voraussetzung, dass unser Wissen, als Wissen, irgend etwas seinen Grund habe. Hätte es keinen Grund, d.h. wäre Nichts sein Grund; so wäre auch Nichts wovon wir Etwas wüssten, und wir wüssten also nichts von Nichts, mithin wäre unser Wissen selbst eine Negation.*"

[98] HÜLSEN 1796, 103

Nach dem Wesen einer Synthesis ist in derselben nun die Thesis zwar nicht weiter zu bestimmen, weil man nach dem nicht fragen kann, Wovon man etwas wissen will. Aber dies ist allerdings in einer andern Frage möglich. Jenes Wovon man etwas wissen will, wird in dieser alsdann das, was man wissen will; nur muss nothwendig auch hier wieder etwas schlechthin gesetz seyn, Wovon man es wissen will. So weit daher die Thesis selbst eine Synthesis ist, kann das schlechthin Gesetzte immer wieder bedingt gesetzt werden: und daraus lässt sich einsehen, dass jede mögliche Frage durch regelmässig fortgesetzte Zergliederung auf dasjenige zurückgebracht werden kann, wonach schlechtherdings kein Fragen weiter Statt findet; sondern Wovon vielmehr alles Fragen schlechthin ausgehen muss.[99]

According to Hülsen, the Absolute I can never appear under the form of an answer-content. The Absolute I is a purely self-identical, an unconditioned (*un-bedingte*) agent, that is, an agent that cannot be *objectified*. That is the reason Hülsen concludes that the Absolute I can never appear in the logical-historical sphere of synthetically determined counter-positing, that is, answered questions.[100]

Progressing reason attains for Hülsen the status of a questioning I (*fragende Ich*).[101] Hülsen so determines the exact systematic location and explains the transcendental possibility of a vague logical-historical feature of Reinhold's early *Elementarphilosophie*. All judging activity is a developing asking-answering activity. Its regulative goal is reason's mediated self-positing of itself as reason. Inquiry into the transcendental possibility of a question as such enables determination of the *only possible developing question* that can be asked and answered in philosophy: how a system of knowledge, *Wissenschaftslehre*, is possible. The possibility of asking non-systematically determined questions can now be avoided, including Reinhold's "disputing questions" (*streit Frage*) as the causes for philosophical disputes. Hülsen so takes another step towards the establishment of universal self-determined consensus, critical philosophy.

---

[99] Hülsen 1796, 106-7
[100] See: Hülsen 1796, 107-8
[101] See: Hülsen 1796, 108

3.7 The Origins of Systematic Philosophy

According to Hülsen, the first discursive synthesis results in a higher discursive thesis (unification). Qualitatively, the self-reflecting faculty of judgment does not develop any further. Quantitative development, intentional expansion, is what this faculty pursues until the emergence of the self-conscious judging act of critical philosophy. The mechanism of judgment enables progressing reason's first *systematic integration* of its intuited plurality of objects (nature). Judging syntheses result in a developing ability to conceptualize nature's plural character, which emerges under consciousness' discursive unity (*Einheit des Bewusstseyns*).[102]

Durch fortgesetzte Synthesis entstand die Intelligenz, die das Mehrere zu Einem zusammenfasst, nun selbst im Bewusstseyn, und dadurch im ganzen Umfange der Urtheile auch Einheit des Bewusstseyns. Aber Einheit des Bewusstseyns, als Einheit der Urtheile im Bewusstseyn, ist **Systematische Einheit***, und diese also, trozt der möglichen Sprünge und Inkonsequenz, schon nothwendig ein lebendiger Versuch zur Philosophie als Wissenschaft von der Möglichkeit alles Wissens.*[103]

This first possible discursive synthesis is the foundation for all subsequent *systematic philosophy*. Each new synthesis enhances progressing reason's ability to unify natural plurality. Synthetic activity is judgment's way to extend its intentional scope and instil *systematic order* in the discursively *undetermined chaos* of natural plurality. As a self-determining procedure, this enables a gradual expansion of human freedom and with it, truth.[104] For the judging subject this striving mechanism is however not yet a *self-aware* mechanism. This demands

---

[102] See: HÜLSEN 1796, 19-20

[103] HÜLSEN 1796, 21 [my bold]

[104] Hülsen's position has implications for a potential skeptic opponent. As Willy FLITNER (1913, 35) comments, "*Wollte man an der Tatsächlichkeit eines ersten Versuches zweifeln, so wäre das ein Zweifel gegen alles Wissen; und gegen jede Skepsis stände dem Peritrope entgegen: auch die skeptische Behauptung wäre ein Versuch zum Wissen.*"

that progressing reason self-reflect on and self-determine for itself the transcendental possibility of the rationally self-grounded asking-answering faculty of judgment. Only the logical-historical emergence of self-consciousness, critical philosophy, can determine this possibility. An entire ascending series of self-posited systems of thought, the entire history of philosophy, Hülsen concludes, will be necessary for progressing reason to reach this stage.

According to Hülsen, all systematizing activity is exclusively personal; it develops only through individual judging or philosophizing. Thetic thought enables progressing reason's ability to self-reflect on an intuited object of representation, say "A". Nevertheless, Hülsen claims, this personal self-determining procedure can potentially refer to other intuited objects, say "B", "C", "D", etc. so that intentionally, intuitional representation can vary from subject to subject. The faculty of judgment's logical-historical development presupposes this particular objective determination.[105] What follows is

Die Natur schuf ihn [i.e., the rational being] *aus ihrer Fülle der Verschiedenheit, und bildete auf die Art, an ihrem Theile, das ganze Menschengeschlecht als ein Mannichfaltiges. So wurde daher nothwendig in verschidenen Subjekten die Kette der Vorstellungen, als Urtheile durch Freiheit, auch demjenigen verschieden, was nicht Freiheit war. In einem jeden also musste die Urtheilskraft in ihrer intensiven Erweiterung einen eigenen Spielraum erhalten. In einem jeden war Einheit aus seinem Gesichtspunkte, und in einem jeden das Daseyn der Welt überhaupt nach eigenen Gesetzen der Reflexion bestimmt.*[106]

All rational beings have the same transcendental constitution. The scope of their intentional contents, the empirical representation of reason's original being, differs however in quantity. For Hülsen this position explains the possibility of different simultaneous philosophical systems; synthetic judgment inaugurates the *history of philosophy*. According to Hülsen, all previous thought is only a "prelude" to this history. The possibility of simultaneous systematic multiplicity opens

---

[105] See: HÜLSEN 1796, 21
[106] HÜLSEN 1796, 22-3

an epoch of practical expansion. Reason is now ready to strive after true philosophical knowledge. The faculty of judgment will create simultaneous, though quantitatively disparate systems. The logical-historical securing of critical philosophy enables that this faculty self-consciously reflect on itself, uncover its universal regulative nature, and strive after an exhaustive self-subsuming of reason's original being.

According to Hülsen, partisan disputes are a result of the logical-historical possibility of systematic multiplicity. All pre-critical were unilaterally determined standpoints. As non-self-conscious stages of the only true possible developing philosophy, each one of these logical-historical stages asserts itself as the exclusive representative of universal truth, and hence disputes.[107] Hülsen's claim is a development and holistic explanation of Reinhold's thesis that reason's logical-historical ignorance of critical philosophy determines the epoch of partisan controversies. A difference between *Preisschrift* and Reinhold's early *Elementarphilosophie* is Hülsen's deduction of pre-critical reason's ability to develop historically.

Hülsen's conclusions paved the way for re-articulating critical philosophy's introduction in a rational history of philosophy. Hülsen's achievement found a philosophical ground for Fichte's historical standpoint. Hülsen so completes Fichte's re-articulating of Reinhold's standpoint. Hülsen's *Preisschrift* provides the reader with the logical-historical tool to uncover his true unending vocation. As in Reinhold's early *Elementarphilosophie*, philosophy's personal securing enables self-determined withdrawal from the sphere of partisan disputes and universal consensus.

3.8 The Systematic Character of Partisan Disputes

Hülsen shares Reinhold's view that philosophical knowledge is teleologically achievable. Hülsen's belief that the *Wissenschaftslehre* is "science" enabled him to amend and improve Reinhold's position. The

---

[107] See: HÜLSEN 1796, 23

emergence of the *Wissenschaftslehre*, i.e., critical knowledge, represents for Hülsen the general-personal *qualitative* end of the rational history of philosophy, the end of reason's empirical development. According to Hülsen, philosophy enabled progressing reason's self-conscious reflection on the unconditionally self-grounded faculty of judgment; exhaustive self-determination of the transcendental, and hence the qualitative possibility of a logically-historically developing system of knowledge. The *Wissenschaftslehre* understood "spiritually" implies an unending striving after a *quantitative* overcoming of the I/Not-I contradiction posited by reason's transformation into a pure-empirical agent. Philosophy's universal qualitative insight enables a personal self-determining recognition of unending striving as the true human moral vocation. Moreover, the *Wissenschaftslehre* enables the rational being to improve his moral performances significantly.

So verstanden fällt nun die Besorgniss von selbst weg, dass uns im Gebiete der Philosophie, als einer vollendeten Wissenschaft, nichts mehr zu thun übrig bleibe. Wir haben nehmlich bis dahin noch nichts gethan, denn wir waren noch gar nicht da. Wir erhalten also mit dem Erkentniss unser selbst erst die Aufgabe von dem, was wir alle Ewigkeit hindurch zu thun haben werden: folglich sind wir durch die Philosophie nur erst in den Stand gesetzt, wirklich anzufangen. [108]

According to Hülsen, the partisan character of all pre-critical thought is determined by the rational being's qualitative inability to recognize his true moral vocation as an unending logical-historical task of quantitative self-conscious striving. Hülsen following Reinhold furthermore claims that critical insight enables a universally self-grounded consensus on the true concept of philosophy. Philosophy as "science" not only assures personal withdrawal from the sphere of partisan disputes, as Reinhold thought, but also self-determined coordination.[109] For Hülsen the establishment of philosophical consensus also requires that its possibility, the transcendental condition of its

---

[108] HÜLSEN 1796, 164-5
[109] See: HÜLSEN 1796, 24, 29-32

historical attainment (*Erreichbarkeit*), be self-determined.[110] Achieving this, Hülsen claims, is tantamount to both justifying the logical-historical emergence and overcoming of the morally adverse epoch of partisan disputes, a critical challenge that Reinhold's early *Elementar-philosophie* did not meet.

Hülsen following Reinhold argued that the history of philosophy is divided in epochs. Hülsen does not discuss the possibility of this division.[111] Instead, he referred to Leibniz whose original effort to transform philosophy into a real "scientific" discipline brought about a new historical level of philosophical inquiry. According to Hülsen, Leibniz's ability to formulate an avant-garde system of philosophy reveals the distinguished degree of his practical self-activity or expand-ing autonomy. For Hülsen, Leibniz is a productive "mastermind", or in his Reinholdian language, a self-thinker (*Selbstdenker*). Still, Hülsen furthermore agrees with Reinhold that the quest for a systematic expression of philosophical truth was a *leitmotiv* of *all* pre-critical thought. Taking Leibniz's system as an example of a pre-critical system of philosophical truth, Hülsen ascribes to it as to all pre-critical systems a disputative polemical character.[112]

Aber eben das thun alle übrigen Selbstdenker, und sie thun es nur aus dem Grunde, weil keines einzigen System gültig seyn kann, wenn alle übrigen zugleich gölten, d.h. ein jeder suchet sein System gegen alle übrigen zu behaupten. Dadurch entsthet nun unter allen ein notwendiger Widerstreit. Wird daher das eine System gesetzt, so sind zugleich auch alle übrigen ihm entgegengesetzt. Aber sie sind ursprünglich alle gesetzt insofern ein jedes für sich ein System ist; mithin sind alle auch gesetzt, insofern irgend eines gesetzt ist, das in einem gewissen Zeitraume wirklich vorhanden ist.[113]

For Hülsen, all disputing systems are non-universal representatives of the only true possible developing philosophy. Disputing systems are self-posited products of philosophizing reason. In different pre-critical

---

[110] See: HÜLSEN 1796, VI
[111] See: HÜLSEN 1796, 131
[112] See: HÜLSEN 1796, 136
[113] HÜLSEN 1796, 137

epochs, reason produces a given number of developing systems. In Leibniz's epoch, Hülsen found a synthetic counter-positing between the *thetically posited* Leibnizian system — the epoch-making system —, and the *anti-thetically posited* systems of his contemporary opponents. For Hülsen the synthetically counter-posited character of these systems is an unnoticed phenomenon of pre-critical (non-self-conscious) thought. Reason was not perceived throughout it as an *infrastructural holistic agent*. Its *synthetically counter-positing* activity was mistakenly understood as an *opposition* or *contradiction* among different mutually excluding systematic positions. Throughout this pre-moral epoch of humanity, the observer can only perceive a persisting state of philosophical disputes, revealing reason's still unsolved heteronomic self-contradiction. Until philosophy becomes *Wissenschaftslehre*, all rationally self-posited systems, thetic or anti-thetic, mistakenly assert themselves as the exclusive representatives of philosophical truth.[114]

In Hülsen's *Preisschrift*, Leibniz's system is the only example of a pre-critically self-posited system of philosophy.[115] Nonetheless, the logical-historical undermining of Leibniz's system allows us to learn the following about progressing reason's *modus operandi* in all other cases. Each thetically posited system inaugurates a new logical-historical epoch, for as a thetic system, Leibniz's system established a higher synthetic form of unity, the object of which was the systematic counter-positing (dispute) of its preceding epoch. Until the *Wissenschaftslehre*, each new thetically posited system is counter-posited by its contemporary systematic opponents. In this way, each system is

---

[114] See: HÜLSEN 1796, 137

[115] Hülsen mentions Spinoza, though only in passing, as the "hero" of the pre-critical history of philosophy. On the one hand, Hülsen rates Spinoza's system, the holistic form of which he shares, as "the papacy of all times and places"; while on the other hand, he criticizes it for its dogmatic foundation, that is, for its assertion of an Absolute Not-I as an original grounding principle. Hülsen's position is that Spinoza's system is right as to its form, but wrong as to its content. Hülsen concludes that no other philosophical system was simultaneously as consistent and inconsistent as Spinoza's system. See: HÜLSEN 1796, 148

transformed into the object of a higher synthetic form of systematic unity.[116]

Hülsen claims that philosophical consensus must be universally valid (*Allgemeingültig*). None of the disputing systems fulfils this demand; all of them are one-sided, subject to refutation. Each disputing system is a developing forerunner of the only possible true philosophy. According to Hülsen, disputes or conflict as such (*Widerstreit überhaupt*) is a *factual* or rather *materially determining* condition of true philosophical thought. Notwithstanding, insight into the efforts of self-thinkers reveals the joint character of their philosophizing activity; all strive to transform philosophy into a rigorous "scientific" discipline. The exposure of logical-historical contradiction (antinomy) is the key for the settlement of partisan controversies.[117]

The way to reconcile contending parties is to begin with what they have in common. As in Reinhold's early *Elementarphilosophie*, the point of convergence is the shared demand of the parties that philosophy be a universal discipline. This common goal shows that their activity is *a joint striving activity of reason* after universal self-determined consensus.[118] Manfred Frank elucidates Hülsen's position.

*Widerstreit kann aber nur herrschen [...], wo es Hinsichtnahme auf ein gemeinsames Ziel — und mit ihm auf ›Geltung‹, ja ›Allgemeingültigkeit‹ — gibt. Denn nur wenn A und B **sich widersprechende** Bestimmungen eines und dasselbe vermeinten Gegenstandes sind, prallen sie aufeinander; handelt es sich nur um **verschiedene** Positionen, so haben sie nicht Kraft zur wechselseitigen Aufhebung und können sehr gut in einem und demselben Überzeugungssystem miteinander koexistieren. So kann Hülsen die nur auf den ersten Blick paradoxe Konsequenz ziehen, daß gerade der widersprüchliche Fort-*

---

[116] This is implied in HÜLSEN's (1796, 148-9) assertion that "*Die Forderung geht demnach auf das endliche und durchaus über allen Widersreit hinausliegende Resultat der philosophierende Vernunft auf ihrem gegenwärtigen Standpunkte; denn das, was wir wissen wollen* [i.e., critical philosphy], *soll demjenigen, was wir schon wissen, durch Synthesis gleich gesetzt werden.*"

[117] See: HÜLSEN 1796, 42, 138-9

[118] See: HÜLSEN 1796, 138

gang der Philosophie ein Negativbeweis dafür ist, alle ihre Einzelpositionen eigentlich auf Konsens aus waren.[119]

Hülsen following Reinhold holds that the state of disputes is the exclusive object or content of a developing history of philosophy.[120] Only critical philosophy opens the road for a justification, or rather self-subsuming explanation of consensus, the resolving of disputes, as progressing reason's teleologically self-posited outcome. According to Hülsen, a philosophical solving of disputes is a necessary condition for self-determining the possibility of consensus. Critical insight, Hülsen argues, reveals the existence of a *rational ground* behind the dissociating state of disputes. From this perspective, all self-excluding systems of philosophy emerge as antinomically developed products of reason. The epoch of partisan disputes constitutes an unavoidable "chapter" of reason's logical history. The rational character of this history provides a consensual ground for the universal unification of all systems of philosophy as necessary evolving stages of an exclusive self-posited critical system. Rational identity, or in Hülsen's own words, pure consensus (*Einverständniss schlechthin*), is the final self-determined outcome of reason's history. Self-determination of the factually self-posited state of disputes enables the critical subsuming of the only possible object of philosophy's history: rational contradiction.[121]

Hat die Vernunft nun den Widerstreit aus ihr selbst als nothwendig, und daher in dieser Relexion für sie als Einverständniss zu erklären; so ist zwischen der Reflexion des Widerstreits und dem wirklichen Widerstreit auch kein anderer Unterschied, als das die Vernunft in jener, als bloss theoretisch, es völlig bestimmt weiss, dass und wie gestritten werde: in diesem aber, als bloss praktisch, das Objekt der Reflexion noch allererst hervorbringt. Im wirklichen Widerstreite ist daher die Reflexion der Vernunft über ihr eignes Produkt d.i. die theoretische Vernunft, oder die Theorie selbst, als eine Wissenschaft, noch gar nicht möglich. Aber eben so wenig bleibt in der wirklichen Reflexion des Widerstreits ein Widerstreit denkbar. Es giebt also

---

[119] FRANK 1998, 912
[120] See: HÜLSEN 1796, 139
[121] See: HÜLSEN 1796, 139-42

auch keinen absoluten Widerstreit, sondern nur einen relativen, denn er hört auf ein Widerstreit zu seyn, so bald er erklärt ist.[122]

Critical knowledge is the first fully self-conscious logical-historical knowledge. The entire history of philosophy, an ascending series of practically self-posited systems, enables philosophizing reason to reach the theoretical standpoint of the *Wissenschaftslehre*. The realization that all *contradiction* is only a theoretical form of *synthetic counter-positing* reveals the relative and therefore surmountable character of logical-historical controversies. The state of disputes, Hülsen holds, is not settled by *negating* its conditioning contradiction. Instead, a self-conscious act of self-subsuming reflection enables *qualitative reformulation* as a contextual act of synthetic counter-positing.[123] In this way, Hülsen explained both the emergence of the state of disputes and the possibility of self-determined consensus, and so was able to solve Reinhold's problem in a critical way.

Hülsen develops the concept of philosophical consensus by discussing three supplementary aspects.

Hülsen believed that he had discovered the conditions which philosophy has to fulfil in order to become a real critical discipline to which no other philosophical system can be counter-posited. Absolute unity (*absolute Einheit*), all-inclusive universality, pertain to critical philosophy as the highest self-subsuming knowledge possible. Hülsen infers from this that every pre-critical disputing must also have claimed a universal grounding.[124]

---

[122] HÜLSEN 1796, 141-2

[123] As Willy FLITNER (1913, 33-4) adds, "*Eigentümlich ist, wie Hülsen den Begriff des philosophischen Widerstreits ausdehnt: er wird überhaupt identisch mit dem Endlichwerden des absoluten Ich. So wird es möglich, das fichtesche Wissen, das die Absolutheit wiederherstellen will, als Reflexion des Widerstreits zu bezeichnen; als Bewußtmachung des Zusammenhangs aller Handlungsweisen, die vom Widerstreit des Ich und Nichtich produziert werden.*"

[124] See: HÜLSEN 1796, 142-3. HÜLSEN counts Reinhold, Schultz, Beck, and Mellin among the most outstanding Kantian proponents of such a universally grounded discipline. Jacobi, Eberhard, and Maas stand out among the anti-Kantians. See: HÜLSEN 1796, 143

Hülsen claimed that the rational history of philosophy, and philosophy's precursor, Greek mythology, reveal such an original ground in a being-in-itself (*Seyn an Sich Selbst*). Such transcendently grounded positions it developed, constitute that discipline which Aristotle named meta-physics. Until Fichte, all philosophical progress was determined by the personal ability to answer the same question: *how metaphysics is possible as a universally grounded discipline.* According to Hülsen, this is the only question, which could be asked and answered in pre-critical thought. The *Wissenschaftslehre* teaches that both this question and its possible answers are self-posited outcomes of reason's asking-answering activity. Logical-historical efforts, holistically individuated acts of self-reflection, were needed, Hülsen claims, to bring on the advent of the *Wissenschaftslehre*. The possibility of the *Wissenschaftslehre* is established exclusively through its emerging reality in history.[125] Metaphysics according to Hülsen is that teleologically developing

---

[125] Hülsen's claim has implications for the skeptic opponents of the *Grundsatz* tradition, and for Paul Johann Anselm Feuerbach in particular, who in his 1795 *Ueber die Unmöglichkeit eines ersten absoluten Grundsaßes der Philosophie* criticized the possibility of founding metaphysics on an absolute *Grundsatz*. According to Hülsen, the *Wissenschaftslehre* has shown that to prove this im-possibility an act of self-reflection is needed. This act, however, can only appear as a necessary asking-answering effort of reason towards the inevitable universal self-grounding of metaphysics. Hülsen therefore concludes that Feuerbach's position is untenable. [See: HÜLSEN 1796, 145]. Moreover, Hülsen's claim about the unconditionally self-grounded relation of each pragmatically self-deter-mined stage of the logical-historical system of knowledge to its preceding condition is an attempt to tackle Feuerbach's criticism. For one of FEUERBACH's (1969, 318-9) claims was that "*Die Vernunft ist das Vermögen zu begreifen, so wie der Verstand das Vermögen zu denken. Ihr Vermögen bestehet also darin sich das Gegründete im Zusammenhang mit seinem Grund, das Bedingte im Zusammenhang mit seiner Bedingung vorzustellen. Kraft dieses Vermögens ist sie im Besitz der Ideen des Unbedingten, die sie als Principien alles Begreifens an die Spitze des Bedingten seßt. Diese Ideen sind aber nich constitutive Principien, sondern lediglich Vorausseßungen der Vernunft zu Regulierung ihres Ge-brauchs.*" Hülsen's strong commitment to the *Grundsatz* tradition, as Manfred FRANK poins out, was a key reason for Fichte's recommendation of *Preisschrift* as an introductory study to his own *Wissenschaftslehre*. See: FRANK 1998, 913

discipline, the expanding possibility of which is self-determined personally by the factual answering efforts of different self-thinkers.[126]

Hierdurch offenbart sich aber bestimmt, dass der Grund des ganzen Widerstreits auch lediglich in dem Urtheile über das Seyn an Sich, oder über das Selbst-Seyn, liege, und das der Widerstreit daher auch im mindesten nicht gehoben würde, wenn gleich alle Welt sich in dem Systeme eines einzigen Selbstdenkers [i.e., the Wissenschaftslehre] vereinigen wollte. Die Thatsache der Uebereinstimmung entscheidet daher noch gar nicht, sondern diese kann sehr zufällig seyn. Ist sie im Systeme gegründet, so muss sie mit dem Fortgange desselben, in praktischer Beziehung, auch nothwendig von selbst kommen. Ist sie das aber nicht; so giebt es kein Mittel weiter, das ein redlicher Selbstdenker zur Verbereitung seines Systems sich erlauben dürfte, als das Selbstdenken.[127]

Synthetic judgment enables all systematic philosophy. Still, according to Hülsen, critical insight reveals that in pre-critical thought, progressing reason was neither aware of the *self-reflective* character of synthetic judgment, nor of its universally self-grounded nature. *Progressing* reason was therefore incapable of self-reflecting on the absolute foundational ground of knowledge, *pure* reason. In no way can reason appear to itself as self-determined content. All judgments appear to the pre-critical observer as mistaken *transitive* judgments, provoking a logical-historical state of disputes in which different systematic positions emerge as *unavoidable errors of judgment*.[128]

---

[126] See: HÜLSEN 1796, 144-6.

[127] HÜLSEN 1796, 147

[128] See: HÜLSEN 1796, III-V. As HÜLSEN (1796, 157) adds the critical establishment of metaphysics, "*konnte nur durch Umkehrung der Prinzipien geschehen. Bisher setzte man das An sich selbst seyn in die objektive Welt und vernichtete also das Ich. Die Wissenschaftslehre zeigt dagegen, dass alles auser dem Ich gesetzte, auch nothwendig Nicht-Ich, und als absolut also genommen, schlechthin Nichts sey. Dieses Nichts ist dem Ich in so fern daher entgegen gesetzt, als das Ich absolutes Selbstseyn ist. Giebt es nun ursprünglich keine andere Realität, als die Realität des Ich, und ist alles übrige schlechthin Nichts; so wird aus diesem Nichts auch nie etwas werden können, ohne das es seine Realität vom absoluten Ich erhalte, und als Etwas daher durch Ich, für das Ich und = dem Ich sey. So wie man diese*

Hülsen's "improved" *Wissenschaftslehre* shows that all non-universally determined standpoints engage in disputes because universal consensus is their necessary logical-historical goal.[129]

Demnach giebt es einen Widerstreit, weil es für die praktische Vernunft ein Ziel giebt, und es soll zugleich um dieses Zieles willen, auch eben so nothwendig aller Widerstreit nicht seyn d.h. das Ziel soll, eben weil es für uns ein Ziel ist, auch durch uns erreicht werden.[130]

Willy Flitner sums up Hülsen's insight into the possibility of settling partisan disputes and reaching philosophical consensus:

Darin liegt eine Ansicht von dem Wesen der Vernunft eingeschlossen, die für die Geschichtsphilosophie entscheidend wird: die Vernunft muß, um zu sich selber zu kommen, sich spalten und durch den Widerspruch hindurchgehen. [...] Die Vernunft hat also eine Geschichte. Sie geht von ihrer ursprünglichen, bewußtlosen Einheit zweckvoll über die Stufe des Widerstreits bis zu der höheren dritten Stufe, wo der Widerstreit eingesehen wird, und die Vernunft wieder Einheit ist, nun aber in vollkommener Weise. [...] Der Irrtum — der mit dem theoretischen Widerstreit zugleich gegeben ist — hat also darin seinen Sinn, daß er sich selbst vernichten und Wahrheit durchdringen will. Eine Folgerung führt zu der weiteren Stufe, den Irrtum zum Zustandekommen der Wissenschaft für notwendig zu erklären. Damit erst wird die Theodicee vollendet. Sie ist aus der fichteschen Lehre vom Bewußtsein herausgeholt: Damit die höhere Reflexion die Einheit der Selbsterkenntnis herbeiführen kann, muß sich das Ich durch ein Nichtich einschränken und spalten lassen. Die Teilung im Ich, der Widerstreit des Nichtichs hat demnach

---

*Idee rein und richtig auffasst, muss sich nothwendig aus unsern Urtheilen auch der **transcendente** Gesichtpunkt verliehren."* [my bold]

[129] See: HÜLSEN 1796, 42-3. As Dieter KLAWON (1977, 193-4) points out, *"Die Forderung nach seiner Überwindung* [i.e., of the state of disputes] *stützt Hülsen mit einer weiteren Überlegung. Wenn Widerstreit gedacht werden kann, so muß notwendig auch sein Gegenteil gedacht werden können, nämlich Übereinstimmung, Harmonie. Logisch Notwendiges aber besitzt für ihn die Garantie der Verwirklichung, auch deshalb ist der Weg zur Harmonie unabänderlich vorgezeichnet."*

[130] HÜLSEN 1796, 43

die Funktion, die höhere Einheit zu stiften, durch welche das Ich erst ein volles (selbstbewußtes) Ich wird. [131]

According to Hülsen, the insight that all forms of judgment are self-reflective and not transitive forms paves the way for an unending quantitative realization of rational self-identity: a condition required to inaugurate an unprecedented epoch of "highest good". Hülsen's initial assertion that the rational being's apparent rejection of his moral vocation is only really an unconscious striving for it is so critically justified. Hülsen reinforced Reinhold's position that the end of the history of philosophy enables a full display of reason's practical potentiality in *the establishment of a new moral order*. Hülsen describes this new "redeeming" epoch as *"die Epoke der Ideen als ewig gültigen Gesetzen für alles, was je durch Vernunft wirklich werden mag"*.[132]

Es gibt nur Ein Ziel, und es ist eine so nothwendige als erhabene Idee, dass es in dem grossen Gebiete der Wissenschaften doch nur Wissenschatf überhaupt und ihre Geschichte geben soll. Jene zeigt uns den Menschen in seiner errungenen Freiheit, während die letztere ihn im Kampfe mit sich selber aufstellt. Beide sind uns aufgegeben in der Idee der Freiheit und des unendlichen Strebens, und diese Idee nur ist es, zu der wir uns auf dem Wege unsers empirischen Fortschreitens irgend einmal erheben.[133]

According to Hülsen, his deduction of philosophical consensus made all past efforts to solve partisan disputes, including Reinhold's effort, obsolete.

Keines der bisherigen Systeme hat dasselbe [i.e., the problem of disputes] *schon lösen können, weil sich noch keines durch die Frage: wie ein Widerstreit selbst möglich sey? über allen Widerstreit hinaushob. Kant legte zwar diese Reflexion seinen Kritiken zum Grunde; aber so wenig bestimmt doch, dass er ihr auch keinesweges getreu geblieben ist. Noch weniger Reinhold. Dieser behauptet vielmehr ausdrücklich: dass die gesammten bisherigen Systeme der Philosophie halb wahr und halb falsch wären; d.h. wahr — in so fern sie mit seiner Theorie übereinstimmen, und falsch — in so fern sie derselben ent-*

---

[131] FLITNER 1913, 34, 33
[132] HÜLSEN 1796, 26
[133] HÜLSEN 1796, 31

gegen stehen. Folglich behauptet er es nur durch einen Widerstreit, und die Theorie des Vorstellungsvermögens löst daher so wenig das Problem von der Möglichkeit eines Einverständnisses in der Philosophie, das sie, [...] doch nur mit in den Umfang des Widerstreits gehört, und hier also selbst noch erst erklärt werden muss.[134]

According to Hülsen, Reinhold was unable to explain the epoch of partisan disputes and their critical resolution as a necessary event of reason's logical history. Implicit is the claim that Reinhold was unable to either determine the material condition required to establish the possibility of consensus, or justify the teleological overcoming of disputes.

3.9 The Concept of the History of Philosophy

In keeping with the "spirit" of Reinhold's early *Elementarphilosophie,* Hülsen argued that all pre-critical systems of philosophy until the *Wissenschaftslehre* are progressing reason's self-posited facts (*Thatsache*). These facts put together constitute a single logically-historically self-posited fact of reason. Reason's mutually excluding products are logical-historical stages of a single reconciling concept of philosophy. Until the *Wissenschaftslehre,* philosophy's self-subsuming activity was unnoticed. This activity alone enables the universal synthetic integration of all apparently atomic facts of reason (systems). Universal unification opens the road for an innovative *systematic articulation* of the history of philosophy as an inherent "chapter" of reason's logical history.[135] The history of philosophy emerges now as

Die getroffene Darstellung des gesammten Fortschreitens der philosphieren-den Vernunft zur Philosophie als Wissenschaft; oder: die Wissenschaft von der werdenden Wissenschaft.[136]

---

[134] HÜLSEN 1796, 141
[135] See: HÜLSEN 1796, 24, 32-3
[136] HÜLSEN 1796, 24

The rational history of philosophy reveals the teleological development of progressing or philosophizing reason. Hülsen's definition seems to tally in part with Reinhold's, for whom reason's history reveals the systematic model of the logical-historical changes that the theory of representation underwent from pre-critical times until its exhaustive articulation.[137] Still, the crucial difference between Reinhold's early *Elementarphilosophie* and Hülsen's *Preisschrift* is that in Reinhold's system a deduction of philosophical historicity was absent. Reinhold could neither explain the logical-historical emergence of partisan disputes, the exclusive *content* of the rational history of philosophy, nor explain the integrative possibility of systematic articulation, history's universal self-determining *form*. According to Hülsen, Reinhold could not explain the possibility of true philosophical consensus.

Hülsen following Reinhold argued that articulation was possible only after the emergence of critical philosophy. Hülsen agrees with Reinhold that lack of critical insight prevents philosophizing reason from recognizing its own teleological direction. No systematic order among philosophizing reason's unilateral, and apparently atomic systems, can be established prior to critical philosophy. The attainment of an adequate idea of reason's historical contextual condition is also impossible.

Zwar hat man sich nirgends so sicher geglaubt, als im Gebiete der Geschichte, sobald nur die Thatsachen Thatsachen waren. Aber man ahndete nicht, das die Wahrheit der Beziehung, worauf doch alles eigentlich ankommt, gar nichts in Thatsachen liege, sondern Urtheilskraft efrordere, und das eben diese für irgend eine Intelligenz, und also bis zum Zeitpunkt der Wissenschaft –noch selbst nur ein historischer Gegenstand war.[138]

According to Hülsen, the history of philosophy ought to be understood as a philosophically self-grounded discipline. As systematised or synthesized outcomes of the same universal logical-historical agent, all

---

[137] "[...] *der dargestellte Inbegrif der Veränderungen, welche die Wissenschaft des nothwendigen Zusammenhanges der Dinge von ihrer Enstehung bis auf unsre Zeiten erfahren hat.*" REINHOLD 1791, 21

[138] HÜLSEN 1796, 32

pre-critically self-posited systems gain an inherent cohesion (*Zusammenhang*). As outcomes of the same unconditionally self-grounded agent, they have a "sceptically immune" certainty (*Gewissheit*).[139] Hülsen's focus on pre-critical systems as stages of an exclusive logically-historically secured philosophy enables an expansion of Fichte's genetic criteria of articulation, innovative application of his deductive method of pragmatic historicity.

Es liegt in die Natur der Sache, dass eine solche Geschichte, als Geschichte des Fortschreitens zur Wissenschaft oder zur Freiheit der Vernunft, pragmatisch sey. [...] Begreift nun die Reflexion in ihrem Resultate die gesammten Handlungen des menschlichen Geistes, durch welche das Ich zur Intelligenz [i.e., self-counscious (in context)] *wird, folglich die Handlungen, durch welche überhaupt ein Wissen Wirklich wird; so ist auch das Resultat, welches nothwendig jene Handlungen als geschehend oder pragmatisch, mithin in ihrer Folge oder systematisch begreift, eine Wissenschaft von der Möglichkeit alles Wissens überhaupt, und also nichts anders als eine Wissenschaftslehre.*[140]

Critical insight, Hülsen holds, makes *systematic* articulation of the history of philosophy as an accurate *methodical* reproduction of philosophizing reason's true logical-historical self-positing course possible. In Hülsen's *Preisschrift, deductive method and system of knowledge are intimately fused.*

Philosophizing reason's self-grounded genesis is the systematic foundation of Hülsen's philosophical approach to the history of philosophy. Hülsen's standpoint completes and corrects Reinhold's approach to the history of philosophy.

---

[139] See: HÜLSEN 1796, 26. In his 1795 *Uebersicht des Vorzüglichsten, was für die Geschichte der Philosophie seit 1780 geleistet worden,* an essay that Hülsen probably knew, the Kantian philosopher of the history of philosophy Wilhelm Gottlieb Tennemann demanded a similar systematic cohesion of all apparently atomic facts of reason (systems). According to Tennemann, philosophical reflection should uncover a rational contextual frame, the grasping of which cannot be immediately perceived in the aforementioned facts. See: TENNEMANN 1795, 328

[140] HÜLSEN 1796, 27, 163-4

Die vielfältigen Versuche, welche biz jetzt über die Geschichte der Philoso-
phie vorhanden sind, müssen vergessen werden. [...] Es gab noch keine
Philosophie als Wissenschaft, noch kein geendetes Fortschreiten der Vernunft
zu ihr selbst. Wie zu diesem Ziele der Gang sich noch winden möchte, war
daher nothwendig unbekannt, und auf diesem Wege also nichts zu anti-
cipieren. Zwar hatte man mit jedem Augenblik eine verflossne Zeit, und also
auch die dahin gehörigen Fortschritte zur Wissenschaft. Aber gerade auch
darum fehlte noch die Intelligenz diese Fortschritte als gerade diese zu
reflektieren, und die momente der Zeit als in aller Zeit des Fortschreitens
genau zu bestimmen. Eine wissenschaftliche Untersuchung, die nicht aus dem
Ganzen in die Theile geht, widerspricht sich selbst, denn sie hat kein Objekt
als Ein Objekt. So war es mit der Geschichte der Philosophie. Noch rang die
Vernunft nur nach ihrer Idee, und was hier daher geschehen ist, muss völlig
vergessen werden.[141]

Reinhold's early *Elementarphilosophie* is not sufficiently consistent and
complete to establish and ground a pragmatic or genetic account for a
rational history of philosophy. Reinhold's system does not allow the
logical-historical stages (unilateral systems) that constitute the object of
philosophy's history to attain a self-grounded certainty and inherent
systematic cohesion. For Hülsen, in a rational history of philosophy,
each developing stage is a necessary result of a monistically self-grounded standpoint. In *Preisschrift*, each stage (part) of philosophy appears as
an inherent self-limited particularization of an ontic-epistemic holistic
agent: pure reason (the whole). A self-limiting movement from the
whole to its developing parts assures that the systematized object of
philosophy's history, reason's mutually-excluding systems, appears as
a self-subsumed or reconciled object (*Ein Objekt* in Hülsen's language).
In Reinhold's early *Elementarphilosophie*, reason is exclusively an epistemic agent. The ground of ontology is a transcendent presupposition.
Reinhold's agent is not an all-embracing agent. Reinhold's system lacks
a logical-historical agent with a truly universal ground. Only a monistic-
holistic approach, can supply the universal ground for the rational self-
limiting movement. Neither Reinhold, nor any other Kantian thinker,
can achieve a critical approach to the history of philosophy.

---

[141] HÜLSEN 1796, 27-8

According to Hülsen, *retrospective insight* enables articulation of philosophy's history as an accurate reproduction of philosophizing reason's productive course. Hülsen, for whom philosophizing reason is a holistically individuated agent, augments Reinhold's *Ueber den Begrif der Geschichte der Philosophie* by discussing the methodical guidelines demanded for articulation. This requires for Hülsen critical knowledge, by definition, a personal outcome.

Alle Geschichte überhaupt stehet nothwendig im genausten Verhältnisse mit dem Menschen. Wie der Mensch, so seine Geschichte. Ist er noch im Werden, noch im Fortschreiten zu sich selber; so giebt es auch für ihn noch keine Geschichte, als wahre Geschichte, sondern nur eine Intelligenz auser ihm könnte sie setzen.[142]

Hülsen following Fichte argues that the attainment of critical knowledge demands a *personal self-reflecting act* of self-knowledge (*Selbsterkenntniss*).[143] Philosophy is a particularized expression of the living spirit (*lebendige Geist*). In it, reason appears as a discursively self-relating agent. Only such an act assures that Philosophy's content, one's own personal representation of reason, emerge as a real content: for Hülsen an indispensable requirement of all theoretical knowledge.

Sie [i.e., the history of philosophy] *soll Wissenschaft seyn, folglich innern Zusammenhang und Gewissheit haben. Mithin muss sie aus dem Geiste des Menschen lebendig hervorgehen. Niemand moge sich also an die Darstellung dieser Geschichte wagen — und wenn er auch von Gelehrsamkeit im Buchstaben strotzte — der nicht vor allen im Spiegel der Selbsterkenntniss die ganze Vergangenheit zurückrufen kann, der in sich selbst also nicht die ersten Keime des Daseyns bis zur gereiften Frucht der Freiheit, bis zum Selbst-Erkennen, zu finden weiss.*[144]

Following Reinhold, Hülsen concludes that the articulation of philosophy's history is a *personal retrospective task* to be pursued exclusively by "scientifically" cultivated individuals. Only critical insight enables apprehension of the true idea of philosophy's history. No self-

---

[142] HÜLSEN 1796, 32-3
[143] See: HÜLSEN 1796, 28
[144] HÜLSEN 1796, 26-7

determination is possible prior to the personal establishment of a self-subsuming order among the disputing outcomes of philosophizing reason. Self-determination demands personal retrospective understanding of the logical-historical relation of philosophy to all its evolutionary stages. Neither autonomy, nor withdrawal from the subordinating sphere of partisan disputes, is possible prior to the personal articulation of the concluding "chapter" of the system of knowledge.[145] This Fichtean insight enables Hülsen's reformulation of another aspect of Reinhold's approach to the history of philosophy.

3.10 The General-Personal Philosophizing Task of the Self-Thinker

Hülsen's deduction of philosophizing reason as a general-personal agent enables the fusion of two unsystematically integrated stems of Reinhold's system: reason's philosophical history and the personal philosophizing labour of the self-thinker (*Selbstdenker*). Fichte implied this integration in *Ueber die Bestimmung des Gelehrten* without making it explicit. Fichte's position was that the logical-historical process that leads to the *Wissenschaftslehre* is a general process, the architects of which are philosophers or scholars. Hülsen's implicit criticism is that Reinhold did not deduce the logical possibility of historical agents; Reinhold's standpoint therefore contains unjustified premises. Hülsen's deduction will establish an innovative connection between the theoretical and the practical divisions of Fichte's early idealism. Hülsen will supply a solution to a problem raised vaguely by Fichte's "improved" *Elementarphilosophie*.

---

[145] See: HÜLSEN 1796, 33. Hans HESS (1926, 265) stresses the intimate character of articulation: "*Der Philosophiehistoriker soll nicht nur die fremden Meinungen äußerlich referieren, sondern er soll sich der innersten Tendenzen der Philosophiegeschichte verstehend bemächtigen. Sentimental, einfühlend ist das neue Verhältnis zur Geschichte, nicht mehr ausschließlich methodologisch, wissenschaftstheoretisch orientiert. Aus der höchsten Kraft der Gegenwart soll die Vergangenheit gedeutet werden. Die lebendige Erfahrung der eigenen Seelengeschichte soll die Vergangenheit lebendig machen.*"

Hülsen begins by commenting on the prize-question of the Berlin Academy. The purpose of the academic authorities is to obtain an exhaustive answer about the progress of metaphysics since Leibniz and Wolf, and so end the controversies around Kant's *Kritik*. Hülsen's position is that most scholars understood Kant's masterpiece dogmatically, for they focused on its letter. According to Hülsen, ignorance of the "spirit" of critical philosophy is a major contemporary cause behind reason's still persisting self-contradiction, behind humanity's morally imperfect situation.[146] Critical analysis of the prize-question reveals that an academic task cannot deal adequately with the personal concept of practical progression. Giving a *"scientific"* or *pragmatic* answer to the academic question requires that this answer emerge spontaneously in personal asking-answering striving. Hülsen's ironical conclusion is that the question asked by the Berlin Academy of Sciences, an institution that intended to supervise officially philosophical progress, was not only a senseless, but also an *"unscientific"* question.[147] Hülsen stresses emphatically the harmful consequences, which a winning nomination would have for the practical purposes of rational beings that strive after critical self-determination.

Aber so unschuldig die Preisfrage der Akademie an sich ist, und so zuträglich es sogar für viele seyn könnte, sich auf eine genaue Beantwortung derselben

---

[146] HÜLSEN (1796, 183-4) focuses on Kant's work from a Fichtean perspective: "*Ich spreche nicht von der Kritik in dem was sie wirklich ist, sondern was sie seyn würde, wenn man von ihrem Geiste abstrahieren und den blossen Buchstaben ergreifen wollte. [...] den Buchstaben von ihr absondern und ihren Geist darstellen, das ist das Geschäft einer Wissenschaftslehre, und zur vollkommen Einsicht in die Kritik durchaus erforderlich.*"

[147] See: HÜLSEN 1796, 37-41, 43, 45. As Karl OBENAUER (1910, 2) comments, Hülsen's position highlights once again the "spirit" of Fichte's idealism: "*Diese, bei aller Ehrlichkeit und Ernsthaftigkeit so seltsam dialektische Polemik, die davon ausgeht, daß dieselbe Frage, von außen gegeben, ohne Sinn, von uns selbst gestellt aber sinvoll sei, setzt die Annahme des philosophischen Idealismus Fichtes voraus, der lehrt, alles im Ich aufzusuchen, und dem die Welt eine die freie Tätigkeit beschränkende Macht ist. Hülsen zeigt, wie sich diese allgemeine philosophische Lehre auf besondere Fälle, bei der Untersuchung über das Wesen einer Frage, konsequent anwenden läßt.*"

einzulassen: so nachtheilig würde es zugleich auch wieder seyn, wenn die Akademie irgend eine an sie ergangene Antwort mit ihrem Beifalle krönen wollte. Dadurch würde das Beste der Wissenschaften nicht nur nicht gefördert, sondern nothwendig gehindert werden; denn es hiesse nichts anders als den Buchstaben heiligen, den der selbstdenkende Gelehrte doch als den Gewaltthäter des Geistes zerstöhren soll. [...] Ein solches Urtheil aber ist ein Machtspruch der Autorität, der dem nach Freiheit strebenden Geiste in seine Fesseln zurückschrekt, und der Fortgang der Wissenschaften dadurch nothwendig aufhält.[148]

According to Hülsen, the intention of the Academy was both "*unscientific*" and *immoral*. Critical philosophy teaches that self-determination requires a personal spontaneous act of self-knowledge. For Hülsen an academic contest obstructs personal freedom; it prevents rational beings that strive for self-determination to reach the standpoint of philosophical consensus. Hülsen hence concludes that the Berlin Academy paradoxically reinforces the partisan controversies that it ostensibly was trying to settle.[149]

Hülsen uses these conclusions to discuss in detail the connection of philosophy's rational history and the personal philosophizing labour of the self-determined scholar (*Gelehrte*) or self-thinker.[150]

---

[148] HÜLSEN 1796, 45-6

[149] See: HÜLSEN 1796, 67. Friedrich JODL reproduces the Berlin Academy's reaction to Hülsen's essay: "*Eine Abhandlung eines gewissen Hülsen, welche bemerkte, so Etwas wie das, was die Herren Fragesteller ,Methaphysic' nannten, existiere eigentlich seit 1781* [i.e., the year Kant's *Kritik* appeared in print] *nicht mehr, hielt man nur für einen Scherz.*" [Cited in: KLAWON 1977, 183]. In opposition to that, Karl ROSENKRANZ (1987, 353) comments: "*Die gründlichste und geistvollste, im unabhängigten Geist geschriebene, ungekrönte Beantwortung der Aufgabe der Akademie gab August Ludwig Hülsen. [...] Er representiert darin den* **Geist der Wissenschaftslehre**, *wie sie sich noch für eine bloße* **Fortsetzung des Kritizismus** *hielt.*" [my bold]

[150] Willy FLITNER (1913, 29) stresses Hülsen's innovation on this point: "*Hier kommt die andere Wurzel der deutschen Geschichtsphilosophie heraus, enthalten in einem neuen Begriff des Menschen. Hülsen ist nun der erste, der in einer selbständigen Untersuchung die beiden Strömungen vereinigt.*"

Hülsen's purpose was to enlighten the scholar's true vocation and determine which type of knowledge is required to enable a moral improvement of the human species. As Hülsen learned from Fichte, recognition of the scholar's vocation demands a preliminary inquiry into the vocation of man. For Hülsen the achievement of human vocation cannot be dissociated from the logically-historically developing concept of philosophy. Otherwise, philosophy's emerging content, a personalized dynamic representation of reason, is a meaningless abstraction. True philosophical knowledge is the concrete product of spontaneous self-activity (*Selbstthätigkeit*)[151] or free expanding spirit; it is grounded *necessarily* on personal practical striving.[152] In Hülsen's *Preisschrift*, Fichte's position that true philosophy is ethical anthropology, a foundation of knowledge according to the metaphysical idea of our practical vocation is augmented historically.[153]

Hülsen learned from Fichte's *Ueber die Bestimmung des Gelehrten* that the scholar's (*Gelehrter*) vocation coincides with the rational being's vocation. According to Hülsen, the task of the scholar, a philosophy expert, consists in ongoing practical self-determination. The scholar should self-reflect or think on his own pure self. He should grasp the practical character of his own productive thought and render it intelligible to himself. Developing Fichte's thought Hülsen maintained that the true vocation of the scholar is *self-thinking* (*Selbstdenken*),[154] and elucidated the intimate relation of the critical concepts "human being" and "self-thinking scholar":

Der Gelehrte als blosser Gelehrte, d.i. als Selbstdenker, ist noch keineswegs der Mensch. Das Gelehrtseyn gehört vielmehr nur zu den Bestimmungen des Menschen, und soll also, wo es ist, im Menschen seyn, d.h. der Gelehrte soll kein Gelehrter, sondern er soll ein Mensch seyn. Nach dem praktischen Begriffe vom Menschen ist es so nothwendig. Der Mensch soll Er Selbst, er soll ein Ganzes seyn. In diesem liegt auch das Gelehrtseyn. Es ist also gewiss: soll

---

[151] This concept ought to be interpreted as (1) a spontaneously self-produced activity, and as (2) an activity of the self or reason.

[152] See: HÜLSEN 1796, 48

[153] See: BAUMANNS 1974, 107 [Hülsen not mentioned].

[154] See: HÜLSEN 1796, 49, 51-2

es Menschen geben, so darf keine Gelehrte geben, sondern dieser Name muss vor dem des Menschen verschwinden. Aber es ist auch gewiss, dass der Mensch, um dem praktischen Begriffe vom ihm entsprechen zu können, seine Bestimmung wissen muss. In so fern ist es wahr, dass wenn der Mensch ein Mensch seyn soll, er vor allen die Anlage zum Wissen in sich entwikkeln, und der Gelehrte oder Selbstdenker also der wahre Mensch seyn soll. Dann aber müssen die Gelehrten auch nur allein nach dem Prädikate vernünftig trachten, und vor dem Menschen in ihnen sich schämen, noch etwas anders als das seyn zu wollen.[155]

Practical self-determination compels the scholar or the self-thinker to keep his own *forum internus*; philosophizing is a personalized self-reflecting activity. As an exclusive self-conscious thinker of his own self, the self-thinker understands himself as the architect of his own practical production. This means that the self-thinker is an independent thinker. Only personal understanding assures attainment of the status of a true self-thinker. Self-conscious insight is the self-thinker's way to realize that only his philosophizing activity, a holistically individuated manifestation of reason, provides philosophy with systematic unity. So Hülsen concludes, philosophical thought appears to the self-thinker as his own intimate spiritual product.[156]

Fichte's influence on Hülsen on this point is unambiguous. In *Ueber den Unterschied* Fichte's position was that philosophical knowledge is grounded exclusively on spiritual activity; no epistemic outcome can be divorced from the personal activity that brings it about. According to Fichte, no printed text can convey this activity. Hülsen was a radical supporter of Fichte's spiritualism. Hülsen's conviction about the practical primacy of spirit explains his short philosophical "career". In *Preisschrift* and in his subsequent short writings, Hülsen stresses the dogmatic risk of mistaking philosophical knowledge (spirit) with printed philosophy (letter).

Das was man uns in Büchern auffstellt ist nie Philosophie, und nie Wissenschaft, sondern nur eines von den vielen Mitteln, welche die Freiheit versucht, um

---

[155] HÜLSEN 1796, 49-50
[156] See: HÜLSEN 1796, 50-1

*den lebendigen Menschen zu erwekken und sich selbst sichtbar zu machen. [...]
Mithin ist dasjenige, was uns Fichte darstellt, auch nicht die Wissenschaftslehre,
ihrem Geiste nach; sondern nur das Instrument für freie und vernünftige
Wesen, dieselbe freie Reflexion auch über sich vorzunehmen, und dadurch
erst den Geist in die gegebene Darstellung hinein zu legen.*[157]

For Hülsen, following Fichte, the printed text of the *Wissenschaftslehre*
was only a formal or abstract tool. Only its personal use, a spontaneous self-reflective entrance into a series of genetically portrayed
stages, leads to self-determining knowledge. Personal insight into one's
own becoming spiritual nature, Hülsen holds, frees our striving spirit
and enables moral improvement. Philosophy is exclusively the spiritual
outcome of personal self-reflecting activity. Hülsen concludes that
philosophy exists only through, for, and by *concrete* rational beings.[158]

*[...] ist die Philosophie nur durch einen jeden für einen jeden Wissenschaft,
und also nur in dem lebendigen Geiste einen jeden; so ist auch vollkommen
klar, was wir unter ihr uns zu denken haben, und was der Verf. des Wissenschaftslehre auch bestimmt genug ausgedrückt hat. Sie ist nehmlich, die Philosophie, schlechterdings nichts weiter als die Reflexion eines vernünftigen
Wesens über sich selber d.i. die bestimmte und vollständige Erklärung seines
eignen Daseyns. Diese Reflexion kann und darf in nichts weiter ihren Grund
haben; in so fern daher ihre Möglichkeit durch die Wirklichkeit gegeben, und
sie folglich absolut ist, ist sie auch der freie und vernünftige Mensch selber,
der in dieser seiner Freiheit und Vernünftigkeit sich weiss.*[159]

Only as a spiritually self-grounded discipline, can philosophical knowledge attain an absolute and hence "skeptically immune" character.
Thus, Hülsen could take later as his philosophical motto the phrase
meine Philosophie ist kein Buch.[160]

---

[157] HÜLSEN 1796, 166, 161
[158] See: HÜLSEN 1796, 159-61
[159] HÜLSEN 1796, 164
[160] HÜLSEN 1796, IX. — HÜLSEN (1796, 210) additionally argued that "*auf Bücher
mich berufen wird nur das Ende meiner Philosphie seyn. Wer nicht so denkt, der
denkt anders von der Wahrheit, und er denkt, nach meiner Ueberzeugung, selbst
noch gar nicht.*"

According to Hülsen, critical insight is the self-thinker's way to un-cover the infinite character of his holistically developing activity and attain knowledge of reason's regulative idea: absolute autonomy (or self-identity). Exhaustive achievement of this idea is the self-thinker's only moral purpose. The idea of reason determines the progressing direction of his striving. Conscious fulfilment of his moral vocation is impossible prior to the personal discovery of critical philosophy. Though conscious or not, practical striving is the self-thinker's un-avoidable vocation.[161]

Ignorance of reason's regulative idea, Hülsen claims, was a distinc-tive feature of pre-critical thought, during which the human spirit lays dormant. Lacking critical insight, Hülsen holds; self-thinkers sought and seek philosophical knowledge in the printed word. Many spon-taneous unsuccessful efforts were necessary for self-thinkers to set their spirit free and change humanity's moral situation. Lacking critical insight, self-thinkers attained theoretical knowledge without knowing exactly how.[162] The immediate result of critical philosophy's discovery is apodictic.

Von da an erkennen wir nur dasjenige für das unsrige, was wir durch Freiheit in uns setzen. Aber wir erkennen zugleich auch, dass ausser uns nichts seyn soll, das nicht das unsrige seyn müsste: folglich dass wir alles Wirkliche und alle Mögliche überhaupt, d.i. eine Welt überhaupt die unsrige nennen und als solche in uns setzen sollen. Jene höhere Reflexion führt uns also zu einer Aufgabe, die wir ohne das Denken unsers Denkens, d.i. ohne Selbstdenken, gar nicht haben konnten. Der Punkt ist gegeben, an dem wir alles zu knüpfen haben: Wir Selbst nehmlich sind es in unserem reinen Wessen, und

---

[161] See: HÜLSEN 1796, 51

[162] See: HÜLSEN 1796, 52. Compare Hülsen's statement with FICHTE's (GA I-2, 143) *Programmschrift* statement that "*Der menschliche Geist macht mancherlei Ver-suche; er kommt durch blindes Herumtappen zur Dämmerung, und geht erst aus dieser zum hellen Tage über. Er wird Anfangs durch dunkle Gefühle (deren Ursprung und Wirklichkeit die Wissenschaflslehre darzulegen hat) geleitet; und wir hätten noch heute keinen deutlichen Begriff, und wären noch immer der Erdkloss, der sich dem Boden entwand, wenn wir nicht angefangen hätten, dunkel zu fühlen, was wir erst später deutlich erkannten.*"

die Aufgabe heisst daher: Uns Selbst in diesem reinen Wesen empirisch zu erreichen.[163]

According to Hülsen, this practical task compels the self-thinker to strive for an absolute self-positing of empirical reality. This implies that *quantity* be self-posited *as such*. This moral goal is absolutely necessary. What is at stake is personal autonomy understood in the strictest sense. Fulfilling this task is an unconditional moral command, which should be accepted absolutely without any further ground. Not to be a self (*nichts Selbst seyn*), Hülsen concludes, is harmful practically. It is tantamount to being nobody or nothingness (*Nichts seyn*): to give up freedom.[164]

According to Hülsen, this highest rational task is posed by the regulative idea of the whole. Its sphere is all-embracing and absolutely conditioning. This task is an exclusively necessary task of reason. Hülsen infers from that that in no moment of his existence, does the self-thinker set himself a random task. Solving such an exclusively rational necessary task of reason requires an exclusively necessary or absolute solution.[165]

Aufgeben überhaupt nehmlich heisst: Etwas setzen, dem etwas anders gleich gesetzt werde. Es muss also durch die Auflösung einer jeden Aufgabe etwas werden, was in und mit der Aufgabe, als bloss solcher, noch nicht ist. Mithin muss bei einer jeden blossen Aufgabe etwas seyn und etwas nicht seyn, und durch die Auflösung also das Nicht-Seyn dem Seyn gleich gesetzt werden, folglich dasjenige, was nicht ist zum Seyn werden. Ist nun unsere höchste Aufgabe; das reine Selbst empirisch zu realisieren; so ist in ihr also gesetzt: 1) das reine Selbst als ein Seyn schlechthin, und: 2) etwas dem reinen Selbst, oder dem Seyn schlechthin Gleichzusetzendes, folglich etwas, das nicht selbst ist, also für sich Nichts ist, sondenr nur ist, in wie fern etwas anderes, nehmlich ein Selbst, ist, dadurch es ist, mithin ein dem Selbst Entgegen-

---

[163] HÜLSEN 1796, 52

[164] See: HÜLSEN 1796, 60

[165] See: HÜLSEN 1796, 53, 59-60, 62-3. In HÜLSEN's (1796, 59) words: *"Aber die Nothwendigkeit einer AUFGABE, die durch die IDEE bestimmt wuerde, ist zugleich auch die Nothwendigkeit ihrer AUFLÖSUNG."*

gesetztes. Demanch liegt in unserm Selbst die nothwendige Aufgabe: das es absolut Alles sey.[166]

The self-thinker's ultimate moral goal is to reach his absolute self empirically. His entire experience must become a manifestation of his pure spiritual being. Reason's highest task must be solved holistically. Solving this task should be the highest determining condition of all practical self-activity. Nonetheless, our finite condition prevents us as empirical beings from solving this task absolutely. Only as a pure rational being, as non-empirical, can the self-thinker think of his posited being as a whole. His absolute freedom and his posited being are congruent in thought. Nonetheless, our empirical existence (*Daseyn*) constitutes a part of our original being (*Seyn*). This compels us to strive for the restitution of our pure being's missing quantity. This is negatively posited in us as an inherent disappearance (*Verschwinden*), determined by pure reason's transformation into a general-personal logical-historical agent. The self-thinker's empirical existence is a spatiotemporal objective becoming (*Werden*).[167] Space and time are inherent constitutive conditions of striving activity. In Hülsen's words:

So lange sich also das Ich Objekte gegenüber stellt, mithin dieselben sich gleich stellt, d.i. das Ich ein Nicht-Ich zu realisieren strebt, sind Raum und Zeit auch die nothwendigen Bedingungen dieses seines Strebens. Sie sind es aber nicht nur bis zu dem ewig von uns unerreichbaren Ziele, sondern sie sind eben so nothwendig auch nur die einziegmöglichen.[168]

For Hülsen, our moral vocation consists in personal teleological striving after the empirical fulfillment of our pure self. The self-thinker should bring about an exhaustive identity between his spatiotemporal existence and his pure or absolute being. He should overcome all those empirical limitations which stand in the way of his attainment of absolute causality (autonomy). Nonetheless, space and time condition the holistic or absolute solution demanded by our supreme moral task.

---

[166] HÜLSEN 1796, 60-1
[167] See: HÜLSEN 1796, 63-4, 53
[168] HÜLSEN 1796, 58

For us this is an unending task; a process that lasts throughout our spatiotemporal eternity.[169]

Hierdurch gehet nun zwar die höchste Aufgabe keinesweges verlohren; aber ihre Auflösung stehet nunmehr unter Zeitbedingungen, indem die Selbstthätigkeit nur streben kann, das absolute Seyn [...] zu realisieren: Es entstehet also durch das Streben ein blosses Werden zum Seyn. [...] Gehet das Streben der Vernunft ihre höchste Aufgabe zu lösen nun in das Unendliche; so erhalten wir durch dies Streben, also durch die unendliche Auflösung, auch eine unendiche Reihe bestimmter Aufgaben d.h die eine und höchste Aufgabe wird durch die wirkliche Auflösung als durch das Streben der Vernunft sie im Momente zu vollenden, unendlich eingeschränkt, und so ist also jede andere Aufgabe, auser der höchsten, selbst diese höchste in einer unendliche Reihe von Bedingungen ihrer Auflösung. Dadurch erhält nun jede Aufgabe in dem unendlichen Progressus nicht nur nothwendig ihren bestimmten Ort; sondern weil sie diesen hat, und also irgend wo auf dem Wege unsers ewigen Fortstrebens liegt; so muss sie am ihrem Orte auch nothwendig gelöst werden: denn sie ist nicht anders, als nur in so fern etwas geschieht, dadurch sie gerade und völlig bestimmt möglich wird. [...] Nur auf die Art schreiten wir unter beständiger Einheit des Strebens auf ein Ganzes auch wirklich fort zu der höchsten Einheit dieses Ganzen.[170]

Hülsen claims that as finite rational beings we cannot solve our supreme moral task as a whole. For us, the unceasingly counter-posited Not-I will never be an absolutely self-determined entity. Nonetheless, regulative morality requires its ideal self-determination. The self-thinker's ultimate moral purpose is to equate all possible counter-posited Not-I (empirical existence) to his own original self (pure being).[171] Pure reason's transformation into a general-personal develo-

---

[169] See: HÜLSEN 1796, 53, 65-6

[170] HÜLSEN 1796, 65-6

[171] See: HÜLSEN 1796, 62. As Manfred FRANK (1998, 915) comments, Hülsen vacillates between two different approaches to reason's regulative goal: "*Einmal benutzt er [i.e., Hülsen] den traditionellen, z.B. Leibnizschen Begriff, wonach Wirklichkeit Vollbestimmtheit eines zunächst Unterbestimmten meint. Und dann kann das ›Werden des Selbst zum Sein‹ im Wortsinne als seine Realisierung verstanden werden [...]. Nach dieser Auffasung ist die Wirklichkeit einfach »die absolute Totalität« ihrer Bestimmungen, deren »Alles Liebe in Einem«. — Anderer-*

ping agent determines the transcendental possibility of an infinitely self-actualizing logical-historical solution to his highest task. In this way, Hülsen deduces the inherent existence of an unending teleological series of correlative tasks, in which each emerges as a self-determined *part* of the only possible task of reason.

For Hülsen the personal understanding by the self-thinker that absolute knowledge has not been yet attained compels him to act. Each act is a step in his infinite positing striving after regulative autonomy. Self-determination of each step is his way to make purposive progress; none can be taken prior to its actual self-positing. Hülsen holds that the self-thinker constantly compares his own progress with his regulative idea of the whole. This comparison enables contrast of his own actual concept of "empirical reality" and his regulative concept of "original being". Self-thinkers thereby attain knowledge of the empirically covered extent of their moral vocation. According to Hülsen, progress demands that the self-thinker focus on his actual empirical standpoint from the perspective of the infinite and seek its self-determination through the regulative idea of the absolute. This persistent gap between the ideal and the real compels the self-thinker to take additional striving steps continually.[172] No teleological striving is possible without reason's regulative idea, as it alone provides the self-thinker with a necessary progressing direction (*Richtung*).[173]

According to Hülsen, philosophizing activity, gradual attainment of logical-historical knowledge, is the self-thinker's way to strive after regulative morality. This ongoing self-determining activity pushes

---

seits wird der Bestand eines reinen Selbst fichteanisch auf eine absolute Thesis gegründet, die ja in der Crusius-Kantschen Tradition mit ›Wirklichkeit‹ einerlei ist, also mit Sinn im modalontologischen Sinne ([...] wo die Wirklichkeit der Selbstsetzung – wie bei Hölderlin – seiner Möglichkeit vorausgehen soll)."

[172] In HÜLSEN's (1796, 203) words: "*Der Ausdrück Ich bin, im absoluten Sinne, gilt daher nur als Aufgabe, in wie fern Nichts dem ich entgegen gesetzt, folglich gleich gesetzt und also Ich seyn muss. Kein Mensch kann sagen: Ich bin! Mit absoluter Identität, sondern wo er es sagt, da denkt er es bloss als den schlechthin nothwendigen Erklärungsgrund seines Strebens.*"

[173] See: HÜLSEN 1796, 53-4, 56-9

philosophizing reason forward and expands, teleologically, the general-personal sphere of human freedom. In this way, Hülsen strengthens his identification or *connection* between *the self-thinker's personal striving activity* and *the rational history of philosophy*. Hülsen's deduction has crucial implications for his critique of Reinhold, for whom also the personal philosophizing activity of the self-thinker and philosophizing reason's ability to progress are connected. Hülsen develops an insight only vaguely asserted in Reinhold's early *Elementarphilosophie*. What is lacking in Reinhold's approach according to Hülsen is a connection between the self-thinker's practical philosophizing activity and philosophizing reason's general-personal ability to develop historically.

Hülsen's *Preisschrift* has a pedagogical function. The task of the self-thinker is to convince concrete rational beings of their true practical vocation, to show reason's unending task, and enable a dramatic improvement of man's moral situation. Hülsen and Fichte do not entirely agree on the pedagogical means demanded for accomplishing this. According to Fichte, moral improvement requires philosophical, historical, and philosophical-historical (logical-historical) knowledge. Together, these three kinds of knowledge constitute scholarship (*Gelehrsamkeit*). Although Fichte seems to stress the predominance of logical-historical knowledge, he insists that to promote moral improvement a joint application of these three types of knowledge is required. Hülsen's deduction of the self-thinker's activity as an exclusive logical-historical activity is a "spiritual" modification of Fichte's position. The trinomial character of scholarship is implicitly for Hülsen a groundless presupposition. Persisting self-determining activity, ongoing attainment of logical-historical knowledge, is the self-thinker's *only* way to make practical progress. As the only possible expression of true philosophical knowledge, logical-historical knowledge must be universal in character. Hülsen's modification of Fichte entails a rejection of pure philosophical versus pure historical knowledge. Hülsen implies that Fichte's system, like Reinhold's, lacks a universal-personal concept of logical-historical progress. Logical-historical knowledge alone is for Hülsen the self-thinker's way to promote moral improvement. Hülsen so established an innovative connection between the theoretical and the practical divisions of Fichte's early idealism. Hülsen provides in this way a solution to a problem left unresolved in Fichte's "improved" *Elementarphilosophie*.

Logical-historical knowledge is the self-thinker's way to strive and approximate regulative morality. Expanding empirical knowledge of his own pure self (self-knowledge), or of freedom as such, is the sole object of his self-determining activity. This means that for Hülsen only a personally self-posited task, an asking-answering self-task (*Selbst-Aufgabe*), has a *true* philosophical meaning. "Reality", an indispensable feature of true theoretical knowledge is, Hülsen claims, a predicate of those correlative question-answer tasks that the self-thinker finds in his logical-historical striving for a solution to reason's necessary task.[174]

The personalized character of all philosophizing activity prevents the self-thinker from acknowledging the "objective" authority of a *forum externus*, say an academy of sciences or any other similar institution. All philosophical objectivity is based on a personal or subjective degree of logical-historical development. Hülsen concludes that each consistent self-thinker is the ultimate judge of his own practical production.[175]

As a practically self-determined being, the self-thinker does not rely on the way other rational beings think. The personalized character of his philosophizing activity prevents this. As the exclusive thinker of his own self, the self-thinker realizes that he is the only source of his own practical production. So for Hülsen following Reinhold, a consistent self-thinker must be a resolutely *independent thinker*. Both Hülsen's

---

[174] See: HÜLSEN 1796, 68-9
[175] As to the contest of the Berlin Academy, HÜLSEN (1796, 68, 69–70) argues: "*Indes lässt sich auch wohl zeigen, dass durchaus kein Gelehrter, der sich die Preisfrage als eine Vernunftaufgabe beantwortet konnte, sie für die Akkademie auflösen werde. Das widerspräche seinem Zwekke. […] Für den Selbstdenkenden Gelehrten hat also die Preisfrage, als solche, gar keine Bedeutung. […] Die Aufgabe der Akademie bleibt also nur bloss für […] Männer und Jünglinge, die noch nie ihre Aufgabe dachten, und die auch die gegenwärtige darum nicht denken können; sondern denen es nur Beruf ist, geschriebene Gesetze zu vertheidigen und als Buchstabe durch Sprüche berühmter Männer zu verbreiten.*"

claim that the self-thinker is the sole judge of his own practical progress, and his rejection of a *forum externum* in philosophy, were inspired by Reinhold's program. The *universal-particular* character of all rational activity is Hülsen's way to realize Reinhold's "enlightened" project of making philosophy concrete, and endowing it with a personal or direct "popular-scientific" grounding. Hülsen learned from Reinhold that philosophical knowledge ought to be made available to the masses. This claim underlies Hülsen's identification of the vocations of the self-thinker (or scholar) and the rational being.[176] For Hülsen as for Reinhold before him, the self-thinker ought to be committed to an autonomous replacement of all "methodological, ethical, religious, and political authoritarianism by a philosophy that can bring about and secure enlightened and universal self-determination".[177]

3.11 The Concept of a True Academy of Sciences

Hülsen's position enabled him to develop Fichte's concept of a true academy of sciences, mentioned in passing in the *1ste Vorlesung. Im Winter-Halbjahr. [von der Bestimmung der Gelehrten]*.

According to Hülsen, the self-thinker or the scholar is an independent thinker. The attempt to determine the will through the imposition of "objective" knowledge, for Hülsen an academic commonplace occurrence, subordinates the self-thinker's spiritual freedom, and even contradicts the moral law: personal self-determination. It also interferes with the autonomous achievement of the self-thinker's practical vocation. Hülsen is an arduous critic of the academic establishment. He calls for its "enlightened" rethinking and reorganization. Hülsen's objection to the Berlin Academy reveals the irrelevance that such outdated institutions now have for true scholars.

---

[176] See: KLAWON 1977, 196 [Reinhold not mentioned]. Although Fichte shares this identification, his position is that scholars should keep their distinctive status of promoters and supervisors of philosophical culture. For Hülsen's further discussion of "popular-scientific" philosophy, see his 1797 *Philosophische Briefe an Hrn. v. Briest in Nennhausen. Erster Brief. Ueber Popularität in der Philosophie.*
[177] AMERIKS 2000, 87 [Hülsen not mentioned].

Er [i.e., the scholar] *soll ein Selbstdenker seyn, und wo er es noch nicht ist, da müssen wir auf seine Selbstständigkeit zwar kräftigst zu wirken suchen; aber gewiss nicht durch Institute, wo die Mündigkeit dekretiert wird. Die Akademie und alle ihr ähnliche Anstalten sind das Werk einer Zeit, die in sich selbst wieder zurükkehrt, sich selbst also beschliesst. Es ist daher gewiss, dass sie in derselben gewirkt, und die Fortschritte des menschlichen Geistes bis zum Ziele seiner selbst gefördert haben. Aber diesen Zirkel einsehen, und ihn beschrieben haben, ist vollkommen eines. Wir sollen ihn also nicht noch einmal durchkriechen, so bald jenes Statt findet; sondern auf besserm Wege Einsicht befördern, und darum in eine Sphäre uns schwingen, wo wir nur durch Unendlichkeit auf uns selbst wieder zurükkomen. Hier erst beginnen die Augfaben der Vernunft durch freie Selbstbestimmung, und mit ihnen der gewise Erfolg unsers Nachstrebens.*[178]

Hülsen learned from Fichte that the scholar ought to be the ethically best man of his time. Guided by the *Wissenschaftslehre*, the scholar is acquainted with the means required to improve our moral performances. As the educator of humanity, the scholar ought to make his fellowmen aware of their true ethical needs. He should also acquaint them with the means necessary for satisfying these needs. This pedagogic task enables the scholar to employ moral means to influence society. On this point Hülsen's agreement with Fichte is unambiguous. Hülsen argues, however, that philosophy cannot be obtained in institutions in which uncritical means are used to coerce practical freedom. Hülsen rejects the teaching of positive or "invasive" knowledge.[179] As purveyors of facts academic institutions are obsolete historical products. In the logical-historical epoch of autonomous self-determination, such training schools in which no true spiritual knowledge can be obtained are no longer necessary. In place of traditional academies and universities, Hülsen presents his own innovative idea of a true academy of sciences.[180]

---

[178] HÜLSEN 1796, 70

[179] Ch. HÜLSEN 1934, 108

[180] *Preisschrift* does not discuss the academic obtaining of critical knowledge. It discusses only the role that modern institutions should have in the unending moral improvement of their members. By 1798, Hülsen rejected an offer to col-

Hülsen used Fichte's pedagogic thought to rethink the concept of a true academy of sciences. In his *1ste Vorlesung*, Fichte exhorted his

---

laborate with Fichte at the University of Jena. Hülsen instead founded his own institute in Lentzke bei Fehrbellin, a small village near Berlin. The purpose of this institution, as Hülsen himself reported to August W. Schlegel on November 15, 1798, and to Mrs. von Rochow (the mother of two of his students) on February 5, 1800, was the philosophical cultivation of young pupils. Hülsen's letters reveals the extent of his anti-positive pedagogic ideas: "*Ich bleibe frey und unabhängig und brauche für das Semestrum kein anderes Lehrbuch, als das der Natur und des lebendigen Menschen. Das äußere Geräusch soll meine Schule nicht empfehlen; aber wohl die Wahrheit, die sich auf Einsicht in die Natur des Menschen gründet. [...] Man kann indeß jungen Männern immer etwas Gutes sagen, wenn man auch ein Lehrbuch in der Hand hat; so bald man sie nur errinert, daß der Mensch eigentlich kein Lehrbuch sey, und daß man doch überall auf ihn zurückkomen müße. Bei solchen Vorlesungen, wie Sie wahrscheinlich wählen, hat die herge-brachte Form den wenigsten Nachtheil. Sie machen ihre Schüler mit der Kraft des Gesanges bekant, und führen sie bis zu seinem heiligen Urquell*" [FLITNER 1913, 100]. "*Den Menschen auf sich selbst führen, dies also ist die Kunst und die einzige Art und Weise, wie unsere Erziehung von gewissen und grossen Erfolgen sein kann*" [Ch. HÜLSEN 1934, 108]. As these passages reveal, the task of the scholar is to promote personal self-determining activity. Some remaining excerpts of Hülsen's letter to Mrs. von Rochow reveal the pedagogic method to be followed. According to Hülsen, the scholar should identify the free, though still dormant spirit of his non-philosophically cultivated pupil, and then instruct him so that he spontaneously self-reflects on it by himself. [See: Ch. HÜLSEN 1934, 108]. The task of the scholar is to help pupils spiritualize their own self-knowledge, make it concrete, and avoid uncritical abstractions [See: Ch. HÜLSEN 1934, 1]. Rudolf LASSAHN (1970, 105) summarizes the philosophical ideas behind Hülsen's peda-gogic position: "*Der Mensch kann nur das Werk seiner selbst sein. Nicht Schule-halten ist Aufgabe des Erziehers, sondern die immerwährende Aufforderung zur freien Selbstgestaltung. [...] Das Geschäft der Bildung muß jeder Mensch selbst vollbringen. [...] Hülsen erkannte, daß das Begreifen der harmonischen Ent-wicklung aller Kräfte dem jungen Menschen noch fehlen muß. Eine Aufgabe des Erziehers besteht deshalb in der notwendigen Vorwegnahme. Aus dem, was ist, muß er schließen auf das, was sein soll. Lebendige Erziehung vollzieht sich in die-sem Spannungsfeld zwischen Sein und Sollen.*" The pedagogic task of the scholar, as Hülsen finally will write to August W. Schlegel on July 8, 1799, is to educate pupils for unconditioned self-education (*Selbstbildung*), for freedom and true morality. See: FLITNER 1913, 103

students to unconditioned or autonomous scholarship. Fichte demanded that academies of sciences, the headquarters of the scholar, assemble self-determined philosophers and so promote "scientific" culture. Such institutions, he claimed, must not be mere schools of theory, but schools of practical action. Only the scholar as self-thinker can transmit "scientific" culture. In any case, the moral law compels the scholar to preserve his practical freedom by avoiding the subordination of his will to academic institutions. Hülsen, as we shall see, takes Fichte's moral concept of purposive coordinated community as his own model for an academy of sciences.

According to Hülsen, every academy of sciences presupposes a community or a society of true scholars (*Gesellschaft von Gelehrten*) as its practical determining ground. Morality demands that a true academy of sciences relates unconditionally to its grounding society of scholars as a determined condition relates to its absolute conditioning ground. The scholars who are members of this unconditionally established institution are themselves self-determined agents. Freedom so furnishes the practical ground of every true academy of sciences; it preserves the rational autonomy of its interacting members.[181] Hülsen takes Fichte's concept of moral community as a model for a true academy of sciences. In it, all fellow members are freely coordinated beings. Subordination undermines the moral foundations of an academy, as it contradicts the moral law. Freedom is the way a scholar affiliates to such an academy. As a universal self-determining condition, freedom assures the independent and the *qualitatively equal moral status* of all academy members. For Hülsen a true academy of sciences is not only an autonomous, but also a *morally non-hierarchical* institution.[182]

Expanding self-determination, logical-historical striving after regulative morality, is the exclusive vocation of the scholar. To make this

---

[181] Hülsen is probably thinking here about the *Bund der freien Männer,* a group of students that he joined in Jena, and which committed itself to the moral-republican implications of Fichte's philosophy. For the moral purposes of the *Bund,* see the *Constitution der Literarischen Gesellschaft zu Jena* in: Marwinski 1992, 2-32

[182] See: Hülsen 1796, 47-9

possible is the premise of a true academy of sciences. Hülsen adapts two additional features of Fichte's concept of moral community: the true human vocation within society: coordinated striving, and communal purposive regulation.

For Hülsen the self-determined integration of the personal striving of the scholars, universal consensus, is possible at a certain logical-historical stage. The *Wissenschaftslehre* has shown that the regulative striving courses of all scholars intersect; all scholars strive after the same single moral perfection. What follows is the self-determined possibility of an unending coordinated striving.[183] This is the foundation of a true "scientific" academic setting, which enables scholars to assemble spontaneously and approximate their supreme moral ideal collectively. Hülsen concludes that the grounding authority of a true academy of sciences, its unconditionally established society of coordinated scholars, is in addition a morally purposive authority.[184]

Critical philosophy is the general-personal consensual result of logical-historical striving. In their strivings, all individuals cover the same rational progressive course. Hülsen holds that each concrete step taken by a leading scholar opens up the road for philosophizing reason's general progress. Attainment of this progress demands personal self-determined evaluation of reason's production; the partial anticipatory solving of reason's supreme task is the avant-garde scholar's way to enable a moral improvement of the human species. Hülsen's argument develops and explains an aspect of Fichte's concept of communal morality: to strive for oneself is tantamount as to striving for one's own fellowmen. The regulative purpose of joint striving is the absolutely coordinated unity of all scholars.[185] To promote a joint

---

[183] As FLITNER (1913, 30) comments: "*Wenn der systematische Zusammenhang bewußt ist, läßt sich das höchste Ziel dieser Generation erreichen, Einigkeit eines jeden mit sich selbst und Ganzheit des ungetrennten Menschen. Der Zusammenhang kommt zum Bewußtsein durch Selbsterkenntnis, durch philosophische Methode. ‚Der Mensch soll Er selbst und er soll ein Ganzes sein, sind [...] zwei völlig identische Sätze'.*"

[184] See: HÜLSEN 1796, 69, 71-3

[185] According to FLITNER (1913, 32), Hülsen's conclusion enables better understand-

achievement of reason's infinite task, Hülsen concludes, is the *raison-d'être* of every true academy of sciences.[186]

According to Hülsen, each step by a self-thinking scholar enables a further progress of reason or humanity. *Self-determined judging evaluation* enhances personal (spiritual) self-knowledge. Hülsen's purpose is to develop Fichte's moral concepts of "giving" and "receiving":[187] two spiritual skills to all coordinated academic activity.

The strivings of all self-thinking scholars intersect. All rational beings are compelled by reason to solve the same task. According to Hülsen, to benefit from rational progress requires the development of the skill of openness or receptivity (*Empfänglichkeit*). Receptivity is a practically *self-cultivated* skill as a means to personal moral improvement. Receptivity alone is not enough to attain progress. The personal reception of philosophizing reason's leading general-personal progress demands that receptivity be supplemented by a self-determined judging ability: free examination (*freie Prüfung*).[188]

---

ing of humanity's pre-critical moral situation: "*Wenn Einigkeit die Bestimmung des Menschen ist, dann ist es sicher, daß die Menschen sich gegen nichts so sehr gesträubt haben als [...] gegen ihre eigene, in ihnen gelegene Bestimmung. Auf Uneinigkeit (Widerstreit) führt Hülsen die Not der Jahrtausende zurück; sie ist der Sitz des Übels. Auf zweifache Art äußert sich der Widerstreit: als Uneinigkeit auf theoretischem Gebiet, wo jeder seine Meinung allen gegenüber durchsetzen möchte; und allgemeiner als Uneinigkeit des Menschen mit sich selber, Trennung seiner Kräfte und Vermögen, Unmoralität überhaupt. Beide Arten werden nicht auseinandergehalten und sind auch nicht zu trennen; wie durch kritisches Wissen jeder an sich selbst verwiesen und damit dem Streit der Ansichten enthoben ist, so wird er mit demselben Wissensakt auch mit sich selbst einig, d.h. sittlich besser.*"

[186] See: HÜLSEN 1796, 72-3, 48

[187] Let us recall that "giving" represents for Fichte the spontaneous ability to perfect one's own moral skills by making use of the formative effect that other rational beings have on oneself. "Receiving" is in turn the personal ability to perfect one's own fellowmen by acting upon them as upon self-determined rational beings.

[188] See: HÜLSEN 1796, 186-7

Alles Objekt der Reflexion muss nach dem Verhältniss des Bedingten zu seiner Bedingung als Unbedingten beurtheilt werden.[189]

According to Hülsen, free examination enables a scholar to self-determine for himself the other scholar's progress; it enables unconditional self-conditioning or critical "appropriation" of someone else's superior standpoint. Free examination allows the *personalized "spiritualization"*, and thereby *self-actualization* of philosophizing reason's progress. Conformation to a particularizing degree of logical-historical development, determines free examination's *individualized outcome*.[190] In addition, free examination enables a self-thinking scholar to spontaneously focus on a philosophical text and establish *a practical limit between its "spirit" and its letter,* a procedure overlooked by Fichte, and without which a *personal "spiritualized" understanding* of his *Wissenschaftslehre* is impossible. Free examination allows *personal non-coercive adequacy* and *incorporation* of the "spirit" of superior systematic truth. It enabled Hülsen, a resolute self-thinker, to apprehend the "spirit" of Fichte's approach, as Fichte himself did with Kant's *Kritik*,[191] modify it normatively, and still call it *Wissenschaftslehre*. As Hülsen acknowledges

Es ist aber darum gar nicht nothwendig, die Wissenschaftslehre anzuerkennen, oder auch so fort keinen Anspruch auf Vernunft zu machen. Nein es ist nur nothwendig, als vernünftiges Wesen die Wharheit zu ehren und unser jedesmaliges Wissen also mit redlicher Ueberzeugung unser bestes Wissen zu nennen, folglich dasselbe auch andern, die es wohl eben so redlich meinen können, nicht aufdringen zu wollen. Das nur fordert die Wissenschaftslehre,

---

[189] HÜLSEN 1796, 187

[190] Although qualitatively no differences are possible, particularization is caused by intentional divergence, by the disparate quantitative insights that finite rational beings gain into reason's original being.

[191] In HÜLSEN's (1796, 196) words: *"Fichte, der mit Kant aus einer Quelle schöpft, aus einer Quelle, die noch den mehresten Kantianern ein Geheimniss zu seyn scheint, dasjenige nur an das Licht bringt, was Kant in den Tiefen seiner Untersuchungen theils wirklich bearbeitete, theils aber nur nachweiss. Daher ist der **Geist** der Kritik selbst die Wissenschaftslehre, oder diese, wie Fichte sich ausdrückt, der durchgeführte kritische idealismus."* [my bold]

*und wo eine solche Gesinnung Statt findet, da wird sich auch ihr **Geist** gewiss fruchtbar beweisen.*[192]

For Hülsen free examination cannot be used prior to a personal veri-fication or justification of its critical suitability as a valid practical means grounded on the human spirit.[193] All true scholars should agree as to free examination's capacity to assert the truth.[194] Free examination is Hülsen's "improved" version of Fichte's concept of "receiving".

Nur unter dem Schutze dieses Gesetzes gibt es für mich eine Vernunft, und darf ich selbst mir eine solche einräumen. Die Voraussetzung ist daher: dass mir objektive kein Absolutes gegeben werden könne, weil es dadurch, dass es nothwendig meine freie Prüfung aufhöbe, auch schlechterdinges nicht in mein Bewusstseyn aufgenommen werden könnte.[195]

Hülsen assumes two different uses of free examination. The emergence of critical philosophy determines the qualitative end of philosophizing reason's history. The scholar can employ free examination either as a *quantitative* means to pursue joint *regulative* striving,[196] or as a *qual-itative* means to reconstruct philosophizing reason's history. As a qualitative means it enables a personal *retrospective* systematization of all logical-historical changes underwent by philosophizing reason.

---

[192] HÜLSEN 1796, 158-9 [my bold]

[193] The circular character of this procedure does not entail an inconsistency, as all rational activity is self-reflective.

[194] See: HÜLSEN 1796, 186-7. For Hülsen free examination also shows that knowl-edge cannot be grounded on an absolute object. HÜLSEN (1796, 137-8) writes: "*Soll aber das aufgestellte Gesetz zur freien Beurtheilung durchaus erforderlich seyn; so kann ein höchstes Prinzip der Philosophie, durch die Zurückführung des Ganzen unsers Wissen auf ihn, auch nichts anders als das Unbedingte, und daher auf keine Weise ein objektives Prinzip seyn. Denn das Objektive stehet noth-wendig in dem Verhältniss des Bedingten zu seiner Bedingung als Unbedingten, oder es ist für die freie Reflexion schlechthin Nichts, und nur als solches erst ein absolutes Objekt.*"

[195] HÜLSEN 1796, 187

[196] Hülsen does not discuss this use of free examination. It however is implied by the fact that morality compels the rational being to an unending striving after absolute coordination.

Free examination enables the actualization of philosophizing reason's progress. Through their personal efforts, all scholars can contribute to the philosophical progress of humanity, an "improved" explanation of Fichte's concept of "giving".[197] "Giving" (or sharing) and "receiving", determine the possibility of a joint regulative striving. These two spiritual skills are the scholar's keys to all purposively coordinated academic activity. The social vocation of the Fichtean scholar is so institutionalized.

3.12 The Systematic Reconstruction of Philosophy's History

Free examination makes a possible critical update or "appropriation" of philosophizing reason's leading progress. Together with "giving" (sharing), it enables a joint regulative striving after absolute identity. For Hülsen, however, academic affiliation is neither a necessary requirement to accomplish these two self-determined activities, nor a condition to be a scholar. "Receiving" and "giving" as personal procedures, transcend the sphere of academic institutions and can develop among non-affiliated scholars. Hülsen also maintains that a historically extended interaction, a mutual "receiving" and "giving", took place among scholars and self-thinkers during the pre-critical development of the *Wissenschaftslehre*. So different historically situated philosophers "appropriated" philosophizing reason's progress, and contributed to its subsequent teleological development. Hülsen clarifies this by expanding his argument about avant-garde philosophizing.[198]

[...] der Mensch ist unter Menschen, und kann nie anders gedacht werden. Die Menschheit ist demnach nur denkbar: durch das Eingreifen der Thätigkeit eines jeden Einzelnen in die Thätigkeit Aller; und jeder Einzelnen [...] soll Antheil an dem Fortschreiten des Ganzen haben, weil das Ganze nur ein

---

[197] See: HÜLSEN 1796, 185-6. The term "giving" does not appear in the text. It is implied by the fact that striving for oneself is tantamount as to striving for all rational beings (reason). See: HÜLSEN 1796, 129

[198] See: HÜLSEN 1796, 185-6, 129

Ganzes durch das Verhältniss seiner Theile ist. [...] Wir streben nur ewig nach der Einen Vernunft, denn ewig stehet die Einheit mit der Mannich-faltigkeit im Kampfe. Hier tritt daher, unter Begünstigung der Natur, stets der Stärke voran, und bezeichnet in irgend einer Beziehung die Stufenfolge des Weges der allgemeinen Menschenvernunft. [...] was diese waren und thaten, das ist Erhebung und Verherligung der Menschheit überhaupt. Auch wir sollen und werden durch Freiheit dahin kommen, denn eine gleiche Fülle der Kraft ist es, die in uns allen wohnt, und die nur unter ungleichen Richtungen und Hindernissen sich entwikkelt. Aber auch sie müssen verschwinden; denn jeder Kampf mit ihnen ist nur ein Sieg der Vernunft mehr. Das sey der Männern gedankt, welche die Wege vor uns hinbahnen.[199]

The personalized activity ("giving") of a number of avant-garde philosophers conditions reason's historical development. In their personal strivings, all rational beings cover the same qualitative progress, the result of which is critical philosophy. Attaining someone else's progress demands personal reproduction ("receiving"). Through a teleological process of "giving" and "receiving", philosophizing reason gradually accumulated and communicated its logical-historical progress. A discussion of such a systematic process is lacking in Reinhold's early *Elementarphilosophie*.

Hülsen discussed only in passing the pre-critical status of "giving".

So lange sich die Philosophie im Progressus noch befindet, ist es lediglich nur die Urtheilskraft welche eigentlich fortschreitet. Je freier daher diese bleibt, je früher muss sie auch zu ihrem Ziele vordringen. Das bezeugt uns allerdings auch die Geschichte der Philosophie. Nur dadurch erhob sich nach oft langen Zwischenräumen ein einzelner Selbstdenker [i.e., Fichte], dass er sich von der gewohnten Vorstellungsart losriss und selbst Gesetztgeber wurde.[200]

As to "receiving", Hülsen says nothing specific. He implies that throughout pre-critical thought both "giving" and "receiving" manifested themselves unconsciously, as the rational being is destined, spiritually, to logical-historical striving and the acquisition of critical philosophy.[201] For Hülsen all philosophers who contribute to philosophizing

---

[199] HÜLSEN 1796, 128, 129, 130
[200] HÜLSEN 1796, 147-8
[201] See: HÜLSEN 1796, 185-6

reason's progress are self-thinkers. Although ignorant of the *Wissenschaftslehre*, their systematic positions nonetheless enabled their practical freedom to expand. Leibniz was for Hülsen one of these pre-critical "productive geniuses". Through "giving" and "receiving", self-thinkers lifted themselves up to a new philosophical level and contributed to philosophizing reason's development.[202] As Dieter Klawon sums it up,

Irrtümer auf der Suche nach Erkenntnis verschlagen hierbei der Sache fast nichts, solange sie im subjektiven Bewußtsein der Wahrheit vorgetragen und bei erweitertem Wissen als solche eingestanden werden. [...] Hülsen nimmt jeden Philosophen ernst, insofern er als „Selbstdenker" (eines seiner Lieblingsworte), d.h. mit Anspuch auf Originalität an der großen Aufgabe mitarbeitet.[203]

According to Hülsen, personal self-determination enables the understanding of the systems whereby philosophizing reason progresses teleologically. It is the personal means necessary to articulate philosophy's history. Hülsen following Reinhold argues that universal consensus is possible only when self-thinkers self-reflect and self-subsume reason's disputing standpoints under their own spiritually attained concept of critical philosophy.

Die Wissenschaft im Geiste ist das ewige Licht, welches in die Unendlichkeit hinausstralt, und uns darum auch die düstern Wege der Vergangenheit erleuchten muss, dass wir sagen können: dieses sind die Fortschritte des Menschengeschlechts. [...] Die Vernunft als Vernunft, kann durchaus nicht anders, als in die Vergangenheit zurückzugehen und sich selbst aufzusuchen. Nur dadurch erst erhält sie ihren bestimmten Standpunkt, denn sie lernt den Menschen begreifen, wie er durch alle Stufen seines Werdens zum endlichen Daseyn hervorging.[204]

Pre-critical philosophy's history is a "chapter" of reason's logical history. For Hülsen the *Wissenschaftslehre* requires the systematic articulation of this "chapter". Retrospective self-conscious insight into

---

[202] See: HÜLSEN 1796, 131-2
[203] KLAWON 1977, 184-5
[204] HÜLSEN 1796, 166

one's own unaware acts of positing is the path to attain universal self-determined knowledge. Only it allows the philosopher to grasp reason's full systematic character by integrating all partisan standpoints with critical philosophy as its highest reconciling standpoint, and so to begin a coordinated striving for regulative self-identity.[205] According to Hülsen, following Reinhold, the history of philosophy ought to take systems of philosophy, investigate them within a rational holistic context, apply to them free examination, and self-determine and re-articulate them. The correct delimitation of each system is for Hülsen a key condition to determine its systematic location within reason's universal logical-historical sphere.[206]

As Hülsen learned from Reinhold, the articulation of philosophy's history demands that all partisan standpoints be deduced from or traced back to the universal concept of critical philosophy. For Hülsen this strategy shows their ultimate identity with the *Wissenschaftslehre.* Subordination allows all disputing standpoints to exhaust their systematic grounds, and to transform themselves into a universally self-grounded discipline, and so find a systematic location within a *synthetically grounded* history of philosophy.[207]

Mithin wäre ihr, als Wissenschaft, schlechthin kein einziges System entgegen gesetzt, sonder sie nur wäre das eine und absolute System. Alle übrigen also könnten nur das Werden der Wissenschaft bezeichnen, und die Wissenschaft müsste folglich das Ziel aller Progressen der philosophierende Vernunft: das

[205] Critical insight shows that the academic task about metaphysics' progress since Leibniz and Wolf must appear in the practical asking-answering course of every single self-thinker. As HÜLSEN (1796, 166-7) writes: "*Die Aufgabe ist also eine nothwendige Vernunftaufgabe. Sie begreift aber als solche nur einen bestimmten Theil der Geschichte. Mithin ist sie durch ihr Verhältniss zum Ganzen bedingt. Der durch Leibniz genommene Standpunkt muss erst fest stehen, und also schon ein Resultat der Untersuchung seyn, bevor wir weiter vorschreiten können. Dies ist wenigstens für die Darstellung des Ganzen nothwendig.*"
[206] See: HÜLSEN 1796, 167
[207] See: HÜLSEN 1796, 158

bestimmte und durchaus unbestreitbare Resultat ihres gesammten philosophischen Nachsterbens seyn.[208]

Philosophy shows the way progress should be determined. Philosophy is the logical-historical result of all previous rational inquiry into its systematic possibility: now a self-determined result of its own reality. Philosophy's self-reflection encompasses reason's full empirical course of progress, summarized in a practically self-posited fact: the *Wissenschaftslehre*. Reason appears in the *Wissenschaftslehre* as the result of what in the past was *reason-in-becoming*. Philosophy's insight, as Hülsen learned from Reinhold, is reason's way to recognize its logical-historical progress, to systematize it as an indisputably unified product of its own striving. Philosophy also shows that the object about which one asks (*etwas*), the history of philosophy, can be equally posited to that from which (*wovon*) or rather whereby one asks: reason. Philosophy's history is so unconditionally self-determined by reason.[209]

Giebt daher die Freiheit sich das Gesetz der Wissenschaft, um das Fortschreiten zur Wissenschaft zu reflektieren, und also die successive Stufenfolge desselben wissenschaftlich zu bestimmen: so kann sie vollkommen sicher seyn festen Trittes fortzuschreiten, denn ihr Gesetz gebietet im Reiche alles menschlichen Wissens. [...] Durch diesen Kreis, den die freie Reflexion geht, stehen nothwendig alle philosophischen Systeme, die sie selbigen vorfindet, unter dem gleichen Schutze der Wissenschaft. Denn was diese ist, das sind sie im werden. Die Reflexion philosophiert also in jedem Momente ihres Kreises mit allen Systemen zugleich, d.h. alle sind in ihr Eines, und mithin bleibt in ihr kein Widerstreit möglich.[210]

Philosophizing takes place exclusively within a *forum internum*. The articulation of philosophy's history is personal. Accordingly, no external objections, even by a sceptic, can obstruct or disqualify personal articulation. Hülsen makes this point by claiming that Self-Being (*Selbstseyn*) is the source and the ultimate goal of all logical-historical striving. The general-personal searching of Self-Being, shows that all

---

[208] HÜLSEN 1796, 152
[209] See: HÜLSEN 1796, 153
[210] HÜLSEN 1796, 153-4

systematic efforts were meant to find an original searching agent (*das Suchende*): reason. With critical philosophy, reason identifies itself as the absolute *qualitative ground* of all knowledge. The self-determined fact that knowledge springs from Self-Being proves as in Fichte's *Wissenschaftslehre* that a system of philosophy can emerge only in, for and by concrete rational beings.[211] What follows is this:

Dem Begriffe zu Folge, den wir durch diese ganze Schrift von der Philosophie als Wissenschaft aufgestellt haben, kann es durchaus nichts verschlagen: ob Fichte oder Cajus, oder wer es seyn möge, als Urheber gennant werde. Sie ist nur Wissenschaft durch einen jeden für einen jeden; mithin nur Wissenschaft überhaupt, in so fern jedes vernünftige Wesen als Urheber gedacht wird. Das vernünftige Wesen aber kann nicht anders als Urheber gedacht werden, als in so fern es sich selbst als Urheber denkt; folglich ist jeder Urheber der Wissenschaft, der dieselbe in sich setzt.[212]

For Hülsen philosophy is an *active product* of the human spirit or reason; it cannot objectively stand by itself. Realizing this is tantamount as to understanding that each concrete rational being is philosophy's *practical producer*. This has implications for the suppression of partisan affiliations. Hülsen following Reinhold claims that philosophy's personal character reveals that all school division (*Schulwesen*) is a "ridiculous pedantry" (*eine lächerliche Pedanterei*). Non-affiliation is a necessary result of all critical thought.[213]

In Hülsen's *Preisschrift* as in Fichte's *Wissenschaftslehre*, developing some of Reinhold's ideas, personal production and critical knowledge are connected. The articulation of philosophy's history is a *personal task* that must be pursued by self-determined individuals only. Self-determination is impossible prior to the establishment of a systematic order among philosophizing reason's practically posited products. Self-determination requires a personal critical understanding of philosophy's logical-historical relation to its evolutionary stages. For Hülsen, reason's suppression of partisan disputes through reconciling self-unity

---

[211] See: HÜLSEN 1796, 155-6
[212] HÜLSEN 1796, 156
[213] See: HÜLSEN 1796, 156-7

determines the ending point of a pragmatic approach to the history of philosophy. With the *Wissenschaftslehre*, all alleged atomically posited systems reach an ultimate limit and achieve a definitive rational-systematic (or contextual) "measurement".[214]

In this way, Hülsen re-articulated the last imperfect aspect of Reinhold's early *Elementarphilosophie*, supplemented Fichte's *Wissenschaftslehre*, and became a co-founder of German idealism.

---

[214] See: FLITNER 1913, 29. — Hans HESS (1929, 265) summarizes these two points: "*Die Philosophiegeschichte gewinnt eine neue Würde. [...] Die zeitlose Vernunft muß die zeitlichen Stufen ihrer Selbstverwirklichung, innerhalb deren sie sich zu immer größerer Vollendung emporarbeitet, kennen lernen. Sie wird überhaupt erst vollständig durch die Geschichte ihres Werdens. ,Die Vernunft als Vernunft kann durchaus nicht anders als in die Vergangenheit zurückzugehen und sich selbst aufzusuchen. Nur dadurch erst erhält sie ihren bestimmten Standpunkt'. Sie besitzt ihre Freiheit nicht anders als durch ,Reflexion ihres empirischen Progressus'.*"

Appendix A

Jakob Sigismund Beck's *Einzigmöglicher Standpunkt*
as a Reconstructive Example of a "Chapter"
of the Systematic History of Philosophy

Hülsen closes with a supplementary section appended on 1796. This section discusses Jakob Sigismund Beck's *Einzigmöglicher Standpunkt, aus welchem die Kritische Philosophie beurtheilt werden muss* (1796), an essay that Hülsen did not know while developing his historically augmented *Wissenschaftslehre*.[1] The discussion of Beck's system provides an example of how to reconstruct, autonomously, a chapter of the systematic history of philosophy. Hülsen's purpose is to show his *free examining reader* how to exhaust the uncritically established foundations of Beck's approach.[2] Comparison and contrast to the universal concept of philosophy is Hülsen's way to correct Beck's misjudgements, and trace his system back to the consensual or non-contradictable standpoint of the absolutely self-grounded I.[3]

Dennoch muss der Versuch des Hrn. B[eck] nicht weniger eben so beurtheilt werden, wie die Kritik d.r.V. Folglich als das, was er wirklich ist, und das andernmal als das, was er seyn würde, wenn man von den höheren Voraussetzungen abstrahieren wollte. Dieses letztere geschiehet nun zum Behufe des erstern, und gehet also auf blosse Berichtigung eines Irrthums im Urtheile.

---

[1] See: HÜLSEN 1796, 171-2

[2] For Hülsen's emphasis on the *personal character* of this free examining task, see: HÜLSEN 1796, 172, 209-10. Hülsen acknowledges that he has reached the standpoint of the *Wissenschaftslehre* without knowing Beck's approach. Still, Hülsen's position is consistent, as the rational history of philosophy represents only a quantitatively disparate general-personal process. Qualitatively, Hülsen implies, Beck's standpoint does not differ from Reinhold's.

[3] See: HÜLSEN 1796, 210, and FLITNER 1913, 45

Jenes erstere aber betrifft die Schrift als ein Produkt der freien Selbstthätig-keit, ohne welche sie […] gar nicht da seyn würde.[4]

The articulation of philosophy's history is *personal*. It is the key to overcome partisan disputes and achieve self-determining coordination. Beck's system has a precise general-personal location within philosophizing reason's logical history.[5] Following Reinhold, Hülsen holds, this comparing-contrasting procedure enables personal critical insight into asking-answering's logical-historical production.

Hülsen's interest in Beck's system is not gratuitous. Beck is for him the only non-Fichtean commentator that has approached the *Vernunft-kritik* from Kant's own standpoint. He therefore is the only commentator that has completely understood Kant.[6] Hülsen assigns Beck a preeminent place in the systematic history of Kantian philosophy.[7]

Hülsen opens with two remarks. (1) Philosophy unifies all rational beings on the same systematic standpoint. (2) Philosophy emerges in one's own general-personal striving, while its exhaustivity is determined by a universal grounding principle. That is why philosophy's standpoint is the *exclusively-possible* (*einzigmöglicher*) standpoint. Non-universally determined judgments provoke divergent and incomplete systematic insights of knowledge's foundational ground. Universal consensus compels rational beings that strive after critical knowledge to rectify their erroneous judgments. Grasping the true form of judgment (*Form der Beurtheilung*), Hülsen will show Beck, reveals that no ultimate divergence among systems and standpoints is possible.[8]

---

[4]   HÜLSEN 1796, 194
[5]   See: HÜLSEN 1796, 33
[6]   See: HÜLSEN 1796, 172
[7]   See: HÜLSEN 1796, 168-9. Guido NASCHERT speculates that Hülsen's interest in Beck can be traced back to 1791. Beck could have been one of Hülsen's philosophy teachers at the University of Halle, where he enrolled in 1785. See: NASCHERT 1998, 115
[8]   See: HÜLSEN 1796, 170-1. It should be recalled that for Hülsen the universal standpoint of the *Wissenschaftslehre* requires a personal self-determining account, or rather, a normative interpretative apprehension of reason's activity.

According to Hülsen, Beck's essay is an attempt at a systematic establishment of the highest or rather the exclusively-possible standpoint of philosophy. If so, Beck's system should determine knowledge's sphere universally. As to the inter-determination of all form and content of knowledge, a substantial condition of critical thought, Beck's approach should express unity as such (*Einheit schlechthin*), neither epistemic, nor ontological dualism, but a monistic realism-idealism. This is the cornerstone of Hülsen's criticism of Beck.[9]

Beck's presentation is divided into four sections. The first discusses the difficulties concerning the "spirit" of Kant's *Kritik*. Beck's own position according to Hülsen was that mistaken discursive insights into the grounding principle of knowledge, the proto-conscious act of representation (*ursprünglich vorzustellen*), prevented a true grasping of the "spirit" of Kant's approach, thus obstructing insight into the true meaning of critical philosophy. Hülsen agrees with Beck and shares his view that a full insight into proto-conscious representation is necessary to grasp the true "spirit" of critical philosophy. Hülsen however claims that Beck omitted the discussion of a crucial topic: the difference between the "spirit" and the "letter" of critical philosophy; only a critically developed insight, a personal ability that the *Kritik* itself should foster, can penetrate the universal "spirit" of critical philosophy.[10] This omission prevented Beck from grounding his system on a universal ground. Beck arrived at the uncritical conclusion that the first principle of knowledge is a transcendental fact.[11] Critical philosophy, Hülsen reminds us, proves that

Das Ich soll nicht nur keine Thatsache seyn, sondern durch dasselbe wird vielmehr alle Thatsache, als höchstes Prinzip, in Anspruch genommen, und als völlig nichtig erwiesen. Ich merke dies nun an, um des Irrthums willen; denn die Wissenschaftslehre selbst habe ich nicht zu rechtfertigen. Sie wird sich selbst rechtfertigen, und wo sie verkannt wird, nach und nach das Erkenntniss schon öffnen. Nur auf diesem Wege hat sie ihre Bestimmung; nur

---

[9] See: HÜLSEN 1796, 173-4

[10] In HÜLSEN'S (1796, 175-6) words: *"Daraus würde sich ergeben haben, das man nur mit Geist in Geist eindringen könne."*

[11] See: HÜLSEN 1796, 174-6, 196-7

durch Selbsterkenntniss will sie aufgenommen seyn, und muthet sich daher Niemanden objektiv an, wie diejenigen Theorien thun müssen, die sich nur durch Widerstreit Eingang verschaffen können.[12]

According to Hülsen, the core of Beck's book is in section two, entiteled "*Darstellung des transcendentalen unserer Erkenntniss, als des wahren Standpunkts, aus welchem die Kritik der reinen Vernunft beurtheilt werden muss*". Its topic is a discussion of The *Grundsatz* of philosophy, the exclusively-possible principle of all knowledge. Hülsen reminds us that every free examining reader ought to demand that Beck's system fulfil the following critical criteria: (1) original representation, for Beck the first possible synthetic unity of consciousness, should provide the system of knowledge with formal and material certainty. (2) As an exclusively-possible principle, it also should hold fully in and by itself; it should attain an absolute systematic status.[13] The critical demands that Beck should satisfy are (1) logical certainty and (2) systematic self-sustainability.

Hülsen claims that Beck's principle is imperfect. Critical contrast reveals that by establishing original representation as the highest principle of knowledge, Beck grounded his system only on one of the divisions of a universal system of knowledge: the theoretical. Moreover, Beck's principle does not fulfil the critical criteria of logical certainty and self-sustainability. For Hülsen the *Einzigmöglicher Standpunkt* fails to discuss the criteria, which its first principle of knowledge should fulfil.[14]

[...] kann es für die Wissenschaft gleichgültig seyn, ob gefragt wird: hier ist für alle Philosophie das einzigmögliche Prinzip; oder: hier ist ein Prinzip, welches den nothwendigen Anforderungen an ein höchstes Prinzip vollkommen entspricht? Dieses letztere setzt voraus, dass man bei der Aufstellung eines solchen Prinzip, einen bestimmten Zwek hatte, welchem Zwekke zu folge das zufindende Prinzip nur in so fern das höchste seyn konnte, als sich der Zwek aus ihm selbst wieder volkommen rechtfertigte, und daher durch

---

[12] HÜLSEN 1796, 197
[13] See: HÜLSEN 1796, 176-7
[14] See: HÜLSEN 1796, 177

seine Gewissheit schlechthin auch das in seiner Aufstellung vorausgesetzte nun völlige Gewissheit erhielt.[15]

According to Hülsen, in Beck's *Standpunkt* the universally self-grounded or self-sustainable principle such as that of the *Wissenschaftslehre* is absent. This oversight has dramatic implications. Only a principle that can furnish the universal ground of logical certainty, can ground the necessary correspondence of the form and the content of all possible knowledge.[16] For Beck, original representation is the exclusively-possible principle of philosophy. His principle is therefore arbitrary. For Hülsen original representation is only an abstraction, or in his own language, a pure assertion (*blosse Behauptung*).[17] For Hülsen this determines the *disputable character* of Beck's principle. An uncritically established principle can be replaced by any other principle of its kind. The consequence is a potential plurality of unjustified "first principles", and hence the impossibility of withdrawing from the sphere of disputes.[18]

Hülsen's next targets both the *formal* and the *material* imperfections of Beck's principle.

Hülsen claims that as self-unaware and therefore unjustified assertions all pre-critical "fist principles" are postulated as absolute in character. Critical insight shows that *qualitatively*, no distinction among them is possible. Hülsen asks which of these "first principles" (including Beck's) can attain the status of the highest principle of knowledge. His answer is none. Beck's principle is formally undistinguishable from other "first principles"; it cannot claim universality as true first principle of philosophy. This compels that we search for distinction in the contents of the principles in question; that we subordinate them according to their functional material advantages.[19]

---

[15] HÜLSEN 1796, 178
[16] See: HÜLSEN 1796, 178
[17] See: HÜLSEN 1796, 178-9
[18] See: HÜLSEN 1796, 179
[19] See: HÜLSEN 1796, 178-80

According to Hülsen, philosophy demands that the "*Grundsätze*" of all possible "first principles" be traced back to a common and universally self-posited fact: the *Wissenschaftslehre*. Hülsen takes Beck's *Grundsatz* (*ursprünglich vorzustellen*) hypothetically as the fact in question, and asks whether it could contain other "*Grundsätze*" within its alleged universal sphere. Beck's *Grundsatz* is formally undistinguishable. Only its content remains to enable a subsuming or subordination of all "*Grundsätze*" under its alleged universality. Using this strategy, provisionally, Hülsen enlightens the full problematic character of Beck's *Grundsatz*. Hülsen asks whether the content (*Behauptung*) of Beck's *Grundsatz*, a determined object of representation, say "A" or "B", can determine the material possibility of other "*Grundsätze*". The *Wissenschaftslehre* has shown that all representational contents are determined products of an act of positing. Positing cannot be determined by original representation. If it could, the following would be the results: (1) positing would only be a derived procedure, and not the act whereby original representation attains the content that enables its hypothetic material assertion as philosophy's *Grundsatz*. (2) It would be impossible to find any other distinguishing content than the one asserted by original representation.[20] Hülsen's concludes by enlightening the material insufficiency of Beck's *Grundsatz*:

In Hinsicht der Behauptung ist demnach das ursprüngliche Vorstellen durchaus nicht weiter als jedes A und B, und darum ist es vollkommen dasselbe, ob A, oder ob B, oder ob beide und noch mehrere, als höchste Grundsätze, behauptet werden.[21]

Materially, Beck's *Grundsatz* cannot claim universality or exclusivity. It does not prevent propositional plurality. Critical insight shows that both formally and materially Beck's principle is imperfect. Taken as philosophy's *Grundsatz*, "original representation" reawakens disputes.

Hülsen uses Fichte's approach in *Grundlage* to develop his discussion of Beck's first principle. All uncritically asserted "first principles" such as Beck's share the same imperfect logical status; they are all

---

[20] See: HÜLSEN 1796, 180-1
[21] HÜLSEN 1796, 181

posited as "originally" counter-posited principles.[22] Ignorance of the act of positing results in the simultaneous "absolute" assertion of two "first principles", "A" and "B". Their "absoluteness" compels both principles to exclude each other and engage in a dispute. For Hülsen the "absolutely" counter-posited character of "A" and "B" presupposes their *previous* particular positing as counter-positable principles. This means that the uncritical assertion of "A" determines its own counter-positable character to "B" and vice versa.[23] Both "A" and "B" are self-contradictable.[24] Hülsen's concludes that

Dieses hat für alle mögliche Thatsachen Gültigkeit, denn [...] das Verfahren im Behaupten ist eines und dasselbe; ist eine und dieselbe blosse Appellation an den gemeinen Menschenverstand. Weil hier nun jede Rechtfertigung eben in der Appellation besteht, so giebt es für den jedesmal behaupteten Satz kein anderes Kriterium der Gewissheit, als das subjektive Fürwahrhalten, wo man bloss zu Folge des Angenommenen nicht einsehen kann, wie wol noch etwas anderes als das Angenommene wahr seyn könnte.[25]

Fichte's insight into the *circular* positing relation of grounding and grounded in *Grundlage* enables the overcoming of such uncritical *linear* efforts.[26]

    Another failure of Beck's system according to Hülsen is that Beck's idealism is a destructive idealism (*zerstöhrenden Idealismus*). As the highest principle of knowledge, "original representation" ought to be that self-determining act whereby all possible reality is originally posited. That is why the *Wissenschaftslehre's* cornerstone, the absolutely self-grounded I, can only appear from Beck's perspective as a *product* of original representation. Beck accordingly cannot determine the Absolute I as a true self-posited agent. In the *Einzigmöglicher Standpunkt* the Absolute I ought to be something determined (*ein Bestimmtes*), something that is because there is something else, original

---

[22] An exclusive feature of critical philosophy is its non-counter-positable character.

[23] HÜLSEN 1796, 182: "*Also: A ist nicht dem B durch A, und B nicht dem A durch B; sondern A dem B durch B, und B dem A durch A entgegengesetzt.*"

[24] See: HÜLSEN 1796, 182

[25] HÜLSEN 1796, 182

[26] See: HÜLSEN 1796, 183-5

representation, whereby it is. Consequently, the Absolute I cannot emerge in Beck's approach as a spiritually self-related agent, as a self. For Beck, the Absolute I ought to be a mere representational object.[27] Hülsen asks:

Aber wo ist nun das Bestimmende, wenn das Ich das Bestimmte ist? und was soll demnach erklären, dass das ursprüngliche Vorstellen ein solches wirklich sey? Aus seiner eignen Realität, sey es ursprünglich oder diskursiv, kann weder mittelbar noch unmittelbar mehr als ein Vorstellen, und nie ein Seyn abgeleitet werden. Wie ist das Vorstellen nun selbst aber zu bestimmen, und wie also überhaupt ein Bewusstseyn möglich?[28]

According to Hülsen, Beck's position is untenable. Beck offers only a determined but not a determining I. Beck posits only an *explanandum*, not an *explanans*. That is why Beck cannot exhaustively answer the question about consciousness' possibility. Critical contrast also shows that Beck's partial "first principle" is a self-contradictory principle; its non-exhaustivity cancels its alleged original condition. The failure of the *Einzigmöglicher Standpunkt* is Beck's omission of a critical account of the original proto-conscious synthesis presupposed by his "original" act of representation. Hülsen concludes that Beck's principle neither grounds, nor explains the possibility of consciousness.[29]

This proves for Hülsen that Beck's standpoint is "destructive idealism". (1) The absence of an original *explanans*-I proves that reality in the *Einzigmöglicher Standpunkt* is not the product of spontaneous positing but of undetermined representation. Beck cannot explain the emergence of an objective world. (2) The absence of an original *self-reflecting explanans*-I leaves the question open: who accomplished the act necessary to ground the act of "original" representation? These two failures reveal the self-contradictory character of Beck's idealism. Critical contrast shows that both formally and materially, Beck's non-exhaustive premise negates or undermines its contention to be critical

---

[27] See: HÜLSEN 1796, 188-9
[28] HÜLSEN 1796, 189-90
[29] See: HÜLSEN 1796, 189-91

philosophy, and hence Hülsen's assessment of it as a "destructive idealism".[30]

Nonetheless, according to Hülsen, Beck came close to understanding the systematic relevance of a self-reflecting *explanans*-I. Beck himself argued that *„das ursprüngliche Vorstellen ist das Objekt der Philosophie als Wissenschaft"*. According to Hülsen, this is what the *Wissenschafts-lehre* teaches. It essentially constitutes a self-conscious explanation of consciousness' foundations, a systematic *representation* of the original proto-conscious acts behind the first possible *representation*. What Beck overlooked is the primacy of the original acts whereby "original representation" is transformed into an object of inquiry. Beck's supporters unavoidably perform these acts, as critical philosophy itself compels their deduction. The self-conscious grasping of these acts is what Hülsen calls *"scientific" philosophizing*.[31]

Hülsen claims that Beck demands from his reader to adopt the standpoint of "original representation". But Hülsen corrects Beck by claiming that transcendental freedom must self-determine itself to self-reflect on "original representation", a spiritual relation must connect transcendental freedom and "original representation". This relation is the unconditional relation of a determined object to its unconditional conditioner (the Absolute I). Beck's overlooking of this proves that his first principle is not exhaustive.[32]

Hr. B[eck] hatte also seine Anforderung: sich auf den Standpunkt des ur-sprünglichen Vorstellens zu versetzen, gar nicht überlegt, da er sonst wahr-genommen haben müsste, dass sich das ursprüngliche Vorstellen gar nicht durch sich selbst erkläre, sondern einen Erklärungsgrund erfordete. Nach

---

[30] See: HÜLSEN 1796, 189, 191

[31] HÜLSEN (1796, 193) reminds us that *"Alle Versuche im Philosophieren gingen nur darauf aus, das ursprüngliche Vorstellen wahr und richtig zu reflektieren. Mithin ist diejenige Reflexion, welche ihrem Gegenstande vollkommen ent-spricht, das endliche resultat aller Versuche, und daher die Wissenschaft von den Handlungsweisen, wodurch die objektiv synthetische Einheit des Bewusstseyns eine solche ist, d.i. eine Wissenschaft von der Möglichkeit alles Wissens, oder eine Wissenschaftslehre."*

[32] See: HÜLSEN 1796, 191-4

seiner Ansicht setzt er Sich Selbst mit seinem ganzen Philosophieren als ein Produkt des ursprünglichen Vorstellens. Wäre dem wirklich nun so; so wäre auch seine Anforderung ganz unstatthaft und sich selbst widersprechend. Nun muss man es umkehren: weil eine solche Anforderung nothwendig ist; so ist jene Ansicht in sich selbst widersprechend und unstatthaft.[33]

In section three, Beck discusses Kant's *Kritik der praktischen Vernunft*. For Hülsen this transition is arbitrary. According to Hülsen, Beck does not even try to justify this transition. Contradicting his own grounding criteria, Beck grounds the practical division of his system on a second "exclusively-possible" principle: practical freedom. To Hülsen's astonishment, Beck holds, this second principle cannot be traced back to original representation. Beck discusses his two principles separately. Inconsistently, Beck presupposes an original duality in the human spirit. Inconsistently, independent treatment is the self-contradictory cause of Beck's focus on each one of these principles as grounding principles. According to Hülsen, critical contrast shows that if Beck's theoretical principle (original representation) were ascribed exhaustive priority, all it could be proved is the formal ability to think (*Gedenkbarkeit*) the principle of practice, but not its reality (*Wirklichkeit*). Beck's system leaves room neither for real freedom, nor for the articulation of philosophy's practical division. If Beck's practical principle were ascribed exhaustive priority, that is, the role of establishing an original spiritual duality, an inconsistency would follow. The systematic determination of this duality would demand its theoretical assertion, its transformation into a determined object of thought.[34] Hülsen's criticism is that considered as two separated, though simultaneously asserted "first principles", the self-complementary principles of theory and practice *relativize* each other and undermine the original condition that Beck ascribes them.

Regarding Beck's concept of moral ought (*sittliches Sollen*), Hülsen's criticism is that Beck assigns this concept the status of an arbitrarily established fact (*Thatsache*), while identifying it with practical reason

---

[33] HÜLSEN 1796, 194
[34] See: HÜLSEN 1796, 200-2

or freedom. This identification allows Beck to characterize moral ought as the highest principle of practice. According to Hülsen, critical philosophy must deduce the possibility of this fact. As an arbitrarily established fact, Beck's concept of moral cannot explain a fundamental feature of critical thought: reason's practical ability to strive. Equally uncritical is Beck's approach to the highest good, which provides a systematic foundation for our necessary belief in God and immortality. According to Hülsen, attainment of the highest good, a full self-conscious fulfilment of our spiritual nature, demands infinite self-reflective striving after regulative self-identity. Hülsen's focus on the highest good as a unitary concept, as a judging synthesis of moral action and happiness, allows a systematic equation of the concepts "reason" and "God". Beck, apart from lacking such a unitary concept, misses the fact that a rationally grounded belief in God and immortality is the rational being's key to regulate his supreme moral task: the exhaustive subordination of all possible Not-I.[35]

Die empirische Erscheinung, welche wir Tod nennen, hat demnach in dem reinen Begriffe von unserer Unsterblichkeit gar keinen Sinn. Haben wir einmal dem Willen seine Aufgabe gegeben; so liegt forthin auf unserm Wege für uns kein Tod mehr, und ihn fürchten heisst eben so viel, als das Fortschreiten zum Vollkommnern fürchten. Der sittlichgute Mensch bedarf also der Ueberzeugung von Gott und Unsterblichkeit jetzt, in diesem Augenblikke, den er will jetzt, un in diesem Augenbikke, schön für die Ewigkeit handeln. [...] Sehen wir nun auf den höchsten Zweck unserer handlungen; so findet sich da nichts von Uebereinstimmung der Glückseligkeit mit der moralischen Würdigkeit, sondern die Glückseligkeit liegt schon als nothwendig in unserm Willen, und der höchste Gegenstand unsers Strebens ist die Vernunft selber. In so fern sie dieses ist, und sich selbst also eine Aufgabe ist, liegt auch Vollendung in der Unendlichkeit in ihrem praktischen Wesen. Seine Aufgabe denken, und die Unendlichkeit in sich ausnehmen ist darum völlig identisch.[36]

The main failure of Beck's system is the absence of a self-conscious insight into the circular relation of philosophy to its exclusive object:

---

[35] See: HÜLSEN 1796, 205-7, 209
[36] HÜLSEN 1796, 207-8

the system of knowledge.[37] Critical insight should show the precise systematic location of *Einzigmöglicher Standpunkt* within a personally articulated rational history of philosophy; it should show how to exhaust, augment, and correct Beck's grounding principle, achieve self-determination, withdraw from the sphere of partisan disputes, and integrate autonomously in a coordinated striving after absolute self-identity.

---

[37] See: HÜLSEN 1796, 204. Hülsen closes without discussing section IV of Beck's essay.

Appendix B: Hülsen's Life

August Ludwig Hülsen was born on March 3, 1765 in Aken an der Elbe, a small village in Saxony-Anhalt. Hülsen was the eighth son of the preacher Paul Gottfried Hülsen and Johanna Dorothea Stutz. Not much about Hülsen's childhood and youth is known, except that he lived in Premnitz, a small village in Brandenburg where his father preached.

On the summer semester of 1785, Hülsen enrolled at the University of Halle to study theology. Instead, he studied classical philology. Friedrich August Wolf (1759-1824) was Hülsen's most important academic teacher. Wolf introduced Hülsen in the interpretation of Homer. Hülsen completed his studies in 1789. This same year he became the private tutor of the Baron Friedrich de la Motte Fouqué (1777-1843), subsequently a romantic writer and poet, and the author of the prologue of Hülsen's posthumously published fragments. Hülsen's pedagogic activity ended in the spring of 1794, when Fouqué became a solider. A strong interest in critical philosophy encouraged Hülsen's enrolment for the 1794 summer semester at the University of Kiel where Reinhold was prominent. Hülsen's purpose was to deepen his knowledge of Kant's and Reinhold's philosophy. Very soon, however, Hülsen found that Reinhold had changed his philosophical position radically. Hülsen's disillusionment with Reinhold motivated his shift to Jena in Easter 1795, where for some months, Fichte was teaching his *Wissenschaftslehre*. In Jena, Hülsen joined the *Bund der freien Männer*, a group of young students that committed itself to the republican implications of Fichte's philosophy.[1] Hülsen's stay at Jena prompted his *Preisschrift* and his first collaboration with Fichte's *Philosophisches Journal*: the *Philosophische Briefe an Hrn. v. Briest in Nennhausen. Erster Brief. Ueber Popularität in der Philosophie.*

---

[1] For a short account of the *Bund's* history see: REK 1983, 577-83 and RAABE 1959, 337-344

From the spring of 1796 and until the autumn of 1797, Hülsen joined some *Bund* members in a journey to Switzerland, where he met the Swiss pedagogue Johann Heinrich Pestalozzi (1746-1827). Hülsen's return to Jena in 1797 prompted his second article in Fichte's journal: *Ueber den Bildungstrieb*, which appeared in print a year later. Fichte's satisfaction with Hülsen's achievements persuaded him to offer Hülsen in 1798 a chair of philosophy at the University of Jena. Hülsen, who saw himself as an independent thinker, rejected Fichte's offer and opened in 1799 an educational institute for boys in Lentzke bei Fehrbellin, a small village near Berlin. Hülsen conceived his institute as a "Socratic school". Hülsen's purpose was to promote introspective self-knowledge through active philosophical debate; his success was short-lived. Although Dorothea Veit planned to send her son Philip to Lentzke, Hülsen's institute closed after one year. On July 1798, Hülsen established his first contacts with the early German romantics; he began corresponding with August W. Schlegel.[2]

In March 1799, Hülsen married Christiane Posern and resumed his literary projects. Friedrich Schlegel invited him to collaborate with the *Athenäum*. This same year Hülsen's *Ueber die natürliche Gleichheit der Menschen* appeared in print. Hülsen's achievement attracted Schleiermacher's interest. Both thinkers began corresponding on October 1799.[3] Hülsen's second *Athenäum* essay, the *Natur-Betrachtungen auf einer Reise durch die Schweiz*, followed in 1800. Notwithstanding the interest and the respect Hülsen's thought received from the early romantics, the *Natur-Betrachtungen* ended Hülsen's collaboration with the *Athenäum*. Hülsen claimed that the *Athenäum* had a scholarly elitist profile, which prevented the promotion of a "popularized" spiritual culture: one of Hülsen's major interests.

Hülsen's wife died in October 1800. Hülsen moved to Seekamp to the estate of his *Bund* friend the Danish philosopher Johann Erich von

---

[2] For Hülsen's correspondence with August W. Schlegel (1798-1803), see: FLITNER 1913, 97-121, and KÖRNER 1937, I 53-64

[3] For Hülsen's correspondence with Schleiermacher (1799-1802), see: HÜLSEN 1913, I-40

Berger (1772-1833). Together with other ex-*Bund* members, Hülsen founded the *Mnemosyne*, a "popular" alternative to the scholarly *Athenäum*. The journal appeared just once. No contributions by Hülsen who planned to take part of the project were included in this only issue. This ended Hülsen's short philosophical career. Notwithstanding Friedrich Schlegel's recurrent collaboration offers, Hülsen remained reluctant to publish.

In 1802, Hülsen failed into a deep emotional crisis, as his relationship with Friederike von Luck, ended badly. His financial situation also became extremely difficult. August W. Schlegel's efforts to intercede on Hülsen's behalf with the Count von Kalkelreuth, formerly Salomon Maimon's benefactor, were unsuccessful. For some months, Hülsen vacillated between Holstein and Berlin. Some years after, Hülsen referred to this period of his life as an epoch of disorientation and existential confusion. Hülsen's situation changed dramatically in the autumn of 1803 after von Berger and some other ex-*Bund* friends invited him to join an agricultural commune they founded in Holstein. This same year Hülsen begun working as a farmer and ended his correspondence with the early romantics. A strong supporter of freedom, Hülsen rejected and criticised severely Friedrich and August W. Schlegel's increasing sympathy to the medieval past, which he considered reactionary.[4]

In the spring of 1804, Hülsen's friends bought him a farm in the village of Wagersrott. The Norwegian philosopher Henrik Steffens (1773-1845), in 1807 a visitor of Hülsen, reported that Hülsen and von Berger became deeply interested in the speculative grounding of the

---

[4] See HÜLSEN's letter to August W. Schlegel from December 18, 1803 in KÖRNER 1937, 55-64. Hülsen's criticism of the Schlegel brothers attracted Walter Benjamin's attention. In his 1938 review of Josef KÖRNER's *Krisenjahre der Frühromantik*, contained in *Der Stratege im Literaturkampf*, BENJAMIN (1974, 541) rated Hülsen's letter as one of the "[...] *seltenen Dokumenten, in denen das Grundmotiv der Aufklärung mit jenem unvergleichlichen Klange vibriert, den es über dem Resonanzboden der Romantik annimmt. Er denunziert die Unmündigkeit des deutschen Bürgertums, die in diesen Krisenjahren zum Verhängnis der Frühromantik geworden ist.*"

new natural sciences; they both conducted several physical experiments.[5] The philosophical fragments that Schelling published after Hülsen's death were written apparently during this time.

In June 1806, Hülsen married Sophie Christine Friederica von Wibel. The marriage did not last long, as Hülsen's wife died in March 1808 after giving birth to a son, who also died a short time after. On March 31, 1809, Hülsen married Maria Elisabeth Wilhelmine Thormälen, his third wife. The couple moved to Stechow *bei* Rathenow, where Hülsen's brother held office as a pastor; a daughter was born on July 1809. A few months after, on September 24, 1809, Hülsen died. After Hülsen's death, Fichte, von Berger, and La Motte Fouqué, supported Hülsen's widow financially. Fichte even offered the widow to take care of her daughter.[6]

---

[5] See: TILITZKI 1983, 125

[6] See: KRÄMER 2001, 138. — For an exhaustive biography of Hülsen see Ulrich KRÄMER's … *meine Philosophie ist kein Buch. August Ludwig Hülsen (1765-1809): Leben und Schreiben eines Selbstdenkers und Symphilosophen zur Zeit der Frühromantik.* Parts of my short account of Hülsen's life were taken from Matthias WOLFES' internet entry in the *Biographisch-Bibliographisches Kirchenlexicon.* See: WOLFES 2000

Bibliography

Primary Sources

BENJAMIN, Walter 1974: *Der Stratege im Literaturkampf.* Zur Literatur-wissenschaft, Frankfurt a. M.: Suhrkamp

FEUERBACH, Anselm 1969: Ueber die Unmöglichkeit eines ersten absoluten Grundsatzes der Philosophie, in: *Philosophisches Journal* einer Ge-sellschaft Teuscher Gelehrten, Reprografischer Nachdruck der Ausg. Neu-Strelitz 1795, Hildesheim: Olms, II, 1969

FICHTE, Johann Gottlieb (GA): *Fichte-Gesamtausgabe* der Bayer. Akad. der Wiss., Stuttgart-Bad Cannstatt: Frommann-Holzboog, 1962 ff.

HÜLSEN, August Ludwig 1796: *Prüfung der von der Akademie der Wissen-schaften zu Berlin aufgestellten Preisfrage: Was hat die Metaphysik seit Leibniz und Wolf für Progressen gemacht?*, Altona: J. F. Hammerich

— 1797: Philosophische Briefe an Hrn. v. Briest in Nennhausen. Erster Brief. Ueber Popularität in der Philosophie, in: *Philosophisches Journal einer Gesellschaft Teutscher Gelehrten*, Hrsg. von J.G. FICHTE und Fr. I. NIETHAMMER, 7. Bd., Heft 1

— 1798: Ueber den Bildungstrieb, in: *Philosophisches Journal einer Gesell-schaft Teutscher Gelehrten*, hrsg. von J.G. FICHTE und Fr. I. NIETHAM-MER, 9. Bd, Heft 2

— 1799: Ueber die naturliche Gleichheit der Menschen, in: *Athenaeum.* Eine Zeitschrift von A. W. SCHLEGEL und Fr. SCHLEGEL, 2. Bd, 1799

— 1800: Natur-Betrachtungen auf einer Reise durch die Schweiz, in: *Athe-naeum.* Eine Zeitschrift von A. W. SCHLEGEL und Fr. SCHLEGEL, 3. Bd, 1800

— 1913: *Briefe August Ludwig Hülsens, J. B. Vermehrens und Fritz Weicharts an Friedrich Schleiermacher*, Berlin, Litteraturarchiv-Gesellschaft in Berlin

— 1971: Philosophische Fragmente, aus Hülsens literarischen Nachlaß, in: *Allgemeine Zeitschrift von Deutschen für Deutsche,* hrsg. von F. W. J. SCHELLING, Bd. 1, Nendeln/Lichtenstein: Kraus-Thomson

KANT, Immanuel *KrV: Kritik der reinen Vernunft*, Riga 1781 (A), ²1787 (B), also in: ww II

— ww: *Werke* in 6 Bdn., hrsg. von Wilhelm WEISCHEDEL, Wiesbaden: Insel 1956-60

MAIMON, Salomon 1969: *Über die Progressen der Philosophie*, Bruxelles: *Aetas Kantiana*

NOVALIS SCH: *Die Werke Friedrich von Hardenberg*, Stuttgart: Kohlhammer, 1977 ff.

REINHOLD, Karl Leonhard 1791: Über den Begriff der Geschichte der Philosophie. Eine akademische Vorlesung, in: *Beyträge zur Geschichte der Philosophie*, vol.1, Züllischau und Freistadt: Frommannische Buchhandlung 1791

— 1794: K. L. Reinhold an seine in Jena zurückgelassenen Zuhörer, in: *Teuscher Merkur*, 1794

— 1963: *Versuch einer neuen Theorie des menschlichen Vorstellungsvermögens*, Wissenschaftliche Buchgesellschaft, Darmstadt, 1963

— 1978: *Ueber das Fundament des philosophischen Wissens.* Nebst einigen Erläuterungen über die Theorie des Vorstellungsvermögens, Hamburg: Meiner, 1978

— 2003: *Beiträge zur Berichtigung bisheriger Mißverständnisse der Philosophen*, 2 Bde., Hamburg: Meiner

— 2005: *Letters on the Kantian Philosophy*, Cambridge: U.P. 2005

SCHELLING, Friedrich W. J. 1971: Nachwort zu den vorhanstehenden Fragmenten, in: *Allgemeine Zeitschrift von Deutschen für Deutsche*, Bd. 1, Kraus-Thomson Organization Limited, Nendeln/Lichtenstein, 1971

— 1985: Vom Ich als Princip der Philosophie oder über das Unbedingte im menschlichen Wissen, in: F.W.J. Schelling Ausgewählte Schriften, Bd. 1, Suhrkamp, Frankfurt am Main, 1985

SCHLEGEL, Friedrich KA: *Kritische Ausgabe seiner Werke*, Paderborn: Schöningh, 1958 ff.

SCHULZE, Gottlob Ernst 1911: Aenesidemus oder über die Fundamente der von Professor Reinhold in Jena gelieferten Elementar-Philosphie: Nebst einer Vertheidigung des Skepticismus gegen die Anmaassungen der Vernunftkritik, Reuther and Reichard, Berlin, 1911

SCHWAB/REINHOLD/ABICHT 1971: *Preisschriften über die Frage: Welche Forschritte hat die Metaphysik seit Leibnizens und Wolffs Zeiten in Deutschland gemacht?*, Darmstadt: Wissenschafliche Buchgesellschaft

TENNEMANN, Wilhelm Gottlieb 1795: Uebersicht des Vorzüglichsten, was für die Geschichte der Philosophie seit 1780 geleistet worden, in: *Philosophisches Journal einer Gesellschaft Teutscher Gelehrten*, Reprograf. Nachdr. d. Ausg. Neu-Strelitz 1795, Hildesheim: Olms II, 1969

Secondary Sources

AMERIKS, Karl 2000: Kant and the Fate of Autonomy: Problems in the Appropriation of the Critical Philosophy, Cambridge: U.P.

— 2003: Reinhold's Challenge: Systematic Philosophy for the Public, in: *Die Philosophie Karl Leonhard Reinholds*, Amsterdam / Atlanta: Rodopi

— 2004: Reinhold on Systematicity, popularity, and the Historical Turn, in: *System and Context / System und Kontext:* Early Romantic and Early Idealistic Constellations / Frühromantische und Frühidealistische Konstellationen, Lewiston / Queenston / Lampeter: Edwin Mellen

— 2005: Introduction, in: Karl Leonhard REINHOLD, *Letters on the Kantian Philosophy*, Cambridge: U.P.

— 2009: Rheinhold, History, and the Foundation of Philosophy, in: *Leonhard Reinhold and the Enlightenment*, Dordrecht: Axel Springer

BAUM, Günter 1974: K.L. Reinholds Elementarphilosophie und die Idee des transzendentalen Idealismus, in: *Philosophie aus einem Prinzip: Karl Leonhard Reinhold*, Bonn: Bouvier-Grundmann

BAUMANNS, Peter 1974: *Fichtes Wissenschaftslehre: Probleme ihres Anfangs*, Bonn: Bouvier-Grundmann

BEISER, Frederick 1987: *The Fate of Reason.* German Philosophy from Kant to Fichte, Cambridge, Ma. / London: Harvard U.P.

— 2002: *German Idealism.* The Struggle against Subjectivism, 1781-1801, Cambridge, Ma. / London: Harvard U.P.

BONDELI, Martin 1995: *Das Anfangsproblem bei Karl Leonhard Reinhold.* Eine systematische und entwicklungsgeschtliche Untersuchung zur Philosophie Reinholds in der Zeit von 1789 bis 1803, Frankfurt a.M.: Klostermann

BREAZEALE, Daniel 1981: Fichte's Aenesidemus Review and the Transformation of German Idealism, in: *The Review of Metaphysics*, 34

— 1982: Between Kant and Fichte: Karl Leonhard Reinhold's "Elementary Philosophy", in: *The Review of Metaphysics*, 34, 5, 1982

— 1994: Circles and Grounds in the Jena Wissenschaftslehre, in: *Fichte. Historical contexts / Contemporary Controversies*, New Jersey: Humanities Press

— 2001: Inference, Intuition, and Imagination: on the Methodology and Method of the First Jena Wissenschaftslehre, in: *New Essays in Fichte's*

Foundation of the Entire Doctrine of Scientific Knowledge, New York: Humanity Books

— 2001b: Fichte's Concept of Philosophy as a 'Pragmatic History of the Human Mind' and the Contributions of Kant, Platner, and Maimon, In: *Journal of the History of Ideas* 62, 2001

BUBNER, Rüdiger 2003: *The Innovations of Idealism*, Cambridge: U.P.

BUHR, Manfred 1965: *Revolution und Philosophie: Die ursprüngliche Philosophie Johann Gottlieb Fichtes und die französiche Revolution*, Berlin: VEB Deutscher Verlag der Wissenschaften

DIETZSCH, Steffen 1990: *Dimensionen der Transzendentalphilosophie*. Studien zur Entwicklung der klassischen bürgerlichen deutschen Philosophie 1780-1810, Berlin: Akademie

FINCHAM, Robert 2005: Refuting Fichte with „Common Sense": Friedrich Immanuel Niethammer's Reception of the Wissenschaftslehre 1794/5, in: *Journal of the History of Philosophy* 43, Baltimore: Johns Hopkins U.P.

FISCHER, Kuno 1900: *Fichtes Leben, Werke und Lehre*, Heidelberg: Winter

FLITNER, Willy 1913: August Ludwig Hülsen und der Bund der freien Männer, Jena: Eugen Diederichs

FRANK, Manfred 1998: *Unendliche Annäherung*. Die Anfänge der Philosophischen Frühromantik, Frankfurt a. M.: Suhrkamp

FRANKS, Paul 1997: Freedom, *Tatsache* and *Tathandlung* in the Development of Fichte's Jena Wissenschaftslehre, in: *Archiv für Geschichte der Philosophie* 79

— 2005: All or Nothing: Systematicity, Transcendental Arguments, and Scepticism in German Idealism, Cambridge, Ma./London: Harvard U.P.

FREYER, Klaus/STAHL, Jürgen 1984: Ansätze des Prinzips der Einheit von Logischem und Historischem in Übergangsfeld der fichteschen Transzendentalphilosophie zum objektiven Idealismus. J. G. Fichte – A. L. Hülsen, in: *Methodologische Konsequenzen Marxschen Denkens*, Jena: Friedrich-Schiller-Universität

FUCHS, Erich 1978 ff.: *J. G. Fichte im Gespräch. Berichte der Zeitgenossen*, Stuttgart-Bad Cannstatt: Frommann-Holzboog

GIRNDT, Helmut 1965: *Die Differenz des fichteschen und hegelschen Systems in der hegelschen „Differenzschrift"*, Bonn: Bouvier

HARTMANN, Nicolai 1960: *Die Philosophie des deutschen Idealismus*, Berlin: de Gruyter

HAYM, Rudolf 1961: *Die Romantische Schule.* Ein Beitrag zur Geschichte des deutschen Geistes, Hildesheim: Olms

HEINZ, Marion 2004: Untersuchungen zum Verhältnis von Geschichte und System der Philosophie in Reinholds Fundamentschrift, in: BONDELLI, Martin / LAZZARI, Alessandro, *Philosophie ohne Beynamen.* System, Freiheit und Geschichte im Denken Karl Leonhard Reinholds, Basel: Schwabe

HENRICH, Dieter 1991: *Konstellationen.* Probleme und Debatten am Ursprung der idealistischen Philosophie (1789–1795), Stuttgart: Klett-Cotta

— 2003: *Between Kant and Hegel: Lectures on German Idealism*, Cambridge, Ma. / London: Harvard U.P.

HESS, Hans 1926: Das romantische Bild der Philosophiegeschichte, in: *Kant-Studien*, Bd. XXXI, Heft 1, Berlin: Pan-Verlag Rolf Heise

HOELTZEL, Steven 2001: Fichte's Deduction of Representation in the 1794-5 Grundlage, in: *New Essays in Fichte's Foundation of the Entire Doctrine of Scientific Knowledge*, New York: Humanity Books

HORSTMANN, Rolf-Peter 1991: *Die Grenzen der Vernunft.* Eine Untersuchung zu Zielen und Motiven des Deutschen Idealismus, Frankfurt a.M.: Klostermann

— 2000: The Early Philosophy of Fichte and Schelling, in: *The Cambridge Companion to German Idealism*, Cambridge: U.P.

HÜLSEN, Christian 1934: *Chronik der Familie Hülsen 1500-1934*, Görlitz: Verlag für Sippenforschung und Wappenkunde C.A. Starke

JAMME, Christoph 1990: Geselligkeit und absolutes Sein: Weisen des Anschlusses an Fichte im Umkreis der Freien Männer, in: *Denken unterwegs.* Philosophie im Kräftefeld sozialen und politischen Engagements, Amsterdam: Erasmus Universiteit Rotterdam

KABITZ, Willy 1968: *Studien zur Entwicklungsgeschichte der Fichteschen Wissenschaftslehre aus der Kantischen Philosophie*, Darmstadt: Wiss. Buchgesellschaft

KLAWON, Dieter 1977: *Geschichtsphilosophische Ansätze in der Frühromantik*, Phil. Diss., Frankfurt a.M., 1977

KÖRNER, Josef 1937: *Krisenjahre der Frühromantik.* Briefe aus dem Schlegelkreis, Brünn / Wien / Leipzig: Verlag Rudolf M. Rohrer

KRÄMER, Ulrich 2001: *... meine Philosophie ist kein Buch. August Ludwig Hülsen (1765-1809).* Leben und Schreiben eines Selbstdenkers und Symphilosophen zur Zeit der Frühromantik, Frankfurt a.M.: Peter Lang

LANGEWAND, Alfred 1991: *Moralische Verbindlichkeit oder Erziehung.* Herbarts frühe Subjektivitätskritik und die Entstehung des ethisch-edukativen Dilemmas, Freiburg/München: Karl Alber

LASSAHN, Rudolf 1970: *Studien zur Wirkungsgeschichte Fichtes als Pädagoge*, Heidelberg: Quelle & Meyer

MARTIN, Wayne 1997: *Idealism and Objectivity. Understanding Fichte's Jena Project*, Stanford: U.P.

MARWINSKI, Felicitas 1992: *Wahrlich, das Unternehmen ist kühn ...* Aus der Geschichte der Literarischen Gesellschaft der freien Männer von 1794/99 zu Jena, Jena/Erlangen: *academia & studentica Jenensia* e.V

MENSEN, Bernhard 1974: Reinhold zur Frage des ersten Grundsatzes der Philosophie, in: *Philosophie aus einem Prinzip: Karl Leonhard Reinhold*, Bonn: Bouvier/Grundmann

NASCHERT, Guido 1998: August Ludwig Hülsens erster Beitrag zur philosophischen Frühromantik, in: *Athenäum.* Jahrbuch für Romantik, Vol. 8, Padeborn: Schöningh

NEUHOUSER, Frederick 1990: *Fichte's Theory of Subjectivity*, Cambridge: U.P.

OBENAUER, Karl 1910: *August Ludwig Hulsen.* Seine Schriften und seine Bezihungen zur Romantik, Erlangen: Junge & Sohn

OESCH, Martin 1979: Hülsens idealistische Romantik, in: *Romantische Utopie – Utopische Romantik*, Hildesheim: Gerstenberg

PERRINJAQUET, Alain 1994: Some remarks Concerning the Circularity of Philosophy and the Evidence of its First Principle in the Jena *Wissenschaftslehre*, in: *Fichte.* Historical Contexts/Contemporary Controversies, New Jersey: Humanities Press

PINKARD, Terry 2002: *German Philosophy: The Legacy of Idealism*, Cambridge: U.P.

PIPPIN, Robert 2000: Fichte's Alleged Subjective, Psychological, One-Sided Idealism, in: SEDGWICK, Sally, *The Reception of Kant's Critical Philosophy.* Fichte, Schelling, and Hegel, Cambridge: U.P.

RAABE, Paul 1959: Das Protokollbuch der Gesellschaft der freien Männer in Jena 1794-1799, in: *Festgabe für Eduard Berend zum 75. Geburtstag*, Weimar: Hermann Böhlaus Nachf.

REK, Klaus 1983: Die Jenaer Gesellschaft der freien Männer 1794-1799, in: *Wissenschaftliche Zeitschrift der Karl-Marx-Universität Leipzig*, Bd. 32, 6, Leipzig

ROCKMORE, Tom 1994: Antifoundationalism, Circularity, and the Spirit of Fichte, in: *Fichte. Historical Contexts / Contemporary Controversies*, New Jersey: Humanities Press

— 2001: Fichte on Deduction in the Jena *Wissenschaftslehre*, in: *New Essays in Fichte's Foundation of the Entire Doctrine of Scientific Knowledge*, New York: Humanity Books

ROSENKRANZ, Karl 1987: *Geschichte der Kant'schen Philosophie*, Berlin: Akademie

STAMM, Marcelo 1995: Das Programm des methodologischen Monismus: Subjekttheoretische und methodologische Aspekte der Elementarphilosophie K. L. Reinholds, in: *Neue Hefte für Philosophie*, Göttingen: Vandenhoeck & Ruprecht

STRACK, Friedrich 1988: Was soll die Schweiz dem Athenäum: Romantische Schönheitsmetaphysik in Hülsens Natur-Betrachtungen, in: *Geschichtlichkeit und Aktualität. Studien zur deutschen Literatur seit der Romantik*, Tübingen: Niemeyer

STOLZENBERG, Jürgen 2003: Geschichte des Selbstbewußtseins. Reinhold – Fichte – Schelling, in: *Internationales Jahrbuch des deutschen Idealismus*, I

TILLITZKI, Christian 1983: August Ludwig Hülsen 1765-1809, in: *Jahrbuch des Heimatvereins der Landschaft Angeln*, Bd. 47

VIEWEG, Klaus 1995: Fichtes Vorlessungen über die Bestimmung des Gelehrten von 1794, in: *Fichtes Wissenschaftslehre 1794. Philosophische Resonanzen*, Frankfurt a. M.: Suhrkamp

VON SCHÖNBORN, Alexander 1999: Karl Leonhard Reinhold: "... Endeavoring to keep up the Peace *mit unserem Zeitalter*", in: *The Emergence of German Idealism*, Washington, D.C.: The Catholic University of America Press

WEISCHEDEL, Wilhelm 1973: *Der frühe Fichte: Aufbruch der Freiheit zur Gemeinschaft*, Stuttgart-Bad Cannstatt: Frommann-Holzboog

WOLFES, Matthias 2000: *Hülsen, August Ludwig*, in: *Biographisch-Bibliographisches Kirchenlexicon*, http://www.bautz.de/bbkl/h/huelsen_a_l.shtml

ZHIXUE, Liang 1991: Interpersonalität beim jungen Fichte, in: *Fichte-Studien*, Bd. 3, Amsterdam / Atlanta: Rodopi

EuKlId

Europäische Kultur und Ideengeschichte

(ISSN 1867-5018)

Herausgeber: Bernd Thum, Hans-Peter Schütt

Institut für Philosophie, Karlsruher Institut für Technologie (KIT)

Die Bände sind unter www.ksp.kit.edu als PDF frei verfügbar oder als Druckausgabe bestellbar.

Band 1   Ulrich Arnswald (Hrsg.)
          In Search of Meaning. Ludwig Wittgenstein on Ethics, Mysticism and Religion. 2009
          ISBN 978-3-86644-218-4

Band 2   Luis Miguel Carrujo Covas
          Worte am Werk. Wittgenstein über Sprache und Welt. 2008
          ISBN 978-3-86644-291-7

Band 3   Christian Hoffstadt
          Denkräume und Denkbewegungen. Untersuchungen zum metaphorischen
          Gebrauch der Sprache der Räumlichkeit. 2009
          ISBN 978-3-86644-378-5

Band 4   Ulrich Arnswald, Hans-Peter Schütt (Hrsg.)
          Thomas Morus' Utopia und das Genre der Utopie in der Politischen Philosophie. 2010
          ISBN 978-3-86644-403-4

Band 5   Ezequiel L. Posesorski
          Between Reinhold and Fichte. August Ludwig Hülsen's Contribution to the
          Emergence of German Idealism. 2012
          ISBN 978-3-86644-861-2